THAT CAT
WON'T FLUSH

Wallace O. Chariton

Wordware Publishing, Inc.

Library of Congress Cataloging-In-Publication Data
CIP available, Reference Number 90-23139

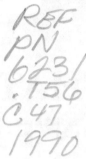

ISBN 1-55622-175-4

10 9 8 7 6 5 4 3 2 1
9010

All inquiries for volume purchases of this book should be addressed to
Wordware Publishing, Inc. at the above address. Telephone inquiries
may be made by calling:

(214) 423-0090

Contents

Introduction

Some wise old sage once remarked that there never had been a movie sequel as good as the original, which I suspect is correct. That same sage, however, continued by suggesting that there never had been a book sequel that was as good as the original. I certainly hope that isn't true because this is book is a sequel of sorts since it is my second entertaining dictionary dealing with country language.

The language used by country folks is actually a lot more than just an accumulation of words. Country talk is pictures set to words. If I said it is very cold outside, that would be a milk toast sort of language. But, if I said it was so cold outside that my teeth were chattering and they were in a glass on the dresser, then you would get a strange image of an impossible situation but you would also know it was, indeed, very cold outside.

I've been collecting the colloquialisms and unique sayings that are so common to country people since I was about ten years old, and that was more years ago than I care to remember. Every time I heard a saying I dutifully wrote it down in a small notebook to preserve it and save it for another day. Through the years my collection has grown considerably, but there was also a problem growing right along with it.

As a native Texan, I've spent all my life rattling around the Lone Star State. I roamed from the Panhandle to the Gulf coast and from East to West Texas and back again. About the only time I was ever out of Texas was during a period when I thought corporate America was for me, which it wasn't. Whenever business took me to Boston or Chicago or Los Angeles, I always made it a point not to stay any longer than absolutely necessary.

Because of such limited horizons, I naturally assumed that the language of Texas was totally unique. After all, I didn't have much to compare it to because I was never in any other place long enough to really get to know the people and learn how they talked. That assumption eventually got me into trouble.

When I finally spit out the hook and abandoned life in corporate hell, I took up the mouse on my Apple Macintosh and started writing. My intention was to write the great Texas novel, but thanks to some friends, I got sidetracked. Those friends had read my notebooks full of Texas sayings and they encouraged me to publish them. I finally caved in and a book entitled *This Dog'll Hunt* was the result.

The Dog book, as it has come to be called, was an instant hit and an instant problem all rolled into one ball of wax. While my intention was to produce the book for Texans, it seems a lot of people in Texas were purchasing copies and sending them to Aunt Martha in Maine, Uncle Fred in Kansas, brother Bob in Boston, or to sister Sue in England. As an author I naturally didn't mind the sales but I wasn't quite prepared for what followed. A lot of those non-Texans who received the book took up paper and pen to write to inform me that I was ever so slightly mistaken about the language in the book being totally unique to Texas.

As it turned out, I heard from people in almost all the United States and a fair amount of foreign countries and the theme was almost always the same. Phrases like "My grandfather in Iowa invented that saying" or "I've been saying that all my life and I've never been closer to Texas than northern Oklahoma" were common. Although I didn't do any formal survey, the consensus of opinion was that Texans didn't have anywhere near a lock on colorful language and interesting sayings. To back up that supposition, a lot of people sent me their favorite sayings with a sort of underlying message that went something like "see, we talk country too."

After reading all the letters and doing a lot of soul searching, I have come to the conclusion that Texans are not the only ones who use country talk as a part of everyday life. As a staunch Texan, however, I stand pat in my belief that, taken as a group, Texans more frequently use the word pictures than almost any other single group of people. I got plenty of letters from Texans to back up that position.

The common thread in the use of colorful language seems to be country roots. Most people I heard from or that I have talked to seem to have some country connection. For example, I didn't hear from a single person who grew up and lived his entire life in New York City but I did hear from several country folks who had moved to New York in an effort to find the end of the rainbow. One man who was born and raised in Chicago admitted that his colorful sayings came from his grandfather who was a farmer in Iowa. The very few people I heard from that didn't have specific country roots did express a desire to make some, which means they couldn't wait to get out of the city and into the country. I hope they make it.

My original intention with the Dog book was to include all the country sayings in existence. However, as Ann Richards pointed out in her introduction for the book, that will never happen. There are too many old sayings for any one person to know and there are more being invented every day. For example, a friend from Georgia called the other day and happened to mention that he had been out drinking some "stealth" whiskey. When I asked what that was, he replied, "It's whiskey that is so strong that after three drinks you believe you can fly and that no one can see you." Even though stealth is a modern word, the old boy that gave me the saying is so country you could smell cord wood on his breath.

It eventually became clear that there are hundreds, maybe thousands, of sayings that didn't make it into *This Dog'll Hunt*. So, thanks to everyone who contributed more material, I decided to complete a sequel and include all the new material. Appropriately, while the Dog book was an entertaining Texas dictionary, this is an entertaining *country* dictionary. A lot of the sayings are from Texas but many are from country people around the nation. Whether you are in Paris, Texas; Paris, Tennessee; or Paris, France, you may find phrases, definitions, and word pictures that either sound like you or someone you know. If you happen to have any favorite sayings that you've used for years (or that you made up yesterday) I'd like to hear from you if you care to share them. Who knows, if the cards and letters keep coming in, there may even be a third volume someday. Write to me care of Wordware Publishing, 1506 Capital Ave., Plano, Texas 75074.

Even if you don't want to send me your sayings, space has been provided in the book for you to record your own favorites. I would encourage you to do that because sooner or later the grandfather or uncle or father whose country talk you enjoy will be gone. If you write the sayings down in the book, you'll always have something to remember them by and that's important. Of course, once you have them written down, it wouldn't take much to send me a copy now would it?

I hope you enjoy this book half as much as I enjoyed bringing it to you because if so you're in for a darn good time. Until we meet again, I leave you with a wish: May your bankroll get bigger, your problems get smaller, you honey get sweeter, and all your kids be born naked.

From a parking lot next door to the Alamo

Wallace O. Chariton

Dedication

As promised, this book is respectfully dedicated to the following: Grace Arianoutos, Mary Beesinger, Mark Betts, Genny Dorsett, Lou Griffin, Stan Hall, Ken Herr, Sally Hogan, Sue Hogge, Todd Lillian, Tracy Maloney, Casey Malarcher, Mickey Short, Evelyn Stark, Wade Stewart, Charles Taylor, Susan Tolar, Pat Trimble, and Will Varner. Together, they helped love ride the rails. Sorry folks, the picture didn't turn out good enough to print. Maybe next time.

Acknowledgements

A lot of folks had a hand in the production of this book, whether they knew it or not. There were so many, in fact, I doubt if I could ever acknowledge everyone's participation. I will, however, give it a try and apologize in advance to anyone who was not included.

I send a big thank you to the following: Donnis Baggett, Steve Bartlett, Joe Barton, Glyn Beesley, Kent Biffle, Thurman Bisher, Ben Boothe, Bobby Bragan, David Brenner, Jerry Brooks, Dave Brownfield, Liz Carpenter, Donald Carter, Lillian Carter, Gage, Jennifer and Judy Chariton, Dan Cook, Mary Margret Davis, Ron Davis, Spike Dykes, Charlie Eckhardt, Mary Lee Edwards, Jerry Glanville, Stan Hall, Dick Hitt, Lou Holtz, Harry Jackson, Hal Jay, Jerry Jones, Randy Galloway, Pete Gent, Jack Glover, Mary Goldman, Eddie Gonzales, Leon Hale, Skip Harless, Paul Harvey, Jim Hightower, Sally Hogan, Sue Hogge, Joe Holstead, Tommy Lasorda, Gib Lewis, Kevin McCarthy, Alan and Martha McCuller, Tim McEvoy, James B. McSheehy, Dr. Billy Mills, Dick Motta, Linda Mylis; Glen Owen, Travis Parks, Dolly Parton, Minnie Pearl, Gilbert Perez, Raddie F. Perry, Paul Peterman, T. Boone Pickens, Edwin Pope, Billy Porterfield, Paul Pryor, Glenn Raines, Michael Ray, Jim Reeves, Joe Reynolds, Ann Richards, Paul Richards, Ken Rigsbee, Frank Rohner, Roy Rogers, Darrell Royal, Joseph E. Scuro, Jr., Dick Seigel, Blackie Sherrod, Dwight "Paddlefoot" Sloan, Evelyn and Craig Stark, Russell Stultz, Tanya Tucker, Big Ed Wilkes, Clayton Williams, Charles Wilson, Justin Wilson, Ben Wilson, Jim Wright, Kevin Young, and Richard T. Young.

A posthumous thanks to Tallulah Bankhead, Judge Roy Bean, Davy Crockett, Hondo Crouch, W. C. Fields, John Nance Garner, Texas Guinan, Phil Harris, Sam Houston, Lyndon Johnson, Abraham Lincoln, Alice Roosevelt Longworth, Elvis Presley, Sam Rayburn, Will Rogers, George Bernard Shaw, Harry S. Truman, Mark Twain, Bigfoot Wallace, John Wayne, and Mae West.

Finally, thanks to all the folks who contributed and either did not want their name mentioned or whose name I never knew.

AMAZED — his eyes bugged out like a frog stepped on by a Clydesdale

A

ABANDONED As an Arkansas still when a Treasury agent comes calling. Somehow those ol' moonshine boys just always seem to know when trouble is on the way.

ABILITY, NATURAL He took to that like a duck takes to water (or a jackrabbit takes to runnin').

ABILITY WITHOUT BRAINS He has plenty of go but he don't know when to say whoa □ he's got the speed but he lacks control

ABLE He's got what it takes to get what there is to be got.

ABLE BUT UNWILLING He puts his lamp under a bushel basket. Like a lot of country sayings, this one has its roots in the Bible (fifth book of Matthew). It means that someone has a lamp but instead of putting it on top of the basket so all can share, he hides it under the basket.

ABSENT MINDED He could lose a bar of soap inside a wash rag □ he could lose his keys in his vest pocket.

ABSOLUTE HONESTY Improves your character and ruins your fishing trip

ABSOLUTELY Would a ten-foot chicken lay a big egg? □ Would a two-ton hog make a lot of bacon? *See also Believe Me, Yes*

ACCEPT IT You gotta grab a root and growl □ somebody has to have the hard seat □ just cinch up your belt and go get dirty

ACCEPT RESPONSIBILITY It's better to pass gas and bear the blame than to not pass gas and bear the pain.

ACCEPT THE INEVITABLE Texan T. Boone Pickens said: "I hate to fail but when it's time to take a bath, I get in the tub." *See also Inevitable*

ACCURATE As an echo □ as a mirror □ on the level as

in "Those figures are on the level."

ACCUSATION That's a chicken snake callin' a hound dog an egg sucker ❏ you're a skunk tellin' a turkey buzzard he stinks

ACE OF SPADES The big digger

ACHIEVEMENT He's found his puddle ❏ he's built his barn

ACHING Hurtin' for certain *See also In Pain*

ACNE SCARS He looks like his face caught fire and someone put it out with a track shoe (or ice pick) ❏ he looks like he was beaten with a barbed wire bat

ACQUAINTANCE, CASUAL Someone you know well enough to talk about

ACQUAINTED, SLIGHTLY We've swapped howdies, which is a variation on the old saying "we've howdied but we ain't never shook."

ACQUAINTED, SOMEWHAT I know him well enough to borrow from but not well enough to loan to.

ACQUIESCED He caved in and gave in.

ACT WISELY "When you have got an elephant by the hind legs and he is trying to run away, it is best to let him run." Abraham Lincoln

ACTING BIG He's a bottle fed colt tryin' to act like a stallion ❏ he's got his big boy pants on ❏ he's acting a little too big for his boots (or britches) ❏ he's acting high and mighty

ACTING CHILDISH His diddy pin must really be stickin' in him. *See also Childish*

ACTING FOOLISH You're askin' a blind man to tell you which horse to buy ❏ cuttin' the fool ❏ giving away the store ❏ he's plowin' up snakes ❏ he's ridin' fast and loose, which means he ain't holding on too tight

ACTING POMPOUS He's puttin' on the dog for all the world to see ❏ he's big-eyein' around town

ACTING PREMATURELY You won't catch many calves if you throw the rope before you build a loop.

ACTING STRANGE His clutch is slipping ❏ his tractor ain't gettin' no traction ❑ he's acting like some loco weed got mixed into his feed

ACTION You can sit up and take notice but it won't do any good if you keep sitting.

ACTIONS SPEAK LOUDER THAN WORDS When the tailgate drops, the BS stops. This saying comes from coon hunters who like to brag about their dogs. When they go huntin' the bragging stops when the tailgate drops and the dogs jump out of the pickup to go to work. From that point on the action of the dog speaks volumes more than the voice of the owner.

ACTIONS, MISLEADING He has a heart of gold but then so does a hard-boiled egg.

ACTIVE AS A four-ball tomcat ❑ as a calf in clover ❑ as a bartender's rag on Saturday night

ACTIVE MAN *See Male, Active*

ACTIVE WOMAN *See Female, Active*

ACTOR A puppet without the strings

ACTOR (HAM) He makes a good line greasy.

ADAPTED TO He's a good hand for that.

ADDLED She's gone plumb around the bend ❑ he's teched in the head

ADOLESCENCE He's between grass and hay, which means he's somewhere between boyhood and manhood ❑ he's in never-never land, which means he never wants to do kid things and his parents never let him do anything adult

ADOLESCENT Somebody who has graduated from Humpty Dumpty to hanky panky

ADROIT She's got more moves than a belly dancer on a roller coaster.

ADULT Someone who has stopped growing except in the middle

ADVANCE WARNING According to Gib Lewis, speaker of the Texas House, "prewarned is prearmed."

ADVANTAGE He's fightin' a three-legged bull (or a blind bull) ❑ he's got a leg up on everybody ❑ he's got an ace in the hole. A really big advantage would be having an ace in the hole with Smith

and Wesson engraved on it.
See also Disadvantage

ADVERSARY He's the fly in my ointment, burr under my saddle, nail in my boot, or worm in my apple.

ADVERTISING The only business that makes money without advertising is the mint ❑ if you stop advertising to save money, you might as well stop a clock to save time

ADVICE Never put all your eggs in one basket or all your whiskey in one woman ❑ advice is like a laxative; it's easy to take but you can't never predict the results ❑ advice is like a mushroom; the wrong kind can be fatal ❑ advice is usually only good for passing on ❑ never play poker with anyone named Ace ❑ never eat at a place called Mom's *See also Business Advice*

ADVICE FOR SPEAKERS When you're done pumping, let go of the handle.

ADVICE, SOUND Never buy anything that has a handle, eats, needs painting, or has babies.

AFFLICTED Down in, such as "He's down in his back." *See also Ill*

AFFLICTED, SERIOUSLY Eat up with, as in "My wife is eat up with jealousy just 'cause I had one dance with that little ol' gal."

AFRAID Fraidy cat

AGE Mind over matter: if you don't mind, it don't matter ❑ makes men and whiskey milder

AGREEMENT, CHANGED The pigs ran through it.

AGGRESSIVE He's a loose hoer, which means when he gets to hoeing weeds he can tear up a fair sized pea patch or ruin several acres of cotton. *See also Female, Aggressive or Male, Aggressive*

AGGRESSIVENESS It's better to pick fruit than wait for it to fall ❑ he's got plenty of Billy goat in his blood ❑ a person with push don't need no pullin'

AGREEABLE Might as well, we can't dance and it's too wet to plow.

AIM HIGH Eagles don't chase flies ❑ it's better to aim high and miss than to aim low and hit the target

ALASKA The world's largest snow job

ALCOHOLIC He suffers from Anheuser's disease ❑ his favorite drink is the next one ❑ the only time he ever refused a drink, he didn't understand the question ❑ works his way down from bottoms up ❑ whenever he gets in trouble he tries to use a corkscrew to pull himself out of it ❑ An alcoholic is not one who drinks too much, but one who can't drink enough. *See also Drunk*

ALCOHOLIC ARTHRITIS He gets a lot of pain in the joints.

ALCOHOLISM Panther colic

ALERT He's bright eyed and bushy tailed ❑ he sleeps with one eye wide open and the other one only half closed

ALIKE There ain't a plug nickel's difference between 'em ❑ they were tarred with the same brush

ALIMONY Is like making payments on a pickup truck that got hit by a train ❑ the high cost of leaving ❑ leave home pay ❑ a case of wife and debt

ALL Everything under the sun

ALL MY LIFE All my born days

ALL TOGETHER Everybody is in the same pew (or stew pot).

ALL WORK, NO PLAY It's all hominy and no ham

ALMOST Nearly 'bout as in "I nearly 'bout got caught when I stole those watermelons."

ALMOST, BUT NOT QUITE Pert near but not plumb

ALMOST EMPTY Runnin' on fumes ❑ runnin' on memories

ALMOST OVER You're hoeing the short rows ❑ the fat lady is clearing her throat (or reaching for the song book). When Dick Motta was coach of the Cleveland Cavaliers of the NBA, he was fond of saying, "the opera ain't over till the fat lady sings," so if the fat lady was reaching for the song book, the opera would be almost over. ❑ turn on the air-conditioner in the bus, which means the ball game is all but over and the visiting team is about ready to leave ❑ it's all over but the shouting, which means the outcome is no longer in doubt but the celebration hasn't officially begun

ALONE All by his lonesome ❏ cooking solitary chili, which means he's cooking only enough for one

ALTERNATIVE Instead of biting the bullet, try getting the lead out ❏ the hind tit is better than no tit at all ❏ there's more than one way to dress a calf's head ❏ when you are up to your nose in manure, try breathing through your ears

ALUMNI He's not an athlete but he is an athletic supporter.

ALWAYS THINKING He brought in a dry well and tried to cut up the shaft so he could sell it for post holes.

AMAZED His eyes bugged out like a frog that had been stepped on by a Clydesdale.

AMAZING Now don't that beat all ❏ I've been to three county fairs, two rodeos and a goat roping and I ain't never seen anything like that!

AMBITION Every man has the ambition to outsmart horses, fish, and women ❏ every woman has the ambition to outsmart men, mirrors, and bathroom scales

AMBITION, LACKING A little fish can't bite a big hook but he can be dinner for a big fish. This means that someone who chooses to remain a small fish in the pond won't have to worry about being caught on a big hook but he will have to always be looking over his shoulder for the fish that did choose to grow.

AMBITIOUS He whittlin' with a big knife.

AMNESIA Something friends get when you loan them money

AMOUNT, SMALL Smidgen

ANATOMY The best part of a girl (or man)

ANCESTRY Bark of the family tree

ANCESTRY, CLOUDED He's got some shady branches on his family tree.

ANCESTRY, POOR Even the best family tree has its sap.

ANEMIC He's so anemic, if he cut his finger he'd have to get a transfusion before he could bleed ❏ he's tick proof

ANGER Makes your mouth work faster than your mind ❏ you can't be angry and reasonable at the same time any more than a horse can buck and eat hay at the same time

ANGERS Makes me want to kick a stump barefooted ❏ makes my butt dip snuff (or crochet a button hole) ❏ that chaps my backside

ANGRY Hoppin' mad ❏ as a bobcat in a mud hole ❏ as a sore tailed bear ❏ as an alligator with chapped lips ❏ enough to eat the sights off a six shooter, which means someone is almost angry enough to start shootin' but not quite ❏ she was hotter than a pot of boiling collards ❏ he was so hot under the collar that all the hair on his neck was singed off and his earlobes shriveled up *See also Female, Angry; Male, Angry; Upset*

ANGRY WORDS You're preaching your own funeral, meaning you're about to talk yourself into a fight that will be your last. It is a slight variation to the old saying, "hot words lead to cold slabs."

ANGRY, BUT IN CONTROL He's chewin' his tobacco ninety to nuthin', which means he is very angry but not enough to spit out his tobacco and fight. Instead, he just chews faster and spits more.

ANOTHER HELPING That was so good my tonsils snapped back and slapped the taste right out of my mouth, which is a country way of saying you'd like another helping so you can remember the taste a little longer.

ANT Horned frog food. Even though horned frogs (which are actually lizards) are almost extinct, those that remain prefer a diet heavily laced with juicy red ants.

ANTIQUE Something that has made a round trip to grandma's attic

ANXIOUS He's foaming at the trough ❏ he's chomping at the bit ❏ he's got ants in his pants, which brings to mind the old country saying, you can't cure ants in the pants by sleeping with an ant eater

APOLOGETIC He's got his hat in his hand, which is a reference to the fact that a lot of country boys don't never take off their hat unless they're fixin' to apologize for something.

APOLOGY When somebody apologizes when there ain't no need, then he knows something you don't.

APPEARANCE It's the man that makes the cowboy, not the duds ❑ clothes do not make the man, especially if it's an apron

APPEARANCE, BAD Looks like a stump full of brush frazzled rats ❑ he looks like the offspring of a scarecrow ❑ he looks like he got caught in the gears of a combine and drug for three acres ❑ he looks like death sitting on a cracker ❑ he looks like something the cat drug in ❑ you look like you were drawn through a knothole backwards ❑ you look like you were chewed up, spit out, and stepped on

APPEARANCE, DECEIVING Like a vulture, he looks scary but he's harmless ❑ you can find a lot of thread on a small spool ❑ you can't tell how fast a rabbit can run by looking at his ears ❑ you can put pants on a woman but she's still a woman

APPRECIATE Simply 'preciate to most country boys

APPRECIATION I'd take kindly to it ❑ I'll dance naked at your next wedding if you'll do that for me.

APPREHENSIVE As a doctor operating on a lawyer who specializes in malpractice cases.

ARGUMENT Like a county road, you never know where it will go ❑ when arguing with a fool make sure he ain't doing the same thing

ARGUMENT, STUPID That's about as dumb as two bald-headed men fighting over a fine-tooth comb.

ARGUMENT CLOSE It's time to back the hearse up (or start the hearse). These sayings are used to close an argument you lost because the implication is that disaster is imminent.

ARID LAND *See Land, Dry*

ARIZONA (Ara-zona) According to the old country legend, Arizona ain't no place for amateurs.

ARKANSAS (Ar-KIN-saw) Land of hills, thrills, and stills

ARMADILLO Poor man's pig ❑ Hoover hogs ❑ road targets, which comes from the fact that so many armadillos are killed while trying to cross a highway *See also Jumps*

ARROGANT He's got more crust than a pecan pie factory

ARTHRITIS
(arthur-EYE-tus) The big miseries

ARTIST, POOR He couldn't draw a conclusion

ASLEEP He's looking for light leaks (or pin holes) in his eyelids.

ASLEEP, SORT OF Just restin' my eyeballs as in "How could I have been snoring when I was just restin' my eyeballs?"

ASPIRATION He's just a little pebble, but he wants to be the whole beach ❑ he's just a little tadpole tryin' to be the big frog in the pond

ASPIRATION, LOW If you want to be a lamb, get ready to meet coyotes.

ASSESSMENT I feel about that like a lamp post feels about a dog.

ASSETS, GOOD He's got a pen full of baby donkeys. In the old days, baby donkeys were a great asset because they could either be sold or kept so they could one day replace old donkeys that wore out.

ASSIGNMENT, DIFFICULT You're asking me to change bulbs in a lightning bug.

ASSISTANCE You don't need help falling down, but a hand gettin' up is nice.

ASSISTED, SOMEWHAT I'll lend a hand but I didn't take you to raise.

ASSISTED Propped him up

ASSUME Makes an ass out of "u" and me.

ASSUMPTIONS Won't feed the bulldog

ASSUMPTION, WRONG *See Presumptuous*

AT HIS MERCY He's got me by the short hairs.

AT RISK You're ridin' a short horse in tall brush, which means there's a good chance you'll end up on the ground pickin' stickers out of your backside ❑ you're dancin' with the sheriff's mistress, which means if you get caught you're liable to end up shot or in jail or both *See also Risk Taking*

ATHEISM A fair weather religion

ATHEIST Has no one to talk to when he's alone

ATHLETE, STUPID (ath-a-leet) He can do anything with a football except autograph it. Baseball or basketball can easily be substituted for football. ❑ He don't know the meaning of the word fear, or most any other word.

ATHLETIC SUPPORTER Jewel box ❑ marble sack ❑ nut cup

ATLANTA, GEORGIA (At-lanna) When Jerry Glanville was hired by the Atlanta Falcons after being fired by the Houston Oilers, he was asked what he had learned since joining the Falcons. He replied, "I've learned that if you aren't sleeping in Atlanta, you're just camping out." It is just possible Glanville picked up that phrase in Houston, because Texans for years have said the same thing with Texas substituted for Atlanta. *See also Georgia*

ATTEMPTING THE IMPOSSIBLE You're trying to hit a five-run homer ❑ you're trying to bathe five kids in a two-kid washtub. In the country, if you had a large washtub and two small children, it was possible to bathe both of the little ones at the same time to save water. There never has been, however, a washtub large enough for five kids at one sitting.

Also, you're tryin' to square the circle. This saying originated long ago when mathematicians tried to build a square that would have exactly the same area as a circle. The math boys never made it and generations later we found out why — it can't be done. The saying eventually found its way to the country even though a lot of folks that used it probably never knew exactly what it meant. *See also Impossible*

ATTENTION GETTER That'll get your attention faster than a cross-eyed javelin thrower.

ATTENTION SPAN, SMALL He's got the attention span of a gnat. Mosquito, chigger, housefly, or almost any other small insect can be substituted 'cause none of 'em have a very long attention span.

ATTRACTED TO Like a moth to a flame ❑ like a counterfeit quarter to a magnet

AUCTIONEER A man who can pick your pocket with his tongue

AUTOBIOGRAPHY A book that reveals nothing bad

about the writer except his memory

AUTOMOBILE, FAST It'll pass everything but a gas station

AUTOMOBILE, LARGE Land cruiser ❑ land yacht

AUTOMOBILE, SMALL A beer can on wheels

AUTOMOBILE DENTS, MINOR Whiskey dents, which are the small, unexplained dents and dings you find in your car the morning after a night at the local honky tonk.

AUTOMOBILE REPAIRS *See Solution, Temporary*

AVERAGE Fair to middlin'

AVERAGE PERSON Someone who is as close to the bottom as he is to the top

AVOID You better go around him like you would a swamp at night.

AVOID TROUBLE Don't get between a dog and his bone ❑ if you run your car on chicken manure, you won't have any trouble with siphoners ❑ don't go around kicking sleeping dogs ❑ if you want to avoid really big trouble, never get between a politician and a TV news crew.

AWKWARD As a blind bear in a briar patch

This space is for your favorite sayings.

B

BORING — as a nudist colony without a peep hole in the fence

B

BABY A sucker that gets an even break □ when baby is happy, everyone is happy

BABY, FAT He looks like the world's largest dumpling.

BABY, UGLY *See Ugly Baby*

BABY CHICK Biddie

BABY-SITTER A teenager that gets paid for talking on the phone and eating leftovers

BABY GROWTH CHART As a baby grows it goes through several very identifiable stages. □ Stage One: An Arm youngun, which means the baby is so small it has to be held at all times when not in a crib. □ Stage Two: Lap baby which means the baby has grown enough that you can rest it on your lap for a few minutes at a time. □ Stage Three: Knee baby, which means the little one is big enough to bounce on your knee and almost ready to walk. □ Stage Four: Sit alone baby, which means he's old enough to sit on a pallet all by himself while you cook supper. □ Stage Five: Porch baby, which means the baby has just learned to walk and you can let him wobble around the porch while you sit in the rocker and knit. □ Stage Six: Yard baby, which means the baby has gotten good enough at walkin' that you can let him wander around the yard while you're hoeing in the garden. □ Stage Seven: Teenager

BACHELOR A good ol' boy that's footloose and fiancé free □ he ain't ever married 'cause he's looking for the perfect woman □ he's been turned down more than an army blanket □ his favorite dish is one that is already washed □ a man who leans toward women but not far enough to alter his stance □ One of the mysteries of life is why all bachelors aren't rich.

BACK TO BASICS Go back to the chicken pen and learn how to scratch.

BACKSEAT DRIVER The only person not bothered by

a backseat driver is a hearse driver.

BACKWARDS You got your hind part before your front part ❏ you got your zipper on the wrong side ❏ you got your hindsight first

BAD BREATH *See Breath, Bad*

BAD DRIVER Waiting to be recalled by his maker ❏ he's a little ol' lady in disguise

BAD MOOD Somebody messed in his mess kit.

BAFFLED He don't even know what planet he's on.

BAKE A CAKE Build a cake

BALD HEAD I've seen more hair on a crystal ball ❏ his hair departed in the middle ❏ a hair on the head is worth two in the brush ❏ he parts his hair with a towel ❏ his hair looks like it was parted by a bolt of lightning ❏ God made a few perfect heads, the rest he covered with hair ❏ the advantage to being bald is that you are immune to hair raising stories ❏ bald men are the most discriminated against because they have to pay full price for a haircut *See also Hair Restorer, Good*

BALDING He ain't goin' bald, he's just making room for a new face.

BANDAGE, LARGE Conversation starter, especially if it's on your forehead.

BANGING Like a screen door in a whirlwind

BANK TELLER The only person who can be tall and short at the same time

BANKER A pawnbroker that made good ❏ somebody who'll loan you an umbrella when the sun is shining and want it back when it rains

BANKER, TIGHT He gives you the same amount of credit as a sharecropper gets in a New Orleans whorehouse. *See also Grand Canyon*

BAPTIST A hell expert. It's been said that Baptists learn as much as possible about hell so they'll be familiar with where their Methodist friends go after death.

BAPTIST, BACKSLIDER His dippin' didn't take. Or he was dipped in muddy water.

BAPTIST, DEVOUT A hard-shell, foot washing Baptist ❏ deep water baptist ❏ somebody who ain't in the army of the Lord, he's in the navy ❏ very devout Baptists never make love standing up for fear someone might think they were dancing

BAPTIST, DRINKER A closet drinker ❑ if you play golf with a Baptist, always play with at least two. If you play with only one, he'll drink all the beer.

BARBECUE, GOOD *See Fried Chicken, Good*

BARBECUE SAUCE Correction fluid ❑ has covered up more mistakes than a maternity dress

BARBER SHOP Clip joint

BAREFOOT Barefooted ❑ clear footed ❑ "soleless"

BARELY MADE IT Made it by the skin of my teeth as in, "I was safe at second by the skin of my teeth."

BASEBALL CATCHER, GOOD He could catch a BB at midnight.

BASEBALL CATCHER, POOR The only thing he can catch is chicken pox.

BASEBALL HITTER, STRONG He can hit one out of any park, including Yellowstone, which is how Paul Richards once described Harmon Kilabrew.

BASEBALL PITCHER, INEPT He worked two years to straighten out his curve.

BASEBALL PITCHER, STRONG He throws so hard, the baseball looks like an aspirin ❑ he could throw a lamb chop past a wolf ❑ Tommy Lasorda once said of Fernando Velenzuela, "He can throw a baseball through a car wash and not get it wet."

BASEBALL PITCHER, WILD He's been known to hit batters while they were still in the on deck circle.

BASEBALL PLAYER, SLOW He could be thrown out at first base tryin' to stretch a double into a single, which is how writer Stanley Frank once described Lou Boudreau.

BASHFUL It makes him blush every time he remembers he was in bed naked with a woman the day he was born.

BATHTUB, LARGE Big as a dippin' vat

BATTERY, STRONG You could use that thing to jump start a nuclear submarine.

BE ALERT Keep one eye out for snakes and the other eye out for hornets ❑ the shrimp that sleeps gets taken away by the current

BE APPRECIATIVE Don't bite the teat you're nursin' on, which is country for "Don't bite the hand that feeds you."

BE CALM *See Calm Down*

BE CAREFUL Everything that comes from the cow ain't butter so watch what you spread on your bread ❑ don't ever step between a man and his spittoon ❑ put all your eggs in one basket and then watch that basket very carefully ❑ before you take a bite out of something, make sure it won't bite you back ❑ you can't always tell which dog'll bite you ❑ milk the cow but don't pull the udder off ❑ if it sounds too good to be true it probably is ❑ play 'em close to the vest, which is the best way to play your cards in a poker game *See also Careful*

BE CAUTIOUS Don't celebrate 'till you're out of the woods cause the posse might be hiding behind the last tree.

BE DECISIVE When the snake raises his head it's time to kill it.

BE OBSERVANT You can't tell which way the train went by looking at the tracks.

BE ON TIME Remember, the worm that was ate by the early bird was running late.

BE PATIENT Take a 'tater and wait ❑ let that train go on by 'cause the next one may be loaded with pretty girls ❑ wait and see how high the cat jumps ❑ you can't measure a snake until it's dead ❑ just sit tight, everything will come out in the wash ❑ the Grand Canyon wasn't dug in a day, which is country for Rome wasn't built in a day

BE PREPARED A hook without bait don't catch no fish ❑ if you're gonna run with coyotes, you better learn to like the taste of chicken feathers

BE QUIET Keep your 'tater trap shut ❑ it's hard to put a foot in a closed mouth ❑ a little bird shouldn't chirp much when it's in hawk country ❑ God gave you two ears, two eyes, and one mouth so you ought to be able to figure out which he expected you to use the most.

BE SATISFIED If you get a good omelet, don't worry whether the chicken likes you or not.

BE SELECTIVE Admire a large horse, saddle a small one ❑ feed the horses you ride

BE SMART Keep your head up and your backside down ❑ brains in the head save blisters on the feet ❑ don't send your dog to the butcher shop or your daughter to the mall ❑ hunt where the ducks are, which essentially means don't hunt ducks in a desert ❑ don't store your meat in your brother-in-law's freezer ❑ don't buy a cow when you can get the milk free, which usually means don't get married as long as there are some willin' women left

BE SPECIFIC On January 24, 1990, a member of the Dallas Mavericks entered the game wearing his uniform shorts backwards. Following the game, he told reporters, "I've been praying to the Lord to show me a way to get more recognition. In the future I'll be a little more specific." That goes along with the old country saying "God's mighty smart but he ain't no mind reader."

BE YOURSELF Blaze your own trail. If you follow another man's tracks, you don't know if he knew where he was going or not, which is a slight variation to the old standby "Another man's tracks might just as well lead to hell as heaven."

BEANS Arkansas strawberries

BEARD, HEAVY He could raise rabbits in his beard.

BEARD, LONG He looks like he swallowed a gray horse. If the beard is some color other than gray, substitute the correct color for the horse.

BEAT Clean his plow ❑ wind his watch ❑ give him a what-for lesson

BEATEN BAD He hung my hide on a fence, which means you got beaten badly and everyone knows it ❑ he kicked my butt so hard I could taste boot leather ❑ he knocked me just this side of heaven ❑ he knocked my toenails loose ❑ he hit me so hard my liver turned a cartwheel ❑ he gave me an all-world butt kickin'

BEAUTY MEASURE The Clydesdale Scale, which is the number of Clydesdale horses that would be required to pull you away from a woman. Therefore, if a pretty girl rates a 7 on the Clydesdale Scale, that would mean it would take seven of the giant horses hitched to your back to pull you away from her.

There is also the Reverse Clydesdale Scale, which is the measure of how many Clydesdales would have to be hitched to your butt to drag you over to her house for a free meal. A 1 on the Reverse Clydesdale Scale would mean she is fairly ugly but a darn good cook. Conversely, a 10 would mean she's so ugly she'd make a freight train take a dirt road and her cooking is so bad it ain't fit for slopping hogs. Note: Both the Clydesdale Scale and the Reverse Clydesdale Scale can be used by ladies to describe their preference in men.

BED A night spot

BED, CROWDED They're sleeping heads and tails.

BEER Fertilizer for raisin' hell ❏ kidney wash (or flush) ❏ belly builder ❏ something you don't wanna reload with if your nerves are shot

BEER, BAD Ought to be poured back into the horse where it came from ❏ coyote slobber ❏ panther pee

BEER DRINKER, SERIOUS He can hold more beer than a gopher hole ❏ he

drinks like he was weaned with beer *See also Coffee Drinker, Avid*

BEGIN Get on with the opera or let the opera begin.

BEGINNING Trigger time, which means it's time to pull the trigger and get started ❏ the get go

BEGINNING TO UNDERSTAND I'm beginning to see some daylight, which basically means he's been in the dark but he's finally beginning to understand, so some light is being shed on the subject.

BEHIND You're bringing up the rear like the tail of an old cow.

BELIEVE ME (bleeve me) If I'm lyin' I'm dyin' ❏ if I tell you there will be a dance you can tune your fiddle ❏ if I tell you it's gonna come a rain you can set out the catch barrel ❏ if I tell you it's Halloween, you can put on your mask *See also Absolutely; Yes*

BELLY, LARGE Banjo-belly

BETRAYED She let down her milk to the wrong man. You can't take a cow's milk, she has to let it down to someone she trusts.

BETWEEN THE EYES
Between the runnin' lights

BEWARE The man who
don't like a fast horse, a fat
cow, a firm woman, and foam
on his beer.

**BIG, STRONG, AND
STUPID** He's big as a gorilla,
strong as a gorilla, and about
half as smart as a gorilla.

BIG HEADED His head is
getting too big for his toupee.

BIG MOUTH *See Mouth,
Large*

BIG SHOT A little shot who
kept firing

BIG SPENDER Big butter
and egg man. When Texas
Guinan owned her famous
nightclub in New York, she
often greeted guests with
"Hello, Sucker." One night
she asked a sucker where he
was from and he said he was
a dairy farmer from
Wisconsin. For the entire
evening Texas referred to
him as her "Big Butter and
Egg Man." The saying, which
may or may not have been a
Guinan original, eventually
became a country favorite to
describe a big spender.

BIG TROUBLE *See
Trouble, Big Time*

BIGAMIST He's rasslin' two
alligators at the same time.

BIGAMY Two rites that
make a wrong ❑ one wife too
many, which, some people
believe, can also be used for
monogamy

BIKINI A bait wiggler ❑ a
troll suit

BIKINI, SMALL There ain't
enough material in that
bikini to make a petticoat for
a pissant.

BIRD HUNTER, DUMB He
killed his bird dog by
throwing it up in the air to
see how high it could fly.

BISCUIT, HARD If that
sucker had a sharp edge, you
could cut a diamond with it.

BISCUIT, HEAVY If that
thing was a little bigger, the
Olympic team could use it for
a shot put.

BISCUIT, LARGE Belly
breakers ❑ cathead biscuits
❑ they're so big it would only
take nine of them to make a
dozen

BLACK As the dirt roads in
East Texas ❑ as the inside of
an unopened coffee can

BLAME Fault, as in "You
can't fault him for stealing
that goat 'cause his kids need
milk and they ain't seen

23

their mother since she run off with the preacher."

BLANKET, THIN Hen skin blanket ❑ my blanket is so thin I can lay under it and count the cracks in the ceiling

BLEEDING Like a dehorned cow ❑ like a stuck pig

BLIVIT The sound made when you put ten pounds of manure in a five-pound sack and hit someone with it

BLOODY He looked like he'd been rasslin' a dozen horned toads. A popular legend has it that horned toads can spit blood when excited. The truth is, they expel the blood through their eyes. No matter how they do it, if you handle a horned toad, you may come away looking like you were in a knife fight with an octopus. *See also Knife Fight Victim*

BLOW, MISDIRECTED A mislick, as in "I swung hard at ol' Billy Fred but it was a mislick. He then proceeded to whup the fire out of me."

BLUFF He could bluff a buck deer out of his antlers ❑ he could bluff a big dog out of his bone.

BLURRY As a new moon in a thick fog

BLUSH The only thing that cannot be counterfeited ❑ man is the only animal that can or needs to blush

BMW Yuppiemobile

BOAT The two happiest days in a man's life are the day he buys a boat and the day he sells it.

BOLD He'd French kiss an ugly frog

BOLD AS A blind burglar ❑ as a 400-pound ballerina

BOLT TURNING RULES Righty tighty, lefty loosy

BOOK, DULL It has about as much action as a snake's hips. This saying could also be used for a dull movie or television program.

BOOK, POOR The biggest problem with that book is that the covers are too far apart.

BOOK, SULTRY It can produce more heat than a Mexican cookbook

BOOK, WORN Has more wear on it than a girlie magazine on a troop ship

BOSSIER CITY, LOUISIANA Known as Boozer city because of the number of local taverns, saloons, and honky tonks.

BOOTS, WORN The soles on his boots were so thin you could read a small print Bible through them in bad light.

BORE The only time he lights up the room is when he leaves ❏ he can stay longer in an hour than most people can in a week ❏ he has the personality of an empty glass (or a dishrag) ❏ he's got all the sparkle of a bottle of champagne that's been left open for a week

BORED Here I am, drunk, all dressed up, and nowhere to go.

BORING As a nudist colony without a peep hole in the fence ❏ as a balloon race at night (no one can see what is going on) ❏ downtown dull, which is a reference to there usually being very little to do in the downtown section of a small country community *See also Dull*

BORN LOSER If he was the last man on earth, the last woman on earth would be his sister (or mother-in-law) ❏ if he quit smoking, he'd get hit by a truck ❏ if he bought a pumpkin farm, they'd cancel Halloween ❏ if he bought a Christmas tree farm, they'd cancel Christmas (or Santa Claus would get hit by a 747)

BORROWING Is like scratching an itch, it only feels good for a little while

BOSTON BAWH-stun, never, ever BAAA-stun

BOUNCE That has more bounce than a volleyball game in a nudist colony

BOWLEGGED As a barrel hoop ❏ he couldn't catch a pig in a phone booth ❏ he's so bowlegged he could tie his shoelaces without bending over, which is how Lefty Gomez once described Honus Wagner

BOY Like a canoe, a boy works best when paddled from the rear.

BOY, YOUNG His daddy was a pistol and he's a son of a gun, but he ain't loaded yet.

BRA, LARGE You could use her bra for a bag to carry your bowling ball.

BRAGGART He's trying to build a reputation on what he's planning to do tomorrow ❏ if BS was music, he could play the Philharmonic ❏ he'd even brag about the number of sit-down holes in his outhouse

BRAGGING Before you start tooting your own horn, be sure you have juice in the battery ❏ struttin' your okra ❏ the only time you should blow your own horn is when you're in a band ❑ the hen that lays the biggest egg usually does the least cackling

BRAND NEW Brand spankin' new

BRAVE AS The man who ate the first calf fry. Lamb, pig, or turkey fries can be substituted. It has been said that any Westerner that won't eat calf fries must have lace on his shorts and water in his pistol. Also, the persons who ate the first oyster and the first egg were equally as brave.

BRAVE ENOUGH To marry a woman who's been widowed three times ❑ to break up a fight between two red-headed women

BRAVERY A condition brought on by necessity or a few cold beers ❑ what you have to have when you run out of options

BRAVERY, SORT OF Even a rabbit will kick a coyote when it's dead.

BREASTS, FALSE Hidden persuaders ❑ flat fixers ❑ she's flyin' under false colors, which is derived from ships flying a flag other than the correct one

BREATH, BAD Wolf (or coyote) breath ❑ his breath smells like he used a skunk tail for a moustache ❑ his breath smells like he ordered a cheeseburger and had 'em cut everything but the onions ❑ remember, however, no matter how bad the breath smells, it is still better than having no breath at all

BRIGHT As a pewter button ❑ as a fresh mint penny

BRIGHT PERSON He's so bright we have to put him in the closet to get the sun to come up.

BROKE If it cost a nickel to use the toilet, I'd have to use the sink ❑ if Cadillacs were $10 apiece, I couldn't afford the hood ornament off a Chevette ❑ I'm so broke I can't even entertain a doubt ❑ I had to get an advance from Mastercard to make a payment on my Visa card ❑ I'm as broke as Lazarus and he had a dog ❑ broke is what happens when you have more yearnings than you do earnings *See also Destitute; Poor; Poverty*

BROKE, ALMOST Borderline broke

BROKEN As a busted trace chain ❑ out of whack

BRONC RIDER Needs a light head and a heavy seat

BRONC, WILD The wildest bronc is always the one you rode somewhere else.

BRUSH, THICK The rabbits had to climb a tree to look out.

BUCK-TOOTHED He could eat a pumpkin through a picket fence.

BUDGET Like a girdle, it takes care of the bulge in one place and it pops out somewhere else ❏ like a girdle, there usually ain't enough to cover everything

BUILDING, HAUNTED Voodoo palace

BUILDING, LARGE Big enough to hold an indoor deer hunt

BUILDING, UGLY "This has all the earmarks of an eyesore," said James B. McSheehy.

BUSIER Than a one-armed paper hanger in a poison ivy patch

BUSINESS (bid-ness) A contact sport, according to Jerry Jones, owner of the Dallas Cowboys ❏ those that can do, those that can't become lawyers and go into politics

BUSINESS, BAD I don't even have to lie to the IRS

BUSINESS ADVICE Never enter into a deal with someone who has less money than you have. ❏ Carol Hall may have said it best in "A Lil' Ole Bitty Pissant Country Place" written for the stage production of "The Best Little Whorehouse in Texas." She wrote, "You keep your mind on your work responsibilities, don't let your mouth overload your capabilities, and we can get along."

BUSINESS LOYALTY If you find a good horse, ride him instead of continuing to look for another horse.

BUSINESS OPPORTUNITY, GOOD This business is better than having the neon concession in Las Vegas.

BUSINESS SENSE Bees can't make honey and sting at the same time.

BUSINESS SENSE, POOR He couldn't run a pumpkin stand if you gave him the pumpkins and the sheriff stopped traffic on the interstate ❏ he does precision guesswork

BUSINESSMAN, DECEITFUL If you buy

27

milk from him you better check it for minnows. Roy Bean once sold milk in San Antonio, Texas. When several customers reported finding minnows in their milk, Roy explained that his cows had been drinking from a nearby creek and must have swallowed the minnows. The excuse didn't hold water so Roy quickly headed West to become a judge in Pecos, Texas.

BUSINESSMAN, HONEST He'll tell you in advance that he's gonna cheat you.

BUSINESSMAN, SMALL TIME He's just a peanut operator.

BUST, LARGE The 8th and 9th wonders of the world ❑ she only dates mountain climbers ❑ they call her melon 'cause it looks like she's carryin' a couple of honeydews in her shirt

BUST, SMALL She looks like a bed without pillows ❑ she don't wear an A cup, she wears a saucer ❑ she wears a thimble cup bra ❑ if she got a pimple on one of her breasts it would double in size

BUSY I'm just weavin' and workin,' workin' and weavin.'

BUSY AS A zipper in a tight skirt, which means it has to work all the time just to stay together ❑ as one horse in a two-buggy town ❑ as a cat on castor oil, which means he spends all his time either squattin' or coverin' it up ❑ as a feather merchant in a chicken plucking factory during a whirlwind ❑ as a dog in a fire hydrant factory ❑ as a grasshopper on a red ant bed ❑ as a prairie dog after a big rain ❑ as a one-legged field goal kicker on a frozen field ❑ as a coyote chasin' four different rabbits ❑ as a cranberry merchant ❑ as bees in a honeysuckle patch ❑ as an old hen with a young chick ❑ as a New Orleans bartender during Mardi Gras ❑ as a pair of jumper cables at a county fair ❑ as a termite with a tapeworm ❑ as a long-nosed weevil in a cotton patch ❑ as a cat tryin' to cover up all the manure in a feed lot

BUSY WORK Rat killing ❑ everyday knittin'

BUTT, BIG *See Rear End, Large*

BUZZARDS The county Hygiene Society

C

COLD — it was so cold my teeth were chattering and they were in a jar on the dresser

C

CAFE Beanery ❏ eatery ❏ ptomaine tavern ❏ chili parlor or ranch ❏ grub corral

CAJUN (IN TEXAS) A bugalee

CAJUN COOKING Dip frozen meat in black pepper and throw it into a blast furnace. *See also Toast, Burnt*

CALF FRIES Mountain oysters, prairie oysters, or Oklahoma oysters. The terms are also used to describe lamb, pig, or turkey fries, all of which are the testicles from the animal that are removed during castration.

CALICO FEVER A fatal disease to bachelerhood

CALIFORNIA Although he wasn't too country, W. C. Fields may have said it best with, "California is the only state in the union where you can fall asleep under a rose bush in full bloom and freeze to death."

CALL HIS BLUFF Check his hole card.

CALM She was so calm she could thread a needle in an earthquake.

CALM AND COLLECTED He don't ever turn a hair, which is a saying that comes from horseback riding. After being ridden, a horse's coat will become ruffled and require currying. If a horse isn't ridden he stays calm and his hair doesn't turn.

CALM AS A plate of spit ❏ a boot in the closet ❏ a road kill ❏ a pound of calf liver on a platter

CALM DOWN Turn your burners down ❏ don't get your tail over the dash ❏ it's the switchin' tail that catches the cockleburs ❏ don't bust your bloomers ❏ the man who loses his head is usually the last to miss it

CALORIES Weight lifters

CAN'T BE DONE You can't take back a rock once it's been thrown ❏ you can't reuse a light bulb

CAN'T CHANGE You can put angel wings on a devil but he'll still stick his fork in you.

CAN'T FIND ANYTHING I wouldn't want to be hangin' from a rope he was looking for. The implication here is that if you were hanging from a rope he was looking for, you'd be good and hung before he found it.

CAN'T REMEMBER I've slept since that happened, implying that once you go to sleep you forget everything that has previously happened.

CAPABILITIES, LIMITED *See Limited Capabilities*

CAR *See Automobile*

CARD PLAYER He's luckier with cards than with horses 'cause he don't ever get to shuffle the horses.

CAREFREE He ain't got nothing to do but spit, whittle, and watch the squirrels.

CAREFUL Watch your step when the chips are down ❑ taste the food before you salt it ❑ don't run against the rope *See also Be Careful*

CAREFUL AS A big chested girl in a string bikini ❑ as a

fry cook in a nudist colony ('cause he never knows where splattering grease might land) ❑ as a buck naked cowboy crawling through a barbed wire fence ❑ as a small boy trying to wrap a large scorpion in a Kleenex ❑ as a cat on a marble table ❑ as a weasel suckin' eggs. Theodore Roosevelt once said that a weasel was the only animal that could suck the guts out of an egg without breakin' the shell. *See also Walk Carefully*

CARELESS BEHAVIOR That ain't no way to run a railroad.

CARESS, ROUGH A love lick

CARPENTER, POOR He couldn't drive nails in Jell-O ❑ the only way he can avoid hitting his thumb is if he holds the hammer in both hands and his wife holds the nail

CARPENTER'S LEVEL Whiskey stick

CASH POOR He's land rich, which means he had all his money tied up in real estate before the bottom fell out of the market. Now he's a millionaire on paper but he couldn't loan you a quarter to call a cab.

CASTRATE Steeralize

CAT, MALE A ball bearing mouse trap

CATS Are like Baptists, they raise hell but no one can ever catch them at it.

CATTLE, THIN Those cows are so thin you could use carbon paper and brand three or four at the same time ❑ those cows are so thin that six or seven of 'em would have to stand up at one time to make a single shadow ❑ those cows look like they only got one gut ❑ those cows are so thin we have to tie 'em together with rawhide to keep 'em from fallin' apart

CATTLEMEN There are two types of cattlemen, those who go broke and those who stay broke.

CAUGHT OFF GUARD They ate me up before I knew they were hungry.

CAUSE HIM TROUBLE Drop him in the grease, which basically means put him in a bad situation and let him cook awhile ❑ mix a little misery into his tranquility

CAUSED TROUBLE That muddied up the water ❑ that stirred up the manure

CAUTION Don't rein the horse when he's jumping ❑ never spur a swimming horse ❑ don't believe everything you read on tombstones ❑ never insult an alligator until you have crossed the river ❑ the fewer knots you get on your head the better off you are ❑ give a lyin' drunk a wide berth. There is an old country saying which goes: "The three most fatal things in the Old West were smallpox, bad horses, and ignorance enough to argue with a liar full of whiskey. "

CAUTIOUS Keeps his seat belt on in a car wash ❑ he wears a belt and suspenders ❑ looks both ways before crossing a one way street ❑ as a fat fryer on Sunday morning ❑ he wears a cast-iron athletic supporter

CAUTIOUS, OVERLY He put a safety belt on his commode seat ❑ he'd ride a mile to spit

CELEBRATE We're gonna sing all day and eat on the ground.

CELEBRATED TOO MUCH He really lived it up, now he'll never live it down.

CEMETERY The last resort

CENTER Smack dab in the middle as in "I shot that old boar smack dab between his runnin' lights."

CERTAIN If I ain't right, I'll kiss your backside in a department store window and give you half an hour to draw a crowd and sell tickets ❑ you can write that on the wall in ink ❑ you can paint that on the barn in waterproof paint

CHALLENGING As tryin' to turn a pair of boots back into an alligator ❑ as trying to mate a possum and a porcupine

CHAMBER POT Thunder mug ❑ Arkansas fire extinguisher

CHANCE, FAT *See Chance, Slim,* which raises the question, how come fat chance and slim chance mean the same thing?

CHANCE, SLIM The chance of that happening is about the same as the chance the Baptist church will open a brewery ❑ you got about as much chance of doin' that as Elvis does in makin' it to a football game at the Astrodome ❑ if I were you, I wouldn't hold my breath waitin' for that to happen ❑ you're playin' with a cold deck ❑ you got about as much chance as a grasshopper in a chicken house ❑ as much chance as a red ant at a horned frog convention ❑ as much chance as a hog in a sausage factory ❑ you'll see an iceberg in the Panama Canal before you see that happen ❑ you ain't got a Chinaman's chance, which is a saying that originated during the California gold rush when Chinese workers truly didn't have much of a chance

CHANGE FOR THE WORSE That muddied up the playground

CHANGE SUBJECTS Punch a different button on the jukebox so we can dance to another tune ❑ put the bridle on another horse

CHANGEABLE The ladder works both ways ❑ he changes his mind about as often as a mother changes a sick baby's diaper, which, in case you don't know, is about every five or three minutes

CHANGED HUSBANDS
She found a new dasher for her churn.

CHANGING The tide is turning.

CHANGING TIMES Times must be changing because these days you have to run fast just to stand still.

CHAOS Three truckloads of bean pickers without a foreman

CHAPPED LIPS, SEVERE You look like you been using an Oklahoma credit card (see siphon hose). When you siphon gas, if you get some on your lips they will burn and look like the world's worst case of chapped lips.

CHARACTER What you have left when you've lost everything else ❑ is easier kept than recovered ❑ it's better to go to heaven in rags than to go to hell in a silk suit ❑ like embroidery, is made one stitch at a time ❑ like a glass, even a small crack shows ❑ he's strong enough to bend

CHARACTER, LACKING He'll stand for anything you'll fall for.

CHARMING He could charm a pea out of its pod ❑ he could charm the pants off

the queen mother ❑ he could charm paper off a wall ❑ he could charm the chrome off a bumper hitch ❑ he could charm the gold out of your fillings ❑ he could charm the air out of your tires

CHEAP As an umbrella in a drought ❑ as a Christmas tree in January

CHEAP TO KEEP As a pet clam

CHEAPSKATE Instead of buying Christmas lights, he tied lightning bugs to the branches of the tree ❑ on his honeymoon he drove his wife slowly through an automatic car wash and told her it was Niagara Falls ❑ he wouldn't pay a nickel to see a termite eat a California redwood ❑ he wouldn't have paid a dollar for a box seat at the last supper ❑ he wouldn't pay a dime to see a pissant pull a freight train up Pikes Peak ❑ he never gets a date 'cause he tries to margarine 'em up *See Also Frugal, Miser*

CHEATER A scale thumber, which means whenever he's weighing something he always finds a way to get his thumb on the scale for added weight.

CHECKBOOK One book that always has a sad ending

CHEST OF DRAWERS
Mary Margaret Davis of the
El Paso Times said she was
fourteen years old before she
knew chest of drawers was
not just two words, as in
"chester drawers."

CHICAGO Sha-cargo to a
lot of country folks

**CHICKEN FRIED STEAK,
GOOD** *See Fried Chicken,
Good*

CHICKEN RIB MEAT
Harrikin

CHICKEN Yard bird □ the
difference between chickens
and people is that chickens
sit and lay while people sit
and lie

CHICKEN FRIED STEAK
Simply CFS in most country
cafes

CHIGGERS Red bugs

CHILD Tricycle motor

CHILD, ARROGANT Snot
nosed kid

CHILD, INQUISITIVE He
could take apart a ball
bearing (or pet rock).

CHILD, MEAN He's the
only hell his mamma ever
raised and the worst crop his
daddy ever planted □ he's so
mean his mamma used to
wash him by carryin' him

down to the creek and beatin'
him on a rock.

CHILD, SMALL No bigger
than an uppin' stone. An
uppin' stone was a small
block used by proper ladies
to mount up into a side
saddle.

CHILD, UNAMBITIOUS
When he was young the only
thing he wanted to be was an
invalid.

CHILD, YOUNG Whistle
britches □ one thing that will
always have to be washed by
hand

CHILDHOOD When the
baby grows from an armful
to a handful *See also Baby
Growth Chart*

CHILDISH He wears diaper
pins in his BVDs. *See also
Acting Childish*

CHILDREN When friends
come over, don't brag about
your children. If theirs are
smarter, you'll be
embarrassed. If yours are
smarter, they won't be
impressed. □ When children
are young they step on your
toes, when old they step on
your heart.

**CHILDREN,
WORTHLESS** Their mother
should have stayed a virgin,
which is how Lillian Carter,

mother of Jimmy and Billy, once described herself ❑ their mother has to go to PTA meetings under an assumed name

CHILI, GOOD According to some knowledgeable Texas chiliheads, the chili ain't no good atall if it don't make your ears ring and your nose run. *See Fried Chicken, Good*

CHILI, HOT You have to keep it in the refrigerator to keep from burning down the house ❑ you could use it to loosen bolts ❑ as a mouth full of red ants ❑ if you drop some on your shirt, it'll cauterize your belly button ❑ Sam Rayburn, the longtime Speaker of the House, was once asked why he never went to society dinners in Washington. He replied, "'Cause they never serve chili." ❑ Will Rogers said Texas chili was a "bowl of blessedness."

CHILI, MILD Flame-retardant chili

CHIROPRACTOR Alignment specialist

CHIVALROUS He picks up a woman's dropped hanky even when she ain't pretty. *See also Gentleman*

CHOICE, DIFFICULT The horns of a dilemma as in "I'm on the horns of a dilemma tryin' to decide if I ought to take Betty Sue or Bobby Lu to the dance."

CHORE, BIG You got a big garden and a dull hoe.

CHURCH A gospel mill or doxology works, according to Mark Twain

CHURCH GOER, INFREQUENT He's an ice cream Christian, which means in the summer when the weather gets hot, his desire to go to church melts as fast as ice cream in a cone.

CHURCH, SMALL They pass a saucer instead of a plate.

CIGARETTE A roll of tobacco with fire at one end and a fool at the other.

CITY BOY Raised on concrete

CITY BOY, STUPID He wouldn't know he was in snake country until he had one hooked on his leg by the fangs ❑ he thinks a longneck is a whooping crane ❑ he don't know the difference between Chablis and Charolais

CLARIFY Sand through the varnish and get down to the wood ❑ put a little more butter on that biscuit

CLASS Jerry Jones of the Dallas Cowboys said class is getting up off your knees when you've been knocked down. Judging from the reception he got when he fired Tom Landry, he ought to know.

CLASS REUNION A liar's convention where everyone gets together to see who is falling apart

CLAWS Paw fangs

CLEAN As an old maid's underwear. The last thing any old maid would want would be to get caught with dirty underwear if she had to go to the hospital. ❑ Also, clean as a new barn. It is a scientific fact that the only time a barn is really is clean is when it's brand new and unoccupied.

CLEAN LIVING You ought to live your life so you wouldn't have to worry if the FBI taped your phone line and then played the tapes in church.

CLEAN SHAVEN Bald faced ❑ nekked faced

CLEAN UP YOUR ACT If you can't repent you can quit sinning.

CLINGS Like a dirt dauber's nest to the side of a barn

CLOCK, OLD That clock is so old the shadow of the pendulum has worn a hole through the back of the case.

CLOSE *See Nearby*

CLOSE AT HAND If it had been a snake it would a bit you.

CLOSE CALL That bullet went by close enough to raise a blister ❑ that missed me by a cat hair ❑ I come within a peg of getting hit. Peg comes from old-time dry good stores where yard goods were measured by pegs on a counter that were one inch apart. ❑ I come within a lash of winning. Lash is short for eyelash ❑ he almost got the dollar knife. In the old country carnivals, a pocket knife worth about a dollar was often the best prize. ❑ Of course, close only counts in horseshoes, hand grenades, and dancing.

CLOSE TO THE GROUND He could trip a tumble bug. Any small insect may be substituted.

CLOSE TOGETHER As two fleas on a frozen dog

CLOSED Like a savings and loan

CLOTHES The wife that dresses to please her husband will wear last year's clothes ❑ two reasons a wife won't wear last year's clothes: she doesn't want to and she can't

CLOTHES, FANCY A bib and tucker outfit ❑ he's dressed up like a New Orleans pimp

CLOTHES, SKIMPY She wears barbed wire clothes, which means they protect the property without obstructing the view ❑ she wears dresses that start late and end early ❑ she wears less in public than grandma did in bed *See also Dress, Skimpy*

CLOTHES, TIGHT Her clothes were tighter than a first day bride's. *See also Jeans, Tight*

CLOTHES DON'T MAKE THE MAN It don't matter if you wear boxer shorts or briefs, it's what in them that counts.

CLOUD BURST *See Rain, Heavy*

CLOUDY Clabbered skies ❑ not enough sun to warm a baby rattlesnake

CLUMSY He's like a big, friendly dog in a small room; every time he wags his tail he breaks something ❑ he could get thrown by a stick horse

COCA COLA (Co-cola)

COCKROACHES *See Roaches, Large*

COFFEE Break fluid ❑ tank water ❑ coal oil or coal squeezin's ❑ an experienced country boy knows not to ever wash the coffee mug 'cause it ruins the taste

COFFEE, DECAFINATED Unleaded

COFFEE, STRONG Range coffee ❑ it'll grow hair on your toenails (or saddle horn) ❑ you couldn't drive a nail into it ❑ you couldn't stir it with a stick ❑ so strong you could use it to stop leaks in your radiator

COFFEE, THICK You don't take a drink of it, you take a bite of it ❑ too thick to drink and too thin to plow

COFFEE, WEAK Town coffee ❑ has to have help to get out of the pot ❑ a spoon won't even stand up straight in it ❑ it won't float a horseshoe much less an iron wedge

COFFEE WITH CREAM
Blonde coffee

COFFEE DRINKER, AVID
He'd walk barefooted through a mile long cactus patch for a cup of coffee ❑ he'd rassle the devil himself for one more cup ❑ if he died he'd go to hell if that was the only place they served coffee. Note, these sayings can also be used to described an avid beer drinker or an avid Dr Pepper drinker.

COLD (ILLNESS) Nose runner ❑ some people starve a cold, some people feed a cold, but a lot of others follow the Jack Daniels theory and try to drown it

COLD (WEATHER) It was so cold my teeth chattered and they were in a jar on the dresser ❑ it was so cold the tobacco chewers were spittin' brown ice cubes ❑ it was so cold that four below no longer referred to cows ❑ it was too cold to cough ❑ the only place you could get warm was on the front row of church when the preacher was talking about the flames of hell (or people were going to church just to hear about

the flames of hell) ❑ it was so cold, the hogs had to eat slop through a straw 'cause their jaws were frozen shut ❑ it was so cold the lawyers were standing around with their hands in their own pockets ❑ my teeth were chattering like dice in a crap game

COLD AS An ex-wife's (or ex-husband's) heart ❑ a wart on a Montana well digger's nose ❑ as a mother-in-law's, stepmother's, or witch's kiss ❑ as a possum in a deep freeze ❑ a marble headstone in January ❑ an ice man's shoulder ❑ Wonder Woman's bra ❑ as sheared sheep in a snow storm ❑ as an outhouse on an iceberg

COLD BLOODED PERSON You'd get frostbite on your fingers if you took his pulse.

COLD ENOUGH TO Freeze the balls off a billiard table ❑ to freeze boiling water so fast it'll make warm ice cubes

COLORADO The Kool-Aid state, referring to Coors beer being called Colorado Kool-Aid

COMBINATION, DEADLY
A do-it-yourself man married

to a when-are-you-gonna-do-it woman

COME BACK Ya'll come back now, ya' hear.

COMFORTABLE As a warm bed on a cold morning ☐ as a pair of old boots that know your feet

COMING OF AGE It's struttin' and gobblin' time.

COMMITMENT Sam Rayburn said, "Never commit yourself until you are sure, and once you give your word keep it."

COMMITMENT, LACKING He just won't stay hitched.

COMMITTEE, SMALL A pulpit committee, which is generally a small committee in charge of hirin' and firin' preachers.

COMMITTED He's bound and determined ☐ the difference between being totally committed and just involved is the difference between having bacon and eggs for breakfast. The chicken that provided the egg is involved, the pig is totally committed.

COMMON AS Pig tracks in a barnyard ☐ as cow chips in a pasture ☐ as broken dreams in Hollywood

COMMON KNOWLEDGE Even the chickens under the porch know that.

COMMON SENSE Horse sense ☐ having a lot of horse sense doesn't keep a man from acting like a jackass ☐ Sam Rayburn said, "Having good, common sense ain't enough. You have to exercise it."

COMP TIME Swap work

COMPANY, LARGE It takes a week and a half for gossip to travel from one end to the other.

COMPLACENT You never miss the water till the well runs dry.

COMPLAIN You have heard the old saying, I used to complain about having no shoes until I saw the man with no feet. A different version is, I used to complain about a flooded basement till I saw a man with a flooded attic.

COMPLAINER He'd complain about the service in a self-service cafe.

COMPLICATION That makes the cheese more binding ☐ that woke up the

Indians ❏ the backlog went plumb out. Backlog, in this case, refers to the large log used in kitchen fireplaces before stoves were common in the country. A big log was placed at the back of the stove and it usually burned all night, providing flames for cooking and heat for sleeping. The backlog would smolder all night and even if it burned up completely, there would always be enough embers to start a fire the next morning. Since matches were usually in short supply in those days, if the backlog went completely out and left no embers, it was a major complication.

COMPOSED He's as cool as the center seed in a cucumber. *See also Keep Your Composure*

COMPROMISE Aim high and settle.

CONCEIT Pulps you up but it don't prop you up

CONCEITED When he goes to a doctor, he insists on having his x-rays retouched ❏ he suffers from "I" strain ❏ he joined the navy so the world could see him

CONDOMINIUM Yuppie cage

CONFESSED Fessed up, as in "He fessed up to paintin' those cuss words on the side of school."

CONFIDENCE, LARGE He'd sign up for a fiddle contest and start learnin' how to play as he walked out on the stage.

CONFRONTATION A set to, as in "Blackie and Billy Jack had a real set to and the blood was flowing like beer from a busted barrel."

CONFUSED AS A mosquito in a nudist colony (he knows what to do but he doesn't know where to start) ❏ as a rooster crowin' to the ground ❏ as a mouse in a maze ❏ as Elizabeth Taylor's ring finger ❏ as a fish on a stringer *See also Mass Confusion*

CONFUSING SITUATION Confusion reigned like manure at a horse show.

CONGRESS Is like a country fair, nothing gets more attention than the bull.

CONSCIENCE Is like an old toothless hound dog, it might not bite you but you can't keep it from barking ❏ is like a baby, it has to go to sleep before you do ❏ something that works best when you're being watched ❏

conscience is something that can't be cleaned with detergent

CONSCIENCE, LACKING He don't have any more conscience than a cow in a stampede ❑ he's got about half as much conscience as a tom cat

CONSERVATIVE Like an old cow, he chews more than he bites off.

CONSIDERATE He holds the door open when his wife carries in the groceries.

CONSPICUOUS AS Ballet shoes on a bay mare ❑ as a pimple on a cheerleader's nose ❑ as a rusty link in a chrome chain, which is the only link that gets noticed

CONSULTANT Someone you hire to tell you what you already to know ❑ someone who'll borrow your watch to tell you what time it is

CONTENTED As a hog in mud ❑ as an old dog next to a warm fire

CONTRARY He's so contrary, if he falls in a river and drowns, look for the body up stream.

CONTRIBUTION, POOR She contributed about as much as one poor pullet

would to a trainload of hungry troops.

CONTROL YOURSELF Put a governor on your carburetor ❑ tighten your reins

CONTROVERSY, NON-VIOLENT A cussing or spittin' match

CONVENIENT Mighty (or powerful) handy as in "A pocket on a shirt is mighty handy."

COOK Dough puncher ❑ bean masher ❑ a Cajun cook is a flame thrower 'cause everything he prepares comes out blackened

COOK, INEPT She tried to smoke a turkey but the bird wouldn't stay lit ❑ it takes her an hour to cook minute rice ❑ when she took homemaking classes in school, she dropped out after they covered thawing ❑ she can't open an egg 'cause it don't have no pull tab ❑ she couldn't cut warm butter with a hot butcher knife

COOK, INEXPERIENCED She cooks pea and turnips in the same pot ❑ where there's smoke, she's cooking ❑ when she cooks banana pudding she don't peel the bananas ❑

43

if it wasn't for pepper and ketchup, we'd starve

COOK, POOR Her cooking would gag a sword swallower ❑ you can taste feathers in her chicken fried steak ❑ the best thing she makes for dinner is reservations ❑ she can scorch water trying to boil it ❑ you could use one of her pancakes to patch an inner tube ❑ flies commit suicide in her kitchen ❑ she gave some scraps to a stray dog and it paralyzed him ❑ you could break a tooth on her Jell-O ❑ if you ask her to a party, have someone else make the dip ❑ her pancakes are so thin they only have one side ❑ she has UFOs in her kitchen, unidentified frying objects

COOKIES, GOOD They'd make you hit your grandmother to get another one

COOL As the other side of the pillow

COOL HEAD A cool head may keep you out of trouble but cold feet work much better.

COOPERATION We all can't play the same instrument but we all can play in the same key ❑ we don't all have the same voice but we all sing the same song

COOPERATIVE EFFORT A load is much lighter with several mules carryin' it.

COPPERHEAD SNAKE Diamondmouth copper back

COPULATION Mattress thrashin' ❑ leg rasslin'

CORN ON THE COB Roastin' ears

CORNBREAD Arkansas wedding cake

CORNERED You're like a frog in a blender, you got nowhere to turn to.

CORRECT You're mighty shoutin' right. *See also Yes*

CORRECTIVE ACTION You better put some oil on those troubled waters, which is a reference to oldtime sailors believing that spilling oil on rough sea would calm the water.

COSMETICS Chemical warfare ❑ wife preserver

COTTON, POOR Bumblebee cotton, which is cotton that is so low a bee can stand on the ground to suck a blossom

COUNTERFEIT, POOR QUALITY Couldn't fool a blind man

COUNTRY BOY Redneck ❑ Bubba ❑ he wears boots

because of his roots ❑ he went barefooted so long that when he finally did get a pair of shoes he wore 'em out from the inside ❑ "When someone says he's just a country boy, you better keep your hand on your pocket book," said Lyndon Johnson. What he meant was, just 'cause someone is a country boy, don't assume he's a country bumkin.

COUNTRY BOY, DRESSED UP You can see the hanger creases in his suit, which means country folks don't care to wear suits unless they have to, such as to a marryin' or buryin.'

COUNTRY BOY, SMART He may not eat possum, coon, armadillo, or jackrabbit but he knows where to find 'em if another Depression breaks out.

COUNTRY GIRL Redneck girl ❑ heaven in blue jeans

COURAGE He's got grit in his craw ❑ it don't take no doctor to cure cold feet ❑ something you have till you need it ❑ brave men don't admit courage, cowards don't admit fear

COURT, CROWDED Overdue process of law

COURTHOUSE BENCH (OR STEPS) Liars' bench, which is a reference to the old-timers who don't have much to do but sit on a bench down at the courthouse and tell lies all day.

COURTING Is like dying, you got to do it yourself

COURTSHIP A man chasing a woman till she catches him ❑ the time when a young lady tries to decide if she can do better

COVERED Like a wall under a fresh coat of paint

COWARD The only time he'll stand his ground is if he's buried standin' up ❑ old feather legs, which means he isn't worth much in a fight. The term comes from cockfighting where birds with lots of feathers on their legs are usually not fierce fighters. ❑ he has the guts of the skeleton ❑ he won't wear contact lenses 'cause no one would know he was wearing glasses ❑ he's afraid to kill time ❑ electric socks couldn't warm up his cold feet ❑ someone who thinks with his feet when danger comes calling ❑ if you see a coward with a gun, make yourself scarce

COWARDICE The man without courage better have a fast horse or fast legs or both.

COWARDICE CURE If your knees start knockin,' kneel on 'em.

COWBOY Someone who is paid to out-think a cow ❑ any cowboy that claims he ain't been throwed is a liar

COWBOY, GOOD When he's in doubt, he lets his horse do the thinking.

COWBOY, OLD A cowboy who hands out good advice 'cause he's too old to set a bad example.

COWBOY, POOR He let his alligator mouth overload his jaybird cowboy ability ❑ he'd ride a sore backed horse ❑ the only reason his spurs are rusty is 'cause he wears 'em in the shower

COWBOY, SISSY He don't ride horses 'cause saddles don't come with safety belts.

CRACKED OPEN Like an egg laid by a tall chicken

CRAYFISH East Texas or Louisiana lobsters

CRAZY His genes are loose ❑ he ain't parked too close to the curb ❑ he's a few fish short of having a full stringer ❑ he's a few pickles shy of a full barrel ❑ he's a few peaches short of a full bushel ❑ there's a few spokes missing from his wheel ❑ his biscuit is a little short of baking powder ❑ one of his tires is out of balance ❑ his elevator don't stop at all the floors ❑ he don't have both oars in the water ❑ he's crazy and I can prove it. He lives in New York City and he likes it. *See also Idiot, Strange Person*

CRAZY AS A bullbat. Often in the late afternoon the bullbats fly in various directions giving the impression they are crazy, which they may very well be ❑ as a goat at mating time ❑ as an outhouse rat ❑ as a road lizard ❑ as a March hare

CREEK, FLOODED The water in the creek got so high you had to look up to see the bottom, or you could see under it, both of which imply you were under water. *See also Water, Deep*

CREDIT CARD A plastic mugger

CREDIT, BAD He can't even borrow trouble.

CREDIT, MISAPPLIED Lightning does the work, thunder gets the credit.

CRIME Something that does not pay unless you're a television writer ❑ if people fought crime as much as they fight sin, this would be paradise

CRIME, SMALL Chicken larceny

CRITICISM Is like dynamite, it ought to be handled by experts ❑ remember, criticizing an egg is a lot easier than laying one

CROOK He knows his rights better than his wrongs. *See also Thief*

CROOK, STUPID He held up a post office and then tried to pay his lawyer in stamps ❑ he tried to hold up a savings and loan company with a gun instead of gettin' a job there

CROOKED He could sleep in the shadow of a post hole auger ❑ as a snake in a cactus patch

CROSS-EYED Gotch-eyed ❑ she was so cross-eyed, when she cried the tears rolled down her back ❑ she was so cross-eyed that her eyeballs could swap sockets ❑ he could watch a tennis match without moving his head

CROWDED There was more people there than there was rednecks at the last white sock sale. A lot of good ol' boys who have to work for a living like to wear white socks under their lace-up work boots so they really turn out for a sale. ❑ everyone in the zip code was there ❑ you have to sit on your fist and use your thumb for a back rest if you want to sit down

CRY Spill some tears

CRY A LOT She shed enough tears to short out the jukebox in a honky tonk ❑ she cried more than the onion chopper in a Cajun restaurant ❑ she cried enough to fill a number three wash tub (or a rain barrel) ❑ she was putting out more water than a patio fountain

CUPBOARD Kitchen safe

CUPID George Farquhar said it best when he described Cupid as "a blind gunner."

CURE That'll cure it as sure as an eggshell full of red pepper will cure a dog from suckin' eggs.

CURIOUS He came to town to see the fat lady, which is a reference to the traveling carnival shows that made regular stops in country towns. The carnival always included, among other oddities, a fat woman and it seems the country boys were always curious to see just how fat she was.

CURIOUS AS A kitten in a new room ❑ as a calf in a new pasture

CURLING IRON Beau catcher

CURSE, COUNTRY STYLE I'll see you in hell plowing behind a blind mule in hard ground.

CUSSES A LOT He can cuss a gate off its hinges, a wheel off a wagon, or the feathers off a buzzard ❑ he can cuss bacon into a sizzle ❑ no matter how much he cusses, remember the only time cuss words will blacken your eye is when they're attached to a fist

CUT DOWN Like summer wheat

CUT UP *See Bloody and Knife Fight Victim*

CUTTING HORSE, GOOD Could cut the seeds out of a watermelon and not break the rind ❑ could cut fleas off a mongrel dog

CUTTING TORCH Blue tip wrench

CYNIC He knows everything but don't believe anything.

D

DUMB — he don't have the sense to bring in his head before he brings down the window

D

DADGUMIT damgotit

DAIRY FARMER Owes everything he has to udders

DAMN Day-um, as in "Frankly may dear, I don't give a dayum."

DANCE, ENTICING She's showin' her linen, which means parts of her under-garments are showing while she moves on the dance floor.

DANCER, GOOD He can dance to the national anthem ❑ he likes to dance so much he'd dance barefoot in a thistle patch

DANCER, LARGE He looks like a waltzing rhino.

DANCING A contact sport ❑ hog rasslin' ❑ the difference between rassling and dancing is that some holds are barred in rassling

DANCING AROUND Like a drunk spider. This is an old country saying and yet years of research have failed to uncover a single person who will admit to actually having ever seen a drunk spider.

DANCING CLOSE If you hold that girl any closer you'll be behind her.

DANCING WITH AN UGLY MAN She's rasslin' a hog.

DANCING WITH AN UGLY WOMAN He's rasslin' a pig.

DANGEROUS AS Walking into a lion's cage with a pocket full of pork chops ❑ as a copperhead under your comforter, which means when you crawl into bed you've got more company than you want ❑ as a cock-roach in the control panel of a nuclear power plant ❑ as riding the New York subway naked (or with your clothes on) ❑ as tryin' to put your foot down while it's in your mouth ❑ as sleeping in a waterbed with long toenails ❑ as playing with a cocked cannon ❑ as a walking rocker on a high porch. A walking rocker is one that moves just a smidgen (little bit) each time you rock back and forth. If such a rocker happened to be out on the porch and you happened to be in it and not paying attention, you might just "walk" right off the porch and break something you don't want broke. *See also Risky*

DANGEROUS SITUATION You'd be better off sittin' in the electric chair and prayin' for a power failure ❑ you got a black widow in your boot ❑ you're courtin' the sheriff's daughter ❑ you're skating on warm ice, which is just a couple of shades more dangerous than skating on thin ice ❑ you're walkin' under a Ferris wheel. In the early parts of the 20th century, about the only time county folks had any real fun was when they went to the local county fair, which almost always included some sort of Ferris wheel. The rides were exciting but there was a problem. A lot of country boys chewed tobacco all the time, even when on a ride. Now, if they happened to be near the top of the Ferris wheel when they needed to spit, which was often the case, they naturally just spit out the side of the gondola. Well, if you happened to be walking underneath, you got splattered.

DARING He's got grit in his gizzard and sand in his craw.

DARK You couldn't see your face in front of you ❑ it was so dark, if you struck a match you'd have to turn on a flashlight to see if the match was still lit ❑ it was as dark as it would have been to a blind flea on a black cat under a bushel of wet charcoal

DARK AS The inside of a boot ❑ the inside of a cow (or black bear) ❑ a wolf's mouth

DARK NIGHT It was such a dark night, the raindrops had to ask directions to find the ground ❑ it was so dark the bats stayed home

DAY, GOOD Any day that you wake up with a pulse is a good day. An old-timer once remarked that every day when he woke up, the first thing he did was check the obituaries to see if his name was listed. If it wasn't, he knew it would be a good day. That same man also wondered how people manage to die in alphabetical order.

DEAD AS A wooden Indian ❑ a sardine in a can ❑ a fly in molasses ❑ a bear that's a rug in front of the fireplace

DEADLY COMBINATION
A jealous husband and an
active imagination

DEATH The only known
cure for birth

DEBT The only thing you
can acquire without money

DEBT, BAD You ain't never
gonna see penny one of what
he owes you.

DECEIVING Gib Lewis said
of changing the Texas
constitution: "It's one of
those things that sounds
good and tastes bad."

DECEPTION He pissed in
my boots and told me is was
rainwater.

DECORATOR, POOR If
she'd been a consultant at
the creation, we'd have red
grass and pastel trees.

DEDICATED He likes his
job as much as a chicken
likes working with eggs.

DEFENDER, STAUNCH
He'd stand in the hedge and
take up the gap, which is
how Texan Leon Jaworski
was described in a eulogy
after his death.

DELICATE As frost on a
moonbeam

DELICIOUS Pure dee good
eatin' ☐ chin lickin' good *See
also Taste, Good*

DELICIOUS LOOKING
Looks tasty as a spitted
chicken.

DEMOCRAT Will Rogers,
one of the favorite sons of
Oklahoma, once said, "I am
not a member of any organized political party. I am a
Democrat." ☐ According to
the old country saying, not
all Democrats are horse
thieves, but all horse thieves
are Democrats.

DEMOCRAT, DEVOUT
Yellow dog Democrat, which
means he'll vote the straight
Democratic ticket even if
there is a yellow dog on the
ballot.

DENIAL James B. McSheehy
once said, "I deny the allega-
tions and defy the alligator."

DEPRESSED He's in low
cotton, which is the opposite
of someone doing well being
in high or tall cotton.

DEPRESSION When the
poor house goes bankrupt

DEPUTY (Deppity)

DESIRABLE I'd like to
have that as much as an old
maid would like to have a
Mrs. on her tombstone ☐ I'd

53

give my war pension for it ❏ I'd give my ring finger up to the second knuckle for that ❏ that's worth riding through blisters for. If you start riding and get a blister, the natural inclination is to stop. If you keep riding right through the blisters, you must be after something very desirable.

DESK, LARGE You'd have to be a distance runner to chase a secretary around that sucker ❏ looks like the deck of an aircraft carrier

DESPERATE You're huntin' hungry. If you go hunting when you're hungry, you'll tend to shoot at anything and take chances you might not otherwise take ❏ when you got nothing to lose, try anything

DESPERATION A drowning man will grab at a sword.

DESTITUTE I'm so bad off I couldn't buy a pair of pants for a pissant ❏ I had to fast twice last week to keep from starving to death ❏ I ain't got a pot to pee in or a bed to slide it under *See also Broke*

DETERMINE THE LOSER Figure out whose train got robbed

DETERMINED Dead set on ❏ I'm gonna do it, come hell or high water ❏ I'll do it by hook or by crook ❏ I'm gonna do that even if it harelips every cannibal in the Congo, every mule in Missouri, every Indian in Oklahoma, every goat in Arkansas, every pretty girl in Texas, or every coon in Louisiana. Take your pick. ❏ Davy Crockett said, "I'm determined to stand up to my lick log, salt or no salt."

DETROIT (DEE-troit)

DIAMOND A hunk of coal that made good ❏ most girls will tell you that the only thing harder than a diamond is getting one

DIARRHEA The green apple nasties ❏ the Mexican water trot or Mexican two-step ❏ Arkansas travels ❏ the backdoor trots, which obviously is a reference to trotting out the back door and heading to the outhouse in a hurry

DID THE IMPOSSIBLE He caught lightning in a bottle.

DID YOU EVER (Jevver), pronounced as one word

DIED He roped a cloud and rode off to the great beyond ❏ the fire went out in his boiler or his pilot light went out

DIET A woman will go to any length to change her width.

DIFFERENT As night and day ❑ as snakes and snails

DIFFERENT SITUATION That's another bucket of possums.

DIFFICULT As tryin' to freeze a musical note ❑ as eatin' Jell-O with chopsticks ❑ as eatin' soup with a hole in your spoon ❑ as frog-gigging in maple syrup ❑ as chugalugging a hot beer ❑ as pushing noodles through a keyhole ❑ as raising corn in a concrete field ❑ as tryin' to get a drink out of a fire hose ❑ as digging a ditch in the ocean ❑ as sneezing with your eyes open ❑ as trying to fly a paper kite in a whirlwind ❑ as picking up mercury with a pair of tweezers ❑ as flaggin' down a runaway freight train ❑ as catchin' a house fly under a teacup (which usually results only in a broken teacup) ❑ as shooting pool with a calf rope ❑ as picking rat droppings out of a pepper mill ❑ as getting a Hereford cow out of quicksand ❑ as tryin' to strike a wet match ❑ as

puttin' socks on a rooster ❑ as tryin' to outrun a bull in a fresh plowed field ❑ as trying to swim up a waterfall ❑ as shoving melted butter up a bobcat's behind with a knitting needle ❑ that's a hard crop to plant (or grow)

DIFFICULT SITUATION You're on a panty raid in the athletic dorm ❑ you're swimmin' upstream blindfolded ❑ he's starving to death in the land of plenty ❑ There are, of course, many difficult situations but the most difficult I ever heard about was the ol' boy whose wife caught him cheating on her. When he went to sleep, she got a couple of tubes of super glue and fastened his private parts to his leg. Later that night when her husband got up to go to the bathroom he found out real quick that he was truly in a difficult situation.

DIFFICULT, SOMEWHAT It's just a little harder to make a banker out of a horse thief than it is to make a horse thief out of a banker.

DIFFICULT TO OPEN Nothing is harder to open than a closed mind.

DIGNITY One thing that cannot be preserved in alcohol

DILEMMA Whether you die from the chills or the fever, you're still dead.

DIMWIT His coil ain't wrapped too tight ❑ she took an umbrella to a baby shower ❑ if he went to a mind reader, he'd only be charged half price ❑ the only time he really knows where he is going is when he takes castor oil ❑ he has the mental range of a windshield wiper ❑ you could pull a slow one on him ❑ his roof ain't nailed on too tight (or is short a few shingles) ❑ there ain't no light on in his attic ❑ if brains were dynamite he couldn't blow his nose ❑ if he knew half of what he thinks he knows he'd be dangerous ❑ he undertakes vast projects with half vast ideas

DINNER CALL Come and get it before the grease sets.

DIPLOMACY Lying in state ❑ the ability to dive into a cesspool and not make a splash ❑ the art of saying things in such a way that no one knows what you said

DIPLOMAT Can put all his cards on the table without showing his hand ❑ can make his wife believe she'd look fat in a mink coat ❑ he can tell you to go to hell and make you look forward to the trip ❑ he remembers a lady's birthday but forgets her age ❑ he can let you do all the talkin' while he gets what he wants

DIRECTION "To know where we are going, it's important to know where we have been," said Sam Rayburn.

DIRT ROAD *See Road, Dirt*

DIRTY As an Indian's horse blanket in a drought. The implication here is that the only time an Indian's horse blanket got washed was when it rained.

DISADVANTAGE Jim Reeves of the *Fort Worth Star Telegram* said Jimmy Johnson, coach of the Dallas Cowboys, was "working with a short stick" which meant he was at a disadvantage. After going 1 and 15 his first year, Johnson actually didn't have much of a stick at all ❑ we weren't playing on a level field. This comes from the world of football. If a football field was not level, the theory is that whoever had the lower end most of the time would be at a disadvantage because they would be playing uphill most of the time. Although this saying is generally used by the losing team, it could also be used by the winning team to mean advantage, such as the case of a big underdog pulling a major upset for no apparent reason. In the 1960 Bluebonnet Bowl, Clemson defeated a much larger, much heavier, highly favored team from Texas Christian University. Following the game, Clemson's Frank Howard explained, "Those other boys were so big they tilted the field and we were able to play downhill all the way."

DISADVANTAGED A cat wearing gloves won't catch any mice.

DISAPPEARED Faster than a plate of fried chicken when the preacher comes over for Sunday dinner ❑ like a short beer ❑ he's got the coon and gone

DISAPPEARED SUDDENLY Absquatulated. This term, used by country folks up until about the turn of the century, has become archaic but it is too good a word to be totally forgotten. If you can find a way to work it into a conversation you have a whole story to tell.

DISASTER, EMINENT The firing squad is oiling their guns.

DISCOURAGING As smelling whiskey through the jail house door ❑ as the bottom check fallin' into the well. A bottom check is used to determine how deep you've dug and if it happens to fall into the well, you have to stop to fish it out before you can proceed, which is, to a well digger, very discouraging.

DISGRACE He stepped in the same cow patty twice.

DISH TOWEL Cup towel

DISLIKE I like that about as much as a Vietnam war vet likes Jane Fonda ❑ I never liked you and I always will

DISMISS Show 'em the gate.

DISORGANIZED He bounces around like a pecan in an empty wagon.

DISORIENTED Addled ❑ as a goose in a hail storm

DISPERSED The hogs scattered ever which a way.

DISQUALIFIED You got both hands on the rigging. In rodeo events such as bronc and bull riding, the cowboy must keep one hand free at all times. If he touches the rigging (or the horse) with his free hand, he is disqualified.

DISTANCE, LONG That's four sights down the road ❏ farther away than you can point two or three pointin's away

DISTANCE, SHORT It's just a rooster step away. A rooster step is an indefinite measure of distance that would be short to a person but might be long to a rooster.

DISTANT Nothing is more distant than a relative with money.

DISTRACTING As a swarm of gnats. When the small insects get to swarming, they have been known to stop baseball games, prevent marriages, and provide drunks with some solid food.

DISTURBED Someone rattled his cage.

DISTURBING SITUATION That like to killed my soul.

DIVERSION Somebody kill a skunk. The theory is that a dead skunk will stink up the place so much that everyone's attention will be diverted.

DIVORCE Holy deadlock ❏ the past tense of marriage ❏ makes strangers of bed-fellows ❏ matrimonial recycling

DIVORCED COUPLE They found out they weren't fit to be tied so they untied the knot.

DIVORCED MAN A gone gander that still has to supply corn to the goose.

DIVORCED WOMAN Born again virgin ❏ the only support she gets is from her panty hose ❏ she found out the knot she tied was a slip knot *See also Changed Husbands*

DO IT CHEAP Poor boy it

DO IT QUICK You better get it done in one-half less than no time ❏ you better get it done in less than two shakes of a lamb's tail

DO IT RIGHT You can't tell how deep the well is by measuring the pump handle.

DO IT RIGHT THE FIRST TIME If you're gonna put a horse in a trailer, you don't put him in once for practice and then take him out for another try.

DO IT YOURSELF The warmest fire is made from wood you cut yourself ❏ skin your own game ❏ you gotta pick your own nose

DO WHAT I SAY If you'll do what I say, you'll be in like a burglar.

DO WHAT YOU CAN If you can't preach, you can pass the plate.

DO WHAT YOU WANT If you're feelin' froggy, jump ❑ if you got an itch, scratch it

DO-GOODER Living with a do-gooder is a heck of a lot harder than being one.

DO-IT-YOURSELFER, EXPERT He could repair the crack of dawn.

DOESN'T MATTER TO ME That don't make me no never mind ❑ that ain't no skin off my backside (or nose) ❑ as long as I don't have a dog in the fight I don't care who wins

DOG (dawg) Flea catcher ❑ a dog is man's best friend because he wags his tail rather than his tongue ❑ you keep a dog but you only feed a cat, which means a dog is faithful but a cat ain't

DOG, GOOD A coon whippin' dog. It takes a good huntin' dog to get a coon up a tree but it takes a better dog to whip the coon ❑ a close tracker, which means he stays on the trail ❑ a meat gitter, which is a dog that

will hunt. A dog that'll hunt helps fill the dinner table, but one that won't hunt is just another mouth to feed. *See also Hunting Dog, Good*

DOG, HARMLESS Never met a man he didn't lick.

DOG, LAZY He has to lean against a fence to bark ❑ wags his tail up and down 'cause it takes less energy ❑ he won't even wag his own tail

DOG, SMART Every dog knows the difference between being tripped over and kicked at ❑ I have a dog that is so smart she knows dinner is ready when the bell sounds on the microwave oven

DOG, STUPID He can get lost under the house.

DOING GOOD Now you're cooking with gas ❑ you're flying with the big birds

DOING IT WRONG You're not holding your mouth right, which is often said to someone who is trying to do something but just can't quite get it right.

DOMINO Bone ❑ rock ❑ stone ❑ tile ❑ seed

DOMINO SPOTS Pips ❑ dots ❑ points

DON'T ARGUE I won't hear of it as in "Don't even try to

pay for the beer 'cause I won't hear of it."

DON'T BLAME ME Don't lay that at my doorstep ❏ don't put my brand on that

DON'T BOTHER ME Why don't you go cry in one hand and piss in the other to see which one gets full first?

DON'T BRAG Let your dog do your barking.

DON'T CARE My giveadamner is broken.

DON'T CRITICIZE You can't sling mud (or manure) and keep your hands clean.

DON'T DELAY Pretty girls and dead fish don't keep.

DON'T DO IT Why don't you quit before you start? ❏ you're just giving the devil a club he can use to beat your brains out

DON'T KNOW Don't rightly know ❏ I have no more idea than a dead snake has fleas (or than a hog knows when it's Tuesday)

DON'T LOOK BACK Keep your face to the sunshine and you'll never see shadows.

DON'T LOOK FOR TROUBLE There is always someone ready to help you

scratch an itchy trigger finger.

DON'T NEED IT I need that like a hen needs singing lessons ❏ I need that like a frog needs a face-lift ❏ I need that like a sinkin' ship needs water *See also Unwanted*

DON'T OVERREACT Don't use a sledge hammer to crack open an egg.

DON'T TALK BAD If you shovel manure uphill, some of it'll roll back in your face.

DON'T TEMPT HIM I wouldn't put it past him if I was you.

DON'T UNDERSTAND I'm not sure I understand all I know about this.

DON'T UNDERSTAND FULLY I can smell the manure but I can't find the stock pen ❏ I hear the choir singin' but I can't find the church ❏ I can feel the heat but I can't see the flames

DON'T WANT TO I'd rather eat a coil of barbed wire than do that ❏ I'd rather get a root canal than do that ❏ I'd rather have twins than do that ❏ I'd rather kiss the top of your hind leg than do that *See also I Don't Care; Reluctance*

DON'T WORRY About the mule going blind, just load the wagon

DOOMED As a cat in hell with no claws ❑ you're a gone gosling

DOOR-TO-DOOR SELLING Trick or treat practice

DOUBLE JEOPARDY A mother-in-law with a twin sister ❑ one woman teaching another woman to drive. Note: Plain ol' jeopardy would be a woman learning to drive by herself.

DOUBLE TALK Double speak

DOUBTFUL You got about as much chance as that of a cat sittin' on a leaking can of gasoline in hell. *See also Chance, Slim*

DR PEPPER DRINKER *See Coffee Drinker, Avid*

DREAMER Rainbow rider ❑ if you want to make your dreams come true you have to stay up nights

DREAMER, BIG He dreams in technicolor.

DRESS, SHORT If she bent over in that dress you could see all the way to her tonsils.

DRESS, SKIMPY A peek-a-bosom dress, which is one that isn't all there on a woman who is ❑ there ain't enough material in that dress to keep a tick mouse dry in a drizzle ❑ her dress was so skimpy the hemline and the collar were touching ❑ she's wearing a Texas dress, one with plenty of wide open spaces ❑ her clothes represent more dollars than sense

DRESS, TIGHT *See Sweater, Tight*

DRESSED FANCY He looks like he just stepped out of a band box

DRESSED UP Gussied up ❑ dressed up like a poodle in a dog show ❑ dressed better than a Wall Street banker or a Philadelphia lawyer ❑ like a one-eyed jack of diamonds

DRESSES, SLOPPY She wears her clothes as if they were thrown on with a pitch fork ❑ she looks like she tossed her clothes up in the air and ran under them ❑ he's a full grown mess

DRINK, PERFECT Dave Brownfield of Garland, Texas described the perfect drink as one that looks like a mug of beer, smells like fresh

61

coffee, and tastes like a Dr Pepper.

DRINKER, HEAVY Must be a Democrat 'cause there never has been a Republican that can hold more than a pint ❏ he hasn't touched a single drop of whiskey since he discovered the funnel ❏ The late Bobby Layne, of the University of Texas and the Detriot Lions, was a notorious drinker. Teammate Jimmy Orr once said, "You'll run into a million fans who'll claim they once had a drink with Bobby, and none of them are lying."

DRINKERS' ADVICE If you drink like a fish, swim, don't drive.

DRINKING Don't drown your problems, it irrigates them.

DRINKING AND TALKING Jugin' and jawin'

DRINKS A LOT He drinks like he inherited a distillery.

DRIVE WITH CARE Life has no spare.

DRIVER, POOR You can tell he/she believes in God (or life after death). *See also Bad Driver*

DROOLING Your jaw is leaking.

DROPPED Like yesterday's oats in a horse corral ❏ like a bad habit ❏ like spit off a tall building

DROUGHT, SEVERE If you put all the rain we've had in the last three years in a tea cup, there wouldn't be enough water for a flea to skin dive ❏ not only did we have to plow under the cotton, we had to plow under the hogs ❏ it was so dry we had to soak the hogs' heads to get 'em to eat slop ❏ the crows have to lie on their backs to eat the corn ❏ I have a three-year-old catfish that ain't learned to swim *See also Dry and Arid Land*

DRUNK If he got bit by a mosquito it would die of alcohol poisoning ❏ he don't have enough blood in his alcohol system ❏ he got so drunk he tried to take his pants off over his head and made it ❏ he couldn't leave the saloon 'cause it was gettin' too drunk outside ❏ he got so high he had to drink over a net ❏ if he died, he'd have to sober up to fall over ❏ he got dizzy after one drink but can't remember if it was his 12th or 13th ❏ a drunk tongue often tells what's on a sober mind *See* *also Alcoholic; Drunkard, Intoxicated*

DRUNK, ALMOST REFORMED He promised to stop drinking but he never promised to stop lying ❑ he read about the evils of drink and quit reading

DRUNK, VERY Booze blind ❑ loop legged ❑ knee walking, commode huggin' drunk ❑ hymn singing, snot slingin' drunk ❑ he's so drunk, if he died and was cremated it would take the undertaker three days to put out the fire ❑ he was so drunk he grabbed a snake and tried to kill a stick

DRUNK AND STUPID He wanted a stiff drink so he put starch in his beer.

DRUNK COWBOY He was so drunk he couldn't have found a cow if she was in bed with him.

DRUNK DRIVER He puts the quart before the hearse ❑ someone who prefers to drive tight rather than sit tight ❑ he has plenty of hearse power ❑ he drives a drunk car

DRUNK VERSUS ALCOHOLIC The difference between a drunk and an alcoholic is that drunks don't have to go to no meetings ❑

some ol' drunks can never join AA 'cause they are always too drunk to memorize the pledge

DRUNK VERSUS FOOL Drunks eventually sober up, fools never get better.

DRUNKARD He won't be able to die until until the government finds a safe place to bury his liver, which is how Phil Harris once characterized himself ❑ like a horse, you can lead him to water but you can't make him drink it straight ❑ the local blood bank uses his blood to sterilize their instruments ❑ all his friends are in low places ❑ he never gets beaten to the punch ❑ he always wakes up at the crack of ice ❑ he'd rather pull a cork than punch a time clock ❑ he wore out three shot glasses in four years ❑ he only drinks for medicinal purposes but he lives in daily fear of getting sick

DRUNKARD, SINCERE He'd step over half a dozen naked beauty queens to get to a bottle of cheap whiskey.

DRY As a frog covered with desert dust ❑ as a powder keg ❑ as Moses in the middle of the Red Sea ❑ as a sack of Bull Durham ❑ as a wooden

63

leg ❏ so dry the cows are giving powdered milk ❏ the only water you could get was dehydrated

DRY LAND *See Drought; Land, Dry*

DULL (BORING) As ditch water ❏ as rinse water from a Chinese laundry ❏ about as exciting as watching bumpers rust ❏ as watching paint dry ❏ as a fisherman who tells the truth ❏ his idea of excitement is ordering a pizza on his car phone and then trying to beat the delivery man to his house *See also Boring*

DULL PERSON His idea of a good time is to stay home and sort his socks ❏ his idea of excitement is to throw caution to the wind and turn up his electric blanket

DUMB He's about as sharp as a bowling ball ❏ someone gave him a pair of cuff links and he went out to have his wrists pierced ❏ he don't have the sense to pull in his head when he pulls down the window ❏ if brains were dynamite he couldn't blow the wax out of his ears ❏ he was fourteen years old before he could wave good-by ❏ don't know spit from noodles ❏ he'd try to pop the corns on

his feet if he could get 'em in the corn popper ❏ he went deaf in one eye (or blind in one ear) ❏ he's like a pin, his head keeps him from going anywhere ❏ someone asked him to imitate a bird and he tried to fly south ❏ he couldn't scatter manure with a four-dollar rake ❏ he don't have enough brains to pound sand down a rat hole ❏ he couldn't roll a ball down a steep hill ❏ he don't know manure from wild honey ❏ enough to make his doctor the beneficiary in his will *See also Dimwitted, Idiot, Stupid*

DUMB AS A turkey. When it starts raining, a turkey will look up to see where the water is coming from and stand there with his mouth open. If it's a hard, fast rain, the turkey will drown before he realizes what's happening. That's about as dumb as you can get. ❏ dumb as dirt ❏ hair on a barber shop floor ❏ a screwdriver

DURABILITY The post wears out before the hole ❏ that'll last so long you'll swear it must be stuffed with scrap iron

DURATION, LONG That'll take longer than a month of Sundays ❏ long as a coon's age

DURATION, SHORT
That'll last about as long as a rainbow after a spring shower ❑ about as long as an old man's dream

DUST House moss

DUST STORM Oklahoma rain ❑ some people believe that a dust storm means the angels are shakin' out their sheets to get the lice out of heaven

DYING He's fixing to promenade home ❑ he's fixing to gather up over yonder

This space is for your favorite sayings.

EXPECTATIONS — every minnow expects to be a whale someday

E

EARS, DIRTY The only time he washes his ears is when he eats watermelon.

EARS, LARGE His ears are so large he can swat flies with them ❑ his head looks like a loving cup

EARTHQUAKE, SEVERE It shook the hail out of the clouds

EASE UP Give me a little breathin' room.

EASY As slidin' off a greased pig backwards ❑ as fallin' off a rollin' log in the middle of the river ❑ as gettin' up after you sit down on a thumb tack

EASY ISN'T ALWAYS BEST You can grow more cotton in a crooked row than you can in a straight one. Unfortunately a crooked row is harder to plant and harder to plow ❑ if you make your bed hard, you can turn over more often

EASY MONEY The more you chase it the faster it moves.

EASY OBSTACLE That ain't no pond for a swimmer ❑ that ain't no tree for a climber

EASY TO FIND As the pitcher's mound in Yankee stadium ❑ as the deck on an aircraft carrier

EASY WAY OUT As former Texas governor Mark White said, "It's easier to burn down a barn than it is to build one."

EAT A LOT Like a hog's holiday ❑ the only thing he won't eat for dinner is breakfast and lunch ❑ they kicked him out of the army 'cause he ate more than an entire platoon

ECHO A secondhand noise

EDITOR Someone assigned to keep egg off an author's face ❑ he'd edit the sermon on the mount if he found a dangling participle

EDUCATED GUESS He used the SWAG system, which is a scientific wild assed guess. *See also Uneducated Guess*

EDUCATION The only known cure for ignorance

EFFECTIVENESS, POOR That has about as much effect as a BB would have on a bull elephant.

EFFICIENT He's smart enough to build the outhouse on the other side of the woodpile. According to country legend, the smartest country boy would build the outhouse on the other side of the wood pile so when his wife went out on a cold morning, she could stop and pick up some stove wood on the way back and save her husband a trip. ❏ Also, he's so efficient he don't lose nothing but the squeal when he kills a hog. Glen Owen said that when he butchered a hog on the farm, he managed to find a use for just about every part of the carcass. "But," he said, "I never did find anything to do with the squeal."

EFFORT, DIFFERENT The difference between picking corn and cotton is the amount of the stooping.

EFFORT, PRODUCTIVE He's cookin' up some good syrup.

EFFORT, WASTED You're shoveling the sidewalk before it has stopped snowing ❏ you can train a jackass all you want, but it still ain't gonna win the Kentucky Derby ❏ you're looking for gold in a copper mine ❏ your trying to find hen eggs in a rabbit cage

EGG Cackleberry ❏ hen seed ❏ an omelet shell ❏ a whole day's work for a chicken

EGGS, POOR Her eggs aren't cooked, they're vulcanized.

EGGS, SMALL It'd take sixteen of 'em to make a dozen. This saying can be used to describe almost anything small.

EGO Big ideas seldom come from swelled heads ❏ if you get too big for your britches, your hat won't fit either

EGOTIST He was born on third base and thinks he hit a triple ❏ the nice thing about him is that he never goes around talking about other people ❏ a self-made man who worships his creator ❏ he has callouses from patting himself on the back ❏ if you sing your own praises, you'll be a soloist ❏ he can't see anything taller than the smoke from his own chili ❑ he's like a ship in a fog, always blowing his own horn ❑ he don't want a feather for his cap, he wants to wear the whole eagle ❑ she thinks she's the only berry on the bush (or peach on the tree)

ELECTION The only race where most of the people pick the winner

ELECTRICAL SHOCK, MINOR Didn't do as much damage as a shock from a lightning bug

ELECTRICIAN, GOOD He could rewire a lightning bug so it would blink the national anthem in Morse code.

ELECTRICITY 'Lectricity

ELEVATOR MUSIC Wallpaper set to music

EMBARRASSED Egg washes off easier than tar, which means it is better to get a little egg on your face than to be tarred and feathered.

EMBARRASSING SITUATION It even made the moon blush ❑ telling a woman her stockings are wrinkled when she ain't wearing stockings ❑ having your dress tucked into the back of your panty hose ❑

when two eyes meet in the same keyhole from opposite sides of the door

EMBELLISHED He put a little extra mortar on the brick ❑ I think you put a few extra pounds on that fish

EMBROIDERY (em-BRAWD-ry) Needlework

EMOTION *See Overcome with Emotion*

EMPLOYEE RELATIONS Don't muzzle your ox when it is treading out the corn, which could be interpreted to mean let your employee do his job.

EMPLOYEE, POOR He has a sign on his desk proclaiming, "Yes spoken here."

EMPLOYEE, VITAL He's the grease on the wheels.

EMPLOYEE, WORTHLESS If they fired him he wouldn't leave a vacancy.

EMPTY As a Waco dance hall ❑ as a church on Saturday night

EMPTY HEADED His head is so empty he has to talk with his hands to keep from getting an echo.

71

ENCOURAGE Don't belittle, be big.

ENCOURAGEMENT, FIRM A kick in the butt is a step forward ❏ sometimes kicking a man when he's down is the only way to get him up

ENCROACHMENT You're gettin' close to diggin' in my 'tater patch.

END That about puts the rag on the bush. In the country, the rags are washed after all the clothes. Since there usually isn't any room on the clothesline, the rags are "hung" on a handy bush. Therefore, when the rags are on the bush, the washin' is at an end for that day. ❏ quietus (kiw-EAT-us), as in "She found out her husband was fixin' to go huntin' and put the quietus on those plans quicker than a minnow can swim a dipper."

ENDED EARLY It died on the vine like a watermelon in a drought.

ENDING That's all she wrote.

ENDURE IT If you want to see a rainbow you got to put up with some rain.

ENEMIES "A man can't be too careful in the choice of

his enemies," said Oscar Wilde ❏ if you have to pick enemies, pick lazy ones

ENEMY Someone you wouldn't want packin' your parachute

ENJOYABLE I ain't had this much fun since the hogs ate baby sister ❏ I had more fun than a one-eyed tomcat in a fish market ❏ as much fun as skipping stones on a still pond *See also Fishing*

ENTERTAINER, UGLY He's got a face built for radio.

EQUAL TO Even up with

EQUALITY Every man has an equal opportunity to seek his own level ❏ on a gentle horse, all men are expert riders ❏ a blind horse can see equally well from either end ❏ the only time equality counts is being equal to the occasion

ERRED You really pissed in your whiskey this time.

ESCORT Carry, as in "Can I carry you to the barn dance next Saturday?"

ETC Something you use to make people think you know more than you really do

EVERLASTING As Elvis

EVERY MAN FOR HIMSELF Every man has to skin his own skunk.

EVERYTHING IS FINE There ain't a bump in the road, as Glenn Raines might say.

EVERYTHING The whole hide, including the tail ❑ jocks to socks. When Jerry Jones took over the Dallas Cowboys he said he was going to be involved in everything from "socks to jocks." ❑ the whole nine yards. Material would usually come in nine-yard bolts so if you got the whole bolt, you got the whole nine yards.

EVIL MAN *See Male, Evil*

EVIL PERSON The only place he'll make a name for himself will be on a tombstone.

EVIL, SOMEWHAT He's just one good scare away from being virtuous.

EX-HUSBAND A former pain in the neck (or certain other parts of the anatomy) ❑ a man who was given enough rope to skip ❑ a man who'll be reminded of the good times every time he sends a child support check

EX-WIFE A wife lasts for the length of the marriage, an ex-wife lasts forever ❑ if you want to keep the beer real cold, keep it next to the heart of an ex-wife ❑ the only thing more expensive than a wife is an ex-wife

EXASPERATED All put out ❑ as a drummer with the hiccups ❑ you're acting like the pay toilet costs a quarter and you only got a dime

EXASPERATING That makes my backside bite a hole out of the seat in my pickup ❑ that really gets my goat ❑ wouldn't that cock your pistol ❑ that'll rattle your slats (or cage) ❑ that would make a preacher pack his Bible ❑ that rips the rag off the bush ❑ that'll cork your pistol ❑ that'll blow your dress up ❑ that'll take the ink out a your pen ❑ that'll take the starch out of your shorts

EXCEEDING YOUR LIMITS You're boring with a big auger.

EXCELLENT Hard down good ❑ the cream of the crop

EXCITED As a pullet anticipating her first egg (Just think about what an experience that must be.) ❑ he's got his tail over the dashboard ❑ she's hot as a billy goat in a pepper patch ❑ wild as a peach orchard boar ❑ as a spring lizard in a hen house ❑ she's so excited she has to walk sideways to keep from flying ❑ his eyes where shining like two fried eggs in a slop bucket ❑ her eyes were blinking faster than a frog's eyes in a hailstorm ❑ his eyes were big as saucers ❑ his heart was pounding like the devil beatin' tanbark

EXCITING It'll give you a quiver in your liver ❑ not only will it put lead in your pencil, but it will make you forget you were supposed to write home ❑ that'll set your tail feathers on fire

EXCITING AS Tryin' to hitch an ornery mule to a plow

EXCLAMATION Well shut my mouth! ❑ Well toot my horn! ❑ Don't that beat all! ❑ Well, I swan! *See also Oath*

EXCLUDED He was invited not to come.

EXHAUSTED My tired hurts ❑ feelin' mighty white-eyed, which is a reference to the fact that your eyes seem to get bigger and whiter when you are very tired

EXHIBITIONIST She bought clear plastic window blinds and see through curtains.

EXPECTATIONS, HIGH Every minnow figures to be a whale someday.

EXPECTATIONS, LOW If you go hunting with a tom cat, you can't expect to catch nothing but field mice and crippled birds ❑ you can't expect anything from a hog but a grunt

EXPENDABLE Cannon fodder

EXPENSIVE That'll put your savings account on the critical list ❑ that'll knock a hole in your wallet big enough to put your fist through

EXPERIENCE Live and learn or die and forget about it ❑ the best thing to sweat the fat off the brain *See also Wisdom*

EXPERIENCE COUNTS An old coyote knows the shortest way to the chicken coop. Any broom will sweep but an old broom knows where the dirt is ❑ a new hat looks good but an old hat knows the shape of your head

EXPERIENCED It's better to know the country than to

be the best cowboy ❑ he's been to the barn a few times ❑ knows how to use hay hooks ❑ too old a cat to be fooled by a kitten ❑ knows the ropes ❑ he's been to more than one rodeo

EXPERT Someone who knows all the right answers if you ask all the right questions

EXPLAIN IT BETTER Put it down where the calves can get at it ❑ wring out the rag some ❑ chew it a little finer

EXPLANATION Something that ain't necessary for friends and is wasted time on enemies

EXPLODED Like a full beer can that had been in the paint mixing machine down at the hardware store

EXPOSED We been smoked out a' the hole.

EXPRESSION *See Shocked Expression*

EXPRESSION, STRANGE You look like you're passin' a peach pit ❑ you look like you just swallowed a fishing lure ❑ you look like lightning just struck your zipper ❑ you look like you just took your temperature with the baby's thermometer

EXPRESSION, SURPRISED You look like you just reached into your minnow bucket and something slimy wrapped around your hand ❑ you look like you just took a big ol' drink out a somebody's spit can

EXTRA Boot, as in "What'll you give me to boot if we trade horses?" In the old days some country folks used lagnappe (land yap) for boot.

EXTRA EFFORT If you work around here, you better soak your screws. That saying comes from working with wood. If you put forth the extra effort to soak screws in a light lubricant or even thick, soapy water, they will go into hardwood much easier than unsoaked screws. Therefore, anyone who soaks his screws is putting out extra effort.

EXTRAORDINARY A real doozey ❑ a lalapalooza

EXTREMELY Big time, for which there are numerous examples throughout this book

EYES A woman's eyes will often tell you what her mouth can't.

EYES, BEADY His eyes are closer together than an earthworm's.

EYES, RED Your eyes got more lines than a Mississippi road map.

EYES, SHRUNKEN Your eyes look like two rabbit pellets in a snow bank.

EYES, SOFT Her eyes look soft as ribboncane syrup on a tin plate.

EYES, WIDE OPEN Popeyed

EYESIGHT, GOOD He can spot a gnat at fifty yards and tell if it's a male or female.

EYESIGHT, POOR He lost his glasses and couldn't look for them till he found them.

F

FEMALE SUPERIORITY — roosters crow, hens deliver

F

FACADE He's all vine and no 'taters, which is a slight variation to the popular "He's all hat and no cattle."

FACE, LARGE She's got enough chins for three faces.

FACE, SKINNED UP He's got bicycle face. In the late 1800s the bicycle was becoming very popular but a lot of people didn't understand how to ride or how to stop. This prompted many doctors around the nation to report they were treating a new malady they named "bicycle face."

FACE, UGLY He looks like he rang the church bell with his face.

FACE THE MUSIC If you can't face the music you'll never lead the band.

FACT If I ain't tellin' you the absolute truth, well then I'm grass and God's a lawn mower ❑ if it ain't true, there ain't a pretty girl in Texas or Georgia ❑ sure as grass will grow in a crack ❑ you can bet the railroad on that

FACTS It is easier to get facts then to face them.

FAILURE He sat down in his own bear trap ❑ he hitched his wagon to a falling star ❑ his cotton didn't come up ❑ he started out with nothing and has most of it left ❑ he took the path of least resistance ❑ made his mark in the world but someone erased it ❑ he aimed to do right but he was a poor shot ❑ he aimed high but he was shooting blanks ❑ her cake was all dough

FAITHFUL As an old hat. Outside of his horse, there was nothing more special to a cowboy than his hat. He used it as a rain bonnet, sun shield, a fan for the cook fire, as well as an emergency water bucket and feed bag. A cowboy often became mighty attached to his hat and treated it like an old friend. More than a few range riders actually drowned while tryin' to retrieve their favorite headgear after it had blown into a swollen river. One cowboy claimed he had a hat that had outlived a dozen pair of boots, three saddles, and one or two horses. He said the best thing about that old hat was that it never did forget the shape of his head. Because the hat was always ready to go where the cowboy went, never drank any of his beer, never ran off with his best girl, never broke a promise, and never let the cowboy down when the goin' got tough, a lot of old-time cowboys considered their hat to be their most faithful friend. If women, men, dogs, horses, and friends were as faithful as an old hat, the world would be a better place to live in.

FAKE As a three-dollar wig ❑ as eyelashes on a Las Vegas showgirl ❑ as a hooker's affection

FALL, SERIOUS He took a head-over-rain-barrel spill.

FALLEN ANGEL She fell out of heaven and landed in the devil's lap.

FALSE That's nothing but Chamber of Commerce statistics ❑ as store bought

teeth ❑ as entries in a truck driver's log book

FALSE IMPRESSION Anyone can look tall when surrounded by midgets.

FAMILY, LARGE They got enough kids to bait a trot line.

FAMILY, SORRY They vote dry, then move away. In Texas, the drinking laws are about as confusing as Chinese arithmetic. In some places you can drink and in other places you can't. Usually, the right to drink is settled by a local option election, and the sorriest of families would all vote dry even if they knew they were moving away.

FAMILY LOYALTY Blood is thicker than water, which means stand by your family members.

FANATIC Someone who sticks to his guns, whether they are loaded or not

FAR AWAY It's a three-greasin' trip, which means you'd have to grease the wagon three times to get there and back.

FARM LABORER Hoe hand ❑ field hand

FARMER He doesn't have to go to work, he wakes up surrounded by it.

FARMER, EXPERT He knows everything there is to know about cows, sows, and plows ❏ the only thing he can't do around a farm is lay an egg

FARMER, INEPT He got his tractor hung in reverse and unplowed fifteen acres ❏ he don't know if he's plowin' or playin' dominoes

FARMER, LAZY He don't raise nothing but hogs 'cause hogs don't need plowin' or hoein' ❏ he sucks his cow rather than milk her 'cause he's too lazy to carry the bucket

FARMER, LUCKY He raised a bumper crop of sons, which means he'll have plenty of cheap, available labor that won't quit and don't have to keep an eye peeled for the immigration boys.

FARMER, SMALL TIME A wool hat boy, which means he can't afford a felt hat ❏ he's a broadcast farmer, which means he can't afford planting equipment so he has to sow his crops by "broadcasting" the seeds by hand

FARMER, SMART He "signed" his crop. When a farmer in Weatherford, Texas was having trouble with people stealing his watermelons, he decided to sign his crop. He put up a sign for all to see proclaiming: "Beware. One watermelon in this patch has been poisoned." The sign worked and the thefts stopped even though no melon had actually been poisoned. Unfortunately, the plan backfired when the farmer went out one morning and noticed that someone had put up another sign which read: "Now there are two poisoned watermelons." Another farmer "signed" his crop a little differently. He had a vegetable stand next to his truck garden but the traffic went by so fast no one ever stopped. That all changed when he put up a sign proclaiming "Nudist Colony Crossing."

FARMER, STUPID He shot his mule 'cause the cotton rows came out crooked.

FARMER, UNLUCKY He don't ever get nuthin' but bull calves and girl babies, which means he never gets cows to help build his herd and he never gets boys to help out around the farm ❑ his pigs all died from mud sleeping sickness. Mud sleeping sickness is a rare disease that sometimes strikes pigs who spend too much time in the mud. A tiny mud ball forms on their tails and grows slowly as they move around. Eventually, the mud ball gets so large it pulls back the pig's skin so much that the animal can't close its eyes and it dies from lack of sleep.

FARMERS ADVICE If you plant onions next to potatoes, the potatoes will cry their eyes out ❑ crops don't grow by the glow of the moon

FARMING Crime don't pay, neither does farming. Politics, however, looks promising.

FASHION CONSCIENCE She dresses up to do the dishes ❑ she wears high heels to mow the lawn

FAST AS A hen gets on a grasshopper ❑ as chained lightning with a snapped link ❑ as a canned cat, which refers to the country prank of tieing a can on a cat's tail to see him run. It seems when a cat has a can tied to his tail, he thinks the only

way to get away from the noise is to run as fast as possible, which generally only makes his situation worse.

FAST PERSON He can play pitcher and catcher at the same time ❑ he's so fast he can run down a rumor ❑ he can turn off the light switch and get into bed before it gets dark ❑ whenever he stops it takes his shadow fifteen minutes to catch up ❑ he could outrun a six-legged jackrabbit ❑ he can catch his own echo ❑ runs like a scared ghost ❑ he's a bullet with feet *See also Quick*

FAST WORKER He could have bailed fast enough to keep the Titanic afloat.

FAT AS A town dog. In the country, dogs often have to fend for themselves but in most rural towns, there will always be someone willing to share scraps with any old stray dog that happens along ❑ as a prize winning hog ❑ as a full possum ❑ as a coon in a corn field

FAT MAN He has to buy two tickets when he flies (or rides the bus); he suffers from hand to mouth disease ❑ his energy has gone to waist ❑ got a figure like a depot stove

❏ he can pinch an inch on his forehead *See also Male, Fat*

FAT WOMAN Her housecoat would fit around a small house ❏ she's built for comfort rather than speed ❏ if she got pregnant they'd have to use two tables in the delivery room ❏ she has to use two burlap sacks for panty hose ❏ she ain't fat, just short for her weight *See also Rear End, Large*

FATE Some days you get, and some days you get got.

FATE, UNAVOIDABLE A rabbit can hide in the forest, but a fox can always find him, which is a country version of "you can run but you can't hide."

FATHER The parent who has to endure childbirth without an anesthetic

FATTENING FOOD Don't bother to eat it, just apply directly to the hips and thighs

FAUX PAUS (Fox pox)

FAVOR If you'll do that for me, I'll give you the first silver dollar I find rolling uphill with spurs on.

FAVORITISM Plays brother-in-law

FEARLESS He sweats ice water.

FEELING BAD I feel like I was run down, run over, and wrung out ❏ I feel like I was sent for and couldn't come ❏ I feel like I was chewed up and spit out ❏ I feel like I was shot out of a cannon and missed the net *See also Sick*

FEELING GOOD If I felt any better, I'd have to be twins 'cause one person just couldn't stand it ❏ if I felt any better I couldn't stand it and the sheriff wouldn't allow it ❏ I feel good all over more than any place else

FEELING POORLY I feel like I slept in a sack with a wildcat ❏ I feel like I was eaten by a billy goat and puked over a cliff ❏ I feel like I was grabbed by an eagle and dropped out of the clouds

FEELING SORRY FOR HIMSELF He's got his tail beneath his hind legs ❏ his bottom lip is sagging so much he's pickling up gravel as he walks

FEELINGS, HURT That cut me to the quick.

FEELS GOOD As fresh washed sheets on a bed ❏ as takin' off a pair of tight boots after a hard day's work. As the story goes, an old cowboy finally saved up enough money for a pair of hand-made boots. Unfortunately, when they arrived, they were about a size too small. Three or four months later the cowboy ran into the boot maker and told him about the problem. Naturally, the boot maker offered to stretch the boots but the cowboy refused. "After 14 or 15 hours of bustin' horses, punchin' cows, mending fences, and chasing strays, the best thing I have to look forward to is gettin' them damned tight boots off."

FEET Dirt movers, which is an expression that comes from the habit of country folks kicking some dirt while they stand around and chew the fat (talk).

FEET, COLD When he gets under the electric blanket, the street lights short out ❑ when he takes off his shoes the furnace comes on

FEET, LARGE He's got a good understanding ❑ his feet are so big he has to go to a crossroads to turn around ❑ you can't have a big building without a big foundation

FEET, STINKING He put odor eaters in his boots and they evaporated ❑ he always sits on the front row in church 'cause if the sermon runs long, he can take off his shoes and force the preacher to a quick conclusion

FELL Like a flour sack off the back of a wagon ❑ like an eagle in a wind shear

FEMALE Something the world would be a lot worse off without ❑ the best thing on earth to squeeze ❑ someone who's fully armed when she's fully naked

FEMALE, ABLE She can iron all day in high heels with a cold iron. *See Female, Tired*

FEMALE, ACTIVE She keeps her dance card full.

FEMALE, AGE OF A lady's age is like the speedometer in a used car. You know it's been set back but you don't know how far.

FEMALE, AGING She used to get a romantic twinkle in her eye when she was in a romantic mood, but now it just means her contact lens is in backwards.

FEMALE, AGGRESSIVE She comes on like a mouthful of hot gumbo (or red beans).

If you have ever taken a mouthful of very hot gumbo, you know it gets your attention real quick just like an aggressive female does.

FEMALE, ANGRY She's a bitch in the kitchen with no back door ❏ she's madder than an old hen in a wool basket

FEMALE, ANXIOUS (SORT OF) She's itching for something she ain't willing to scratch.

FEMALE, ATTRACTIVE She could make a glass eye blink ❏ she's captured my heart and about three or four other organs ❏ she looks so good she could make a Bishop kick a hole in a stained glass window ❏ she's been hit on more than the back wall in handball court

FEMALE, CONNIVING She always smells tired, which means every day just before her husband gets home she dabs some Pine Sol on her neck and sprays Lysol under her arms so she'll smell like she's been working all day ❏ she ain't lookin' for a husband, she's looking for a diamond mine ❏ she may have a short rope but she can still throw a big loop (and there is always, it seems,

some man who is willing to get caught in it) ❏ she made it to the top because her dress didn't

FEMALE, CRAZY She's a cup and a saucer short of a set.

FEMALE, DANGEROUS She can shoot as well as she cooks ❏ she'd dip her man's boxer shorts in catnip and then buy a mountain lion for a pet ❏ she might turn your head but it would be on a spit over an open flame

FEMALE, DECEIVING If she's an angel she's wearing invisible wings ❏ if she was a hen, she'd eat your feed and then lay her eggs under the neighbor's porch, which is a country version for "she'd let you buy the drinks all night and then go home with the bartender."

FEMALE, DESIRABLE She'd make a cowboy forget his horse ❏ she's so desirable, I'd give an alligator a hysterectomy without antiseptic just for the opportunity to hold her hand ❏ she don't have any trouble findin' a rake to gather her hay crop

FEMALE, EASY They call her Ford 'cause she's the best pickup ❏ she's such a pushover, you can fool her even if you play your cards wrong.

FEMALE, EVIL She'd make Bonnie Parker look like an MYF counselor. MYF is Methodist Youth Fellowship and Miss Parker was the Bonnie in the Bonnie and Clyde crime duo. *See also Male, Evil*

FEMALE, FAT *See Fat Woman*

FEMALE, FLIRTATIOUS She's been in more laps than a napkin, which is how the legendary Mae West once described herself ❑ she never met a lap she didn't like

FEMALE, GENTLE She only hits you with the soft end of the mop.

FEMALE, HARD She is so hard the only thing that will make an impression on her is a diamond.

FEMALE, HIGH SPIRITED If she was a horse, she'd be hard to break to a halter.

FEMALE, IGNORANT Her bra size is about equal to her IQ.

FEMALE, INEPT She bought cosmetics for a make-up exam ❑ she went to the Community Chest for a mammogram ❑ when she puts on her bikini she takes off her brain ❑ she don't think she can be overdrawn at the bank 'cause she still has checks left

FEMALE, IRATE Your butt is crabgrass and she's the goat.

FEMALE, JEALOUS *See Jealous Woman*

FEMALE, JILTED Her heart has been broken more than the ten commandments ❑ her heart broke into more pieces than a crystal ball that was dropped out of an airplane ❑ she took up with the wrong ol' boy and her took he for a short ride

FEMALE, LARGE If she was a stripper, her G string would be as wide as a tow strap ❑ she has to put on a girdle to get into her kimono ❑ she's built like a pillow ❑ she gained so much after having the baby that her stretch marks look like tank tracks

FEMALE, LAZY *See Lazy Woman*

FEMALE, LYING She don't even tell the truth in her diary ❑ she usually starts lying about her age when the mirror starts telling the truth

FEMALE, MADE UP She's got fresh paint on her cheeks, new chalk on her nose and fresh slobber on her spit curls. (Unfortunately, her husband will probably never notice it.)

FEMALE, MEAN *See Mean woman*

FEMALE, MIDDLE AGE She's too young for medicare and too old for men to care.

FEMALE, PROMISCUOUS She sleeps around so much, she'd catch fire if she didn't sweat □ the inscription on her tombstone will read: "The only time she ever slept alone" □ she's a widow woman who always seems to want her weeds plowed under □ she's the original frito lay □ with her you got no chance to be the first one but you stand a good chance of bein' the next one □ she's got round heels, which implies the heels on her shoes have been rounded making it easy to push her over

FEMALE, PROUD She's a real honey but none of the bees know it □ she thinks she's the only peach on the tree

FEMALE, RESPECTABLE She's an all-standing tough ol' gal which, from a country boy, is high praise.

FEMALE, SEDUCTIVE She's got more moves than a water wiggle □ she can give you such a hot feeling it'll melt the fillings in your teeth *See also Walk, Seductive*

FEMALE, SHALLOW She's like an Easter egg, mostly trimmings.

FEMALE, SHAPELY Built like a brick outhouse, which is a common saying although few people built their out-house out of bricks because you often had to change locations of the facilities, especially if the prevailing winds changed □ she's got more curves than a rain barrel full of pygmy rattle-snakes □ like the country song says, nuthin' would sure look good on her

FEMALE, SHY She won't even bend over in the garden 'cause the potatoes have got eyes.

FEMALE, SKINNY She has to wear suspenders to hold up her girdle. *See also Skinny Woman*

FEMALE, SMALL If she was gold plated you could

use her for a watch fob, which is how Roy Rogers once described Barbara Mandrell.

FEMALE, SMART She has horse sense, she knows when to say nay.

FEMALE, STUBBORN She's got a body like a marble statue and a head to match.

FEMALE, STUPID She has to sneeze every now and then to keep the dust from building up on her brain □ they call her the last frontier, 'cause all she has between her ears is space *See also Stupid Woman*

FEMALE, TIRED She looks like she's been ironing all day in high heels with a cold iron.

FEMALE, UGLY She ain't two faced cause if she was, she wouldn't be wearing that one □ she can't help being ugly but she could stay at home □ her necklace ought to be a flea collar □ a dead hog that has been lying in the sunshine for two weeks could beat her in a beauty contest □ she wouldn't be fit for a drunk cowboy to take up with *See also Ugly Woman*

FEMALE, VAIN She's used so many mud packs, she could retread a Louisiana swamp.

FEMALE, YOUNG Better use what mother nature gave her before father time takes it away

FEMALE CONFIDENCE The ability to walk past a mirror and not look

FEMALE DRINKER Men make passes at lasses who drain glasses.

FEMALE EQUALITY As Ann Richards said in her 1988 Democratic keynote address, "Ginger Rogers did everything Fred Astaire did and she did it backwards in high heels."

FEMALE FLORIST A lady who loves to show off her bloomers.

FEMALE JUDGEMENT, POOR There's only two kinds of men in the world, good old boys and the kind she brings home.

FEMALE LIAR *See Liar, Female*

FEMALE MAGICIAN She can, as if by magic, turn any ol' dirty, rundown, ramshackled, rat-infested house into home sweet home. I'd like to see Houdini try that.

FEMALE POWER A woman who can wrap a man around her little finger will never have to twist his arm.

FEMALE STUBBORNNESS If a woman don't wanna see you, there ain't no use looking for her.

FEMALE SUPERIORITY Houston's Liz Carpenter said it best with, "Roosters crow, hens deliver."

FEMALE WARDROBE A woman is like a salad, everything depends on the dressing.

FEMINIST, DEVOUT She's arrow proof, which means she doesn't have to worry about being struck by one of Cupid's arrows.

FENCE, GOOD Hoss high and bull strong

FEVER, HIGH His fever got so high his hair was sweatin' ❑ his fever got so high you could fry an egg on his forehead ❑ his head was so hot his eyes were almost hard boiled

FEVERISH I felt like my hat was full of hot coals or, I felt like I was drug through a pile of hot coals face first.

FIDDLER, BAD He plays the fiddle like the strings were still in the cat. *See also Musician, Poor*

FIGHT, BIG A knock down, drag out fight

FIGHT, SHORT It'll be a two-hit fight: I'll hit you and you'll hit the ground ❑ he had me licked and whipped before he even had time to get good and mad

FIGHTER, POOR He couldn't whip a 90-year-old blind, paraplegic grandmother.

FIGURE, FAIR It's somewhere between "oh boy" and obese.

FILLED UP Like an airline seat holding a 400-pound passenger.

FINALIZE IT Put the last nail in that coffin.

FINANCIAL CONDITION, POOR I'm like a dog chasin' his tail, we're both tryin to make ends meet ❑ I'm runnin' a poor string of horses. This is a saying that comes from cow country where it is said that a ranch is no better than its horses. A ranch with good horses can get by even if the cowboys are only average quality. It follows that a rancher running a poor string of horses is having financial problems.

FINANCIAL GENIUS Somebody who can earn more money than his wife can spend.

FINDERS FEE Bird dog money

FINGER, INDEX Trigger finger ❑ pointer

FINISHED You can stick a fork in him cause he's done ❑ it's over and done with

FINISHING Playing out the string

FIREMAN Smoke eater

FIRE STARTER, POOR He wore out three hats tryin' to get one little ol' camp fire to a blaze.

FIREFLY Lightning bug

FIRM As bed springs in a brand new $100 mattress

FIRM BUT FAIR He's like a watermelon, he's got a big heart but it's hidden under a mighty thick skin.

FIRST THINGS FIRST You can't kill the snake till you get the hoe in your hand ❑ if you're gonna eat pecans

you gotta crack the shells ❑ you can't steal second base if you're not on first ❑ the water won't clear till you get the hogs out of the trough

FISH, LARGE You could use the scales for roof shingles ❑ you'd have to dislocate both shoulders to describe how big it was ❑ it has been proven many times over that the biggest fish are always caught by the tale

FISH, MEDIUM SIZED It's too small for the wall. This saying probably originated by the recent practice of releasing most large fish after they're caught so they live to breed other large fish. A fish too small for the wall is one that is big but not big enough to stuff and hang on the wall as a trophy.

FISHERMAN, ACTIVE His trotline never gets dry ❑ his hooks never rust in the tackle box

FISHERMAN, AVID He's a foaming-at-the-mouth fisherman. Foaming at the mouth is a reference to someone having rabies, which means they are sure enough crazy. Therefore, someone who is a foaming-at-the-mouth fisherman is thought to be just plumb crazy about fishing. The foaming mouth analogy can be be used for anything.

FISHERMAN, CLEVER
He fishes with drunk worms. A really clever fisherman would dip his worms in tequila until they got good and drunk. Then when he put the worm on the hook it would be so brave that it would bite the fish! ❏ An equally clever fisherman "fishes with chewin' tobacco." He simply feeds the tobacco to the fish and then knocks 'em over the head when they come up to spit.

FISHERMAN, EXPERT
He's completed the graduate program at the Oklahoma school for fish hook baiters which makes him a Master Baiter.

FISHERMAN, ILLEGAL
He talks to the fish, which is a reference to using electricity to stun the fish so they quickly float to the surface. In some places men who use the tactics are said to be fish pickers cause they "pick" their catch off the top of the water much like a cotton picker might pick cotton.

FISHERMAN, INEPT He couldn't catch a fish in a baited hole (or at Sea World)

❏ he couldn't catch fish in a power company discharge pond. Power companies generally discharge recycled water that is warmer than the rest of the water in a lake, which is something minnows like. As the minnows gather, so do the bigger fish. If you can get close enough to a discharge pond, you can almost always catch fish, unless you are an inept fisherman.

FISHERMAN, LAZY He never married 'cause he couldn't find no rich, good lookin' woman willin' to clean fish, which means he was also a stupid fisherman 'cause no rich, good lookin' woman ought to have to clean fish.

FISHERMAN, LUCKY He was born with a silver hook in his mouth ❏ he could catch a fish with a rotten line and no bait on the hook

FISHING The most fun you can have with your clothes on ❏ a bad day fishing is better than a good day working ❏ the best excuse on earth for drinking in the daytime ❏ the best way to separate men and truth

FISHING, GOOD The fish are so hungry that you have

to hide behind a tree to bait your hook to keep the bass from jumping out of the water and taking the worm out of your hand.

FISHING, POOR Even the biggest liars weren't catching anything.

FISHING TRIP, LOUSY The only fish we caught were the Dolphins (Dawh-fins) on TV.

FIST Arkansas soup bone

FIT As a fiddle *See Out of Shape*

FIT, GOOD Fits like a hand in a glove □ like hot lead in a bullet mold

FIT, LOOSE Fits about as snug as a choir robe on a skinny person. In case you have never sung in the choir, the robes generally come in one-size-fits-all variety which means they'll fit you whether you weight 103 pounds or 301 pounds.

FIT, POOR Fits like a daddy's hat on the head of a patch-seated kid □ like a big ring on a little finger □ fits like socks on a rooster □ fits like a hog in a saddle

FIT, TIGHT As wax in a candle mold □ as ski pants on a fat woman

FLAPPING Like a runaway window shade

FLATTERY Artificial sweetener □ is like French toilet water; it smells good but you ain't supposed to drink it □ is like chewing gum, enjoy it for a while but don't swallow it □ resembles friendship about as much as a wolf resembles a dog □ John Wayne said it best when he described flattery as the "phony express"

FLEW APART Like a $2 suitcase in a train station

FLEXIBLE He can dance to whatever tune the band is playing.

FLIMSY As a cheesecloth socks

FLIRT Wishful winking □ attracts a man before he's married, distracts him afterward

FLIRTATIOUS, INNOCENT It don't matter where you get your appetite so long as you take your meals at home.

FLOOD *See Creek, Flooded and Water, Deep*

FLORIDA (Flar-dah)

FLY SWATTER Emergency tea strainer □ fly brush, which was a homemade brush used by many country folks to shoo the flies off the food

FLY, OPEN *See Zipper, Open*

FORT WORTH (Foat-Wurth)

FOG, THICK So thick you couldn't cut it with a chainsaw ❑ so thick the farmers had to mount fog horns on their tractors

FOOD, BAD Would make a buzzard gag ❑ would make a maggot puke ❑ could be used as a fly repellant *See also Taste, Bad*

FOOD, GOOD That's the best I ever lapped a lip over, as in "Her biscuits are the best I've lapped a lip over in a coon's age." *See also Taste, Good*

FOOL You can educate him but you can't make him think ❑ you can teach sense to a smart man but not to a fool ❑ if you have to be a fool, be a rich one

FOOLING ME You're passing gas and tryin' to blame the dog ❑ you're tryin' to sell me possum hide for rabbit fur ❑ you're tryin' to sell me a black cat with a white stripe down his back

FOOLISH He'd jump into the river to get out of the rain.

FOOTBALL Elbert Hubbard said, "A sport that bears the same relation to education that bullfighting does to farming" ❑ a three-hour commercial with occasional interruptions for play

FOR SURE Sure as the world, as in "I'm gonna get my wife a job next week sure as the world." *See also Absolutely, Certain*

FOREIGNER (Furiner) ❑ he can't even laugh in English

FOREVER As long as pigs go barefooted ❑ until there's enough frost in hell to kill snap beans on the vine

FORGET IT Kiss it off like the old maid you keep locked in the attic 'cause she won't leave the mailman alone.

FORGETFUL Ron Davis always said his daughter Evelyn was so forgetful that she had an automatic twine loser for a brain.

FORGOT He misremembered it.

FORTUNATE She always toted her ducks to a good market.

FOUR-WHEEL-DRIVE VEHICLE What I'd like to be buried in 'cause I ain't never seen the hole they couldn't get you out of.

FRAGILE As a hand blown glass bulb ❏ as a sopapia

FRECKLES He's got more freckles than a turkey egg (or guinea egg).

FREEDOM Like cheap soap, loses its strength when it's watered down

FRIED CHICKEN, GOOD It's so good it'll straighten your teeth, smooth your skin, and make childbirth a pleasure. This description, or something similar, can be used to describe good barbecue, chili, chicken fried steak, or gravy.

FRIEND Someone who will talk about your faults in private ❏ someone who has never heard your story before ❏ former Speaker of the House Jim Wright, at his welcome home party in Fort Worth, Texas said, "A friend is someone who knows your faults and doesn't give a damn." ❏ a real friend will tell you when you have broccoli on your teeth or when your zipper is open ❏ you can't cultivate a friend by diggin' up dirt around him ❏ God takes care of the relatives but you pick your own friends

FRIEND, BEST He'll help you out when both of your arms are broken and in casts and your nose needs picking. Of course, the very best friend of all is the one who'll help you out when your arms are broken and Mother Nature calls you to the necessary room. Now that's true friendship.

FRIEND, FAIR WEATHER Some friends are like your shadow, you only see 'em when the sun shines, which is a newer version of "fair weather friend."

FRIENDLESS He's a one-buggy man, when means when he dies the only buggy in his funeral procession will belong to the undertaker. A more modern version would be "one-car man" which means one car would be more than enough to take all his friends to his funeral.

FRIENDLY ADVICE Don't buy friendship, you might lose it to a higher bidder ❏ friendship is like a dollar, hard to get, easy to throw away

FRIENDLY, SOMEWHAT He's friendly only up to the pockets, which means he'll be your friend but he won't loan you money so he ain't much of a friend after all.

FRIENDS They get along like two pups in a basket ❑ they were so close they used the same toothpick

FRIENDSHIP Ain't something you get, it's something you give

FRIENDSHIP, QUESTIONABLE He's friendly as a bootlegger. In most cases a bootlegger will only be your friend as long as you're buyin' whiskey from him.

FRIGHTENED He come down with a case of the runs and he did ❑ he was scared witless *See also Scared*

FRIGID His (or her) side of the waterbed froze solid as a glacier.

FRUGAL He gets out of the bed to turn over to save wear and tear on the sheets ❑ he has a three-legged dog 'cause they don't run as fast so they don't get as hungry ❑ can squeeze a dollar till George Washington's nose starts to bleed ❑ if he had a cold, he wouldn't give you a germ ❑ he's a close chewer and a tight spitter ❑ he always breathes through his nose to save wear and tear on his store bought teeth ❑ he's so tight, when he grins his outy belly button is drawn in ❑ when he blinks his eyes, his toes curl up ❑ he's so tight he names all his dollar bills like pets ❑ he still has his elementary school lunch money ❑ he's so tight, when he blinks his knee caps move ❑ he takes long steps to save shoe leather ❑ he learned braille so he could read after dark without turning on a lamp ❑ he throws quarters around like they were manhole covers *See also Cheapskate, Miser*

FRUGAL, BUT COURTEOUS He's quick to tip his hat to a lady but slow to tip anyone else.

FRUSTRATED As a pickpocket in a nudist colony ❑ as a rubber nosed woodpecker ❑ as a mule at a crowded trough ❑ as a small hog in the big hog's pen, which means the big hogs would crowd out the little hog when it came time to go to the trough ❑ as a chicken snake in an empty coup ❑ I can chew but I can't swallow

FRUSTRATING As eatin' soup with a fork

FULL It's as full of that as an egg is of chicken ❑ I'm so full I could bust a beetle on my belly ❑ as a bloated toad

FUN The older you get the more it costs

FUNERAL PARLOR The only business with a permanent layaway plan

FUNNY I laughed so hard I almost popped a gizzard string (a supposed tendon in the stomach).

FUTILE You're shootin' spit wads at a battleship ❑ you're bear hunting with a broomstick ❑ as arguing with a mother-in-law ❑ as a bird hunting for worms on Astroturf ❑ as talking Chinese to a deaf pack mule. Davy Crockett once said, "I might as well have sung Psalms over a dead horse."

FUTILITY A bull snake tryin' to make love to a buggy whip ❑ a turtle tryin' to mate an army helmet ❑ you're just warmin' up leftover snow

FUTURE, UNCERTAIN The only thing he can count on is his fingers.

G

GRINNING — like a cat that ate an eagle

G

GAMBLER, INEPT He once lost ten dollars in a stamp machine ❏ he loses money on instant replays *See also Poker Hand, Worthless*

GAMBLING The best way to get nothing for something ❏ if you can't afford to lose, you can't afford to play

GARDENER, INEPT He'd fertilize Astroturf ❏ the only thing he can grow in his garden is tired ❏ he couldn't grow pole beans in a pile of horse manure

GARDENER, SMART Never plants more garden than his wife can hoe

GENIUS A crackpot that hit the jackpot

GENIUS, ALMOST He had a spark of genius but he suffered ignition problems.

GENIUS VERSUS STUPIDITY The difference between being a genius and being stupid is that genius has its limits and stupidity has none.

GENTLEMAN No true gentleman has ever heard the other person's joke ❏ a real gentleman is one who'll help an old, ugly woman across a busy street when no one is looking *See also Chivalrous*

GENTLEMAN FARMER The only thing he raises is his hat when a pretty girl walks by.

GEORGIA (Jaw-ja) The land of tall girls and virgin pines. This saying is used to describe several states as well as East Texas.

GET BUSY You can't plow a field by turning it over in your mind ❏ a coyote don't catch no rabbits while sittin' in the shade ❏ don't worry about the mule goin' blind, just load the wagon ❏ get up and git instead of sittin' down an sittin' ❏ you'll never get a hit with the bat sittin' on your shoulder

GET CONTROL Stop the hemorrhage ❏ teach 'em to fly in formation ❏ get everybody dancing to the same tune (or singing out of the same song book) ❏ you better flag down the train ❏ cut the ground out from under 'em

GET CONTROL OF YOURSELF Get a choke hold on your temper.

GET GOING Pull the trigger ❏ John Wayne might have said, "head 'em up and move 'em north"

GET IT DONE QUICKLY Let's get past the house before some ol' cur dog starts barking, which basically means you want to get something done before someone starts complaining. An example might be "Let's get that tax increase bill past the house before some taxpayin' dog starts barking."

GET LUCKY Every now and then you cut a fat hog.

GET OUT OF HERE, QUICKLY You better cut the chain on the anchor and row so fast the friction makes the water boil.

GET REVENGE, SORT OF Wet in his well. Such a form of revenge gives you the satisfaction of knowing you did it but the other person never tastes the difference.

GET RID OF HIM Loan him some money. According to the old country saying, the best way to get rid of someone is to loan him some money that you expect to be repaid.

GET SERIOUS Let's talk turkey ❏ let's get down to the nut cuttin'

GET STARTED Drive a stake. In almost any construction job, the first thing you do is drive a stake to provide a starting place.

GET IT OUT IN THE OPEN Put some smoke down that hole.

GET TO THE BOTTOM OF IT Get down to where the water hits the wheel ❏ get down to where the hogs are gruntin'

GET TO THE POINT Don't tell me about the labor pains, just show me the baby ❏ quit coyotin' around the rim ❏ quit dancing me all over the floor ❏ skip the gristle and get to the bone ❏ go around that pig and get to the tail

GET TO WORK The bee that makes the honey doesn't hang around the hive ❏ a mosquito don't get slapped on the back till he gets to work

GET UP Hoist your carcass ❏ cool that chair, which is a reference to chairs getting warm when you sit in them ❏ you'll never stumble over anything worthwhile when sitting down

GETTING ANGRY His sap's rising ❏ his blood is simmering, which indicates it's about to boil

GETTING OLD He's feeling his corns more than his oats ❏ he can still paint the town but he can only give it one coat at a time ❏ he had to stop having birthdays 'cause he couldn't find a cake that could stand up under the weight of the candles

GIFT, PERFECT Give a gift that keeps on giving — a female cat.

GIRDLE Pot holder ❏ waist basket ❏ an aid for over-developed areas ❏ holds a woman in when she goes out ❏ a lot of women claim that taking off a girdle after a hard day is the second best feeling in the world

GIRL *See Female*

GIRL, CUTE She could make you jump a nine-rail fence, rassle a boxcar load of bobcats, and dance across Texas with a grizzly bear ❏ a

girl with a future ought to avoid a man with a past *See also Female, Desirable*

GIVE HIM A CHANCE Let him alone and he'll come home to his milk.

GIVE IT UP Fork it over.

GIVE ME THE FACTS Tell it with the bark on.

GLASSES, THICK His glasses are so thick he looks like he's staring at you through the walls of an aquarium.

GLISTENS Like hoarfrost in the morning sunshine. Hoarfrost is a country word for frozen dew that coats the ground and plants with a thin layer of ice crystals. It glistens in the morning sun like a basket full of diamonds.

GLOWS Like foxfire at midnight. Foxfire is a fungus that forms in decaying wood which causes a strange, often eerie glow.

GO AHEAD AND DO IT It's easier to get forgiveness than permission.

GO FOR IT Don't settle for half a shebang, get the whole shebang.

GO GITTER A cowboy who forgot to hobble his horse,

101

which means he'll have to go get it 'cause it wandered off

GO SLOW Better to be last in a traffic jam than first in a funeral procession.

GOES TOGETHER Like rum and coke ❑ like biscuits and molasses ❑ like cowboys and country music ❑ like lips and lipstick

GOING NOWHERE He's soap-tracked and spinning his wheels.

GOING TOO FAST He's hung in overdrive.

GOLD DIGGER She's a violation to the law of gravity 'cause it's easier to pick her than it is to drop her.

GOLF The game that turned the cows out of the pasture and let the bull in ❑ a game where the player's lie can correct the lay of the ball

GOLFER, HONEST One that's being watched

GOLFER, LUCKY He could hit into a sand trap and grass would grow under his ball before he got there.

GOLFER, UNLUCKY He could putt toward a hole and it would heal over before the ball arrived.

GOOD Shiny, as in "The way I rode that bull wasn't too shiny but it worked." ❑ whale, as in "He's a whale of a horse."

GOOD DEED The smallest good deed is bigger than the largest good intention.

GOOD EXAMPLE The hardest thing on earth to put up with

GOOD FENCES *See Neighborly*

GOOD INTENTIONS Bricks in the highway to ruin ❑ he tried to make hay while the moon was shining

GOOD OLD DAYS When a stocking would hold all a kid wanted for Christmas

GOOD SPORT The worst thing about being a good sport is that you have to lose to prove it.

GOOD TIMES It'll be a great day when schools have all the money they need and the air force has to have a bake sale to buy a bomber.

GOSSIP Murder by tongue ❑ clothesline talk ❑ tongue exercise ❑ the difference between news and gossip is whether you're hearing it or telling it ❑ gossip travels faster over grapevines that are sour ❑ is like slinging fresh manure at a clean white wall. It may not stick but it leaves its mark.

GOSSIP (PERSON) She has a keen sense of rumor ❑ she believes in the old adage that you can't believe everything you hear but you can repeat it

GOSSIP, DANGEROUS When she let the cat out of the bag it turned into a lion and ate her, which means she told something that wasn't true and ended up suffering the consequences ❑ remember, gossips frequently get caught in their own mouthtraps

GOT MARRIED He belled his mare.

GOT MORE THAN I CAN HANDLE I got more ground broke than I can plant ❑ I've caught more fish than I can fry

GOT NO RESPONSE I drew a blank.

GOT THINGS TO DO Like an old chicken, I got scratchin' to do and eggs to lay.

GOT WHAT HE DESERVED His chicken came home to roost, or as Jennifer Chariton said, his chicken came home to roast.

GOVERNMENT Ought to be like your digestive system, when it works properly you hardly know it's there.

GOVERNMENT BUREAU Where the taxpayer's shirt is kept

GOVERNMENT SPENDING George Bernard Shaw said it best with, "The government that robs Peter to pay Paul can always depend on the support of Paul."

GOVERNMENT WORKER, DEDICATED He put a sign on Hoover Dam warning, *Property of the U.S. Government. Do Not Remove.* Unfortunately, taxpayers had to pay for the sign.

GRAB HOLD Grab a holt ❑ cabbage on to it

GRACE Good bread, good meat, good God, let's eat.

GRAND CANYON It's been said the Grand Canyon was dug by a banker who dropped a nickel down a gopher hole.

GRANDCHILD Nothing makes a boy smarter than being a grandson.

GRASS Cemetery carpet, as in "I believe the cut worms are gonna kill the cemetery carpet in our front yard."

GRASS, MEDIUM HIGH Belly deep to a big dog

GRASS, SHORT Belly deep to a ground squirrel

GRASS, TALL Belly deep to a big horse

GRAVE A one-size-fits-all hole in the ground

GRAVEYARD Marble orchard

GRAVEYARD CLEANING *See Party, Dull*

GRAVY Texas butter, so called because Texans will often use gravy in places a lot of other people would use butter, such as on biscuits, bread, mashed potatoes, etc.

GRAVY, GOOD Sloppin' good *See Fried Chicken, Good*

GRAVY, POOR You had to cut it with a steak knife ❑ had more lumps than chunky peanut butter

GREEDY If he had the world by the tail he would let go to reach for the moon.

GREEN As a gourd

GRIN, WIDE He could swallow a banana sideways ❑ he was grinnin' like a cat that ate an eagle

GRINNING Like a barrel of possum heads ❑ from his butt to his eyebrows ❑ like a possum eating dirt out of a hair oil bottle ❑ like a mule eatin' briars. When a mule eats briars he holds his lips apart, which gives the impression he's grinning.

GRIP, UNSAFE A hospital hold

GRITS (gree-uts) Georgia ice cream

GROUND HOG Whistle pig

GROWING FAST As a crack in a frozen windshield ❑ as a fertilized weed ❑ as popcorn in a hopper ❑ he's growin' so fast his shadow can't keep up

GROWING UP He's getting a little hair on his belly.

GUILT A guilty man runs even when no one is chasing him.

GULLIBLE He'd buy hair restorer from a bald barber ❑ he's green as a cut-seed watermelon

GUN COLLECTOR, AVID He's got enough firepower to start a small revolution in a South American country ❑ if Robert E. Lee had had half that many guns you'd be buyin' groceries with Confederate money

H

HAPPY — as a short cowboy dancin' with a tall cowgirl

H

HABITS Are like a half full water bed, easy to get into and almost impossible to get out of

HABITS, BAD Dying is the only sure cure for a bad habit ❑ it's easier to form good habits than to reform bad ones

HAD ALL I CAN STAND I'm at the end of my tether ❑ I've enjoyed about all I can take of that

HAIR RESTORER, GOOD Glen Owen has a bottle of medicine from Canada that he thinks will cure anything. He also says, "It'll grow hair on a door knob."

HAIR When you're young, it is light, then it turns dark, then it turns white, then it turns loose

HAIR, GREASY His hair looks like it was combed with buttered toast ❑ he's got enough oil on his hair to grease a freight train

HAIRCUT, POOR A white sidewall haircut, which occurs when the barber virtually shaves a band all around the head that fully exposes the ears, which then appear to be circled with a white stripe much like a white sidewall tire ❑ you look like you fell asleep in the chair and the barber forgot what he was doin'

HAIRDO, WILD Asylum hair ❑ he looks like he stuck his finger in a light socket

HALF TRUTHS No amount of half truths will make the whole truth.

HANDLE Pig tail

HANDS, QUICK He could steal hubcaps off a moving car ❑ he could steal the needle out of a running sewing machine

HANDSHAKE, FIRM He shakes hands like he's clubbing a snake at a garden party ❑ shakes your hand like it's a pump handle

HANDSHAKE, WEAK His handshake makes you think you holdin' a limp dishrag ❑

107

his handshake wouldn't squash a marshmallow

HANDWRITING, POOR He can't read his own handwriting when it gets cold ❏ he couldn't even be a doctor

HANDWRITING, SMALL He could write the constitution on a matchbook cover.

HANDY As indoor plumbing ❏ as a necessary room on a cross country bus ❏ as a hip pocket on a hog, which gives you something to grab aholt of when trying to move the hog ❏ as a warm fire on a cold night

HANDYMAN, GOOD *See Do-It-Yourselfer*

HANG ON Like a fiddler crab to the underpinning of a boat

HANGOVER I feel like the Baptist bell choir is practicing inside my head ❏ my head is banging like a Chinese gong

HAPPY AS A short cowboy dancing with a tall cowgirl ❏ as a coon in a corn field ❏ as a one-eyed dog locked in a smokehouse ❏ as a wettin' dog with a mile of fence posts ❏ as a colt in clover ❏ as a gopher, ground hog, prairie dog, or armadillo digging in soft ground ❏ as a possum eatin' persimmons ❏ as a cow in a field of belly high clover ❏ as a wet dog behind a kitchen stove ❏ as a blowfly on manure ❏ as a wife who sees a double chin on her husband's old girl friend ❏ as a weasel in a hen house ❏ as a woodpecker in a 10-acre deadening, which is any area, usually around a lake, that has a lot of dead trees. Since the wood in a dead tree is softer than in a live tree, a woodpecker would certainly find the peckin' easier. The number of acres can be adjusted according to the degree of happiness.

HARD AS A frozen cannon ball ❏ as a nine-pound jawbreaker ❏ as Superman's kneecap ❏ as pig iron ❏ as a banker's heart ❏ as a diamond drill bit ❏ as a lightard knot, which is the center of a pine stump that contains a concentration of pine pitch. When fully dried, the center of the stump takes on the characteristics of hardened blue steel.

HARD HEADED Granite or steel headed ❏ if his head had a point he could etch glass ❏ hard as a ball peen hammer ❑ as a Texan. According to the old saying, you can always tell a Texan but you can't tell him much.

HARD LABOR Splittin' gum logs in August with a dull axe. There just may not be any hotter job on earth.

HARD PART'S OVER It's time to lick the calf. If you have ever seen a cow giving birth, you know that by the time she gets around to licking the calf, the hard part is over.

HARD TIMES He's been sandpapered, which means he's had a rough time.

HARD TO DO As nailing custard pudding to a wall. Author's Note: The person who contributed this saying offered no explanation as to why anyone would want to nail custard pudding to a wall.

HARD TO FIND As ears on an earthworm ❑ as third base in a football game

HARD TO HANDLE As a bronc with saddle sores

HARD WORKER He works 365 days a month ❑ he's a goin' Jesse *See also Worker, Good*

HARDHEADED He's unwilling to be confused with the facts ❑ he follows the straight and narrow minded path ❑ you couldn't put a nail in his head with a 22-caliber nail gun ❑ his head is so hard you could turn him upside down and use him for a rock crusher

HARASSING She's bein' ugly with me.

HARVEST Barn it

HAT, SPECIAL My marryin' and buryin' hat, which basically means it is only worn on special occasions, such as a wedding or a funeral. The same expression could also be used for a special jacket, belt, or pair of boots.

HATE Is like water in a dry gulch, the longer it runs, the deeper it digs

HAUGHTY Actin' mighty biggety

HAWAII (Hi-wa-ya)

HAY Horse manure seeds

HEAD, SHAKING Like a dog killing a garden snake

HEADACHE MEDICINE Easin' powder

HEADACHE, SEVERE I had to keep my eyelids shut

to keep my eyeballs from popping out ❑ a diamond cutter ❑ a skull (or brain) crusher ❑ so big it wouldn't fit in a horse corral ❑ so strong it would kill a middlin' sized steer. Rodeo bull, water buffalo, bull elephant, or rhinoceros may be substituted for steer. Sally Hogan once had a headache that she was sure would have killed a small child. Tim McEvoy claims he frequently gets headaches that would kill lesser men.

HEALTH, GOOD Doin' fine as long as I got a pulse and my plot down at the cemetery is still empty.

HEALTH, POOR The doctor said he didn't know what ailed him but that he'd know more after the autopsy.

HEARD ABOUT Got in the wind of

HEARING, GOOD He could hear a termite sneeze in a thunder storm ❑ could hear a worm cough ❑ could hear the sun set or the moon rise

HEARING, IMPAIRED He's deaf in one ear and can't hear out of the other ❑ he couldn't hear a rattlesnake buzzing if he was wearin' it for a necktie ❑ he couldn't hear a pin drop if it was a cattle pen dropped off a cliff onto a tin roof barn

HEARTLESS He can't cross his heart and hope to die ❑ someone gave him a chocolate heart for Valentines Day and someone else had to explain what it was.

HEAVY As a mother-in-law's baggage when she's moving in. *See Light (Weight).*

HELL Heaven's junkyard ❑ Satan Place ❑ there's a way to stay out of hell but no way to get out once you're there

HELL RAISER He raised more hell than an alligator in a dry riverbed.

HELP Hep, as in "You gotta hep me fix this fence."

HELPLESS As a clay pigeon ❑ as a frozen snake

HEREDITY One thing there ain't no cure for

HEROES "We can't all be heroes because somebody has to sit on the curb and clap when they go by," said Will Rogers.

HEROISM Steppin' into the breach ❑ Remember, when there is heroism to be done, someone still has to hold the horses.

HICCUP CURE The best known cure for hiccups is to go to a turkey shoot for blind men.

HIGH AS A Georgia pine ❑ as a hen's behind when she's in a dead run

HIGH HEELS *See Shoes, High Heels*

HIGH RISK Like playing a poker hand with your eyes shut

HIGHWAY Something that is either under construction or being repaired. In Minnesota they have two seasons, winter and road repair.

HIPS, SMALL *See Rear End, Small*

HISTORICAL ACCURACY If you have ever heard two people describing an accident, you'll have serious questions about the accuracy of history.

HISTORICAL EVENT, MINOR An historical speed bump. Paul Harvey, the famous radio newsman who would certainly qualify as a country boy, once did a story about Turkey not supporting the United Nation's sanctions against Iraq after the invasion of Kuwait. Mr. Harvey said the Turkish leaders considered the Iraq situation just "a speed bump in history."

HIT IN THE MOUTH Got kissed in the eyeteeth

HOARD Ground squirrel it

HOLD YOUR OWN Always give back as good as you got in a trade or a fight.

HOLD YOUR TONGUE You don't ever get hurt by words you don't spit out.

HOLDING HANDS Armed up

HOLE, SMALL If you were to crawl through that hole it would be like reliving your birth ❑ about as big as a cat hole, which is the small hole often cut into a door to allow cats to come and go as they please without someone having to get up and open the door ❑ an even smaller hole would be a spit hole, which was often cut into the flooring of cabins to be used to dispose of tobacco juice when no spittoon was available

HOME The only place where you can always scratch where it itches

HOME, CHEAP As a shotgun house which means it was built by firing the nails out of a shotgun rather than using a hammer.

HOME GIRL I've been back under the chicken coop looking for eggs farther than she's been away from home (can also be used for home boy).

HOME REMEDY The poultice has been used by country grandmother types to cure just about anything that might ever ail you. Of course, some grandmothers make "better" poultices than others, but the best that has ever been recorded was the little old lady that "could poultice the hump off a camel's back."

Another grandmother could use a hot Coke bottle to "suck the venom out of a snake through his tail." This comes from an old cure for boils. Someone, usually a grandmotherly type, would heat up a Coke bottle and then slap it over the boil. As the bottle cooled, a vacuum would be created which would draw the poison out of a boil. Speaking as one who has endured the cure, trust me on this one, don't try it.

HOMELY *See Ugly*

HOMEMAKER, INEPT She knows how to press buttons but not clothes.

HOMESICK She's wishin' she was back under mamma's bed playin' with the kittens.

HONEST As a baby's smile

HONEST MAN He plows a straight row ❑ a square shooter ❑ he's so honest he don't have to worry about having a poor memory

HONEST WOMAN She believe mirrors and bathroom scales

HONESTY *See Absolute Honesty*

HONEYMOON The calm before the storm ❑ the period between the bridal toast and burnt toast ❑ the last time the husband gets to work the controls on the electric blanket or the furnace

HONEYMOON END When he finds out he married a big spender and she finds out she didn't.

HONKY TONK (haw-key tawnk) Juke joint *See also Saloon, Dangerous*

HONKY TONK ANGEL An angel who traded in her golden halo for one made of neon ❑ she still wears a halo but it's propped up by her horns

HOPPING AROUND Like drops of water on a hot griddle ❑ like a migrating bull frog

HORSE Something that is uncomfortable in the middle and dangerous at both ends ❑ the hardest thing on earth that is filled with hay ❑ to ride a horse, put one leg on each side and keep your mind in the middle ❑ never ride a horse named Widow Maker, Whiplash, Undertaker, Bone Crusher, or Autopsy

HORSE, FAST He runs so fast he has to keep knockin' the rabbits out of the way ❑ he'd make Man O' War look like a pony in a kid's ride ❑ anybody ridin' that horse ought to take out flight insurance

HORSE, GENTLE He's as easy to ride as a rocking chair (or a stick horse).

HORSE, INDEPENDENT You don't have to give him his head 'cause he takes it when he wants it. Giving a horse his head refers to releasing the pressure on the reins to allow the animal to pretty much do as he pleases.

HORSE, MEAN Cinch buster (a horse that rears and falls backwards, often breaking the cinch) ❑ a bucker and a snorter ❑ he'll throw you so high you'll need a parachute to get back down

HORSE, REAR END Horse's patoot

HORSE, SCARED He's boogered up and bailing out.

HORSE, SCRAWNY He ain't nuthin' but buzzard bait.

HORSE, WELL-TRAINED If he jumped off a cliff, he'd stop three feet before he hit bottom if I yelled whoa.

HORSE, WILD He could buck off a plaster cast or buck you into a plaster cast.

HORSE SENSE Stable thinking ❑ is usually found only in a stable mind ❑ what keeps a horse from betting on people ❑ what keeps a woman from being a nag

HORSEBACK RIDING One thing you have to do by the seat of your pants

HORSESHOER, GOOD He could put iron shoes on a horsefly.

HOSPITAL, EXPENSIVE The only thing they don't charge for is the ink in the pen you use to write the check to pay your bill.

HOSPITALITY Ability to make your guests feel like you want them to stay without interfering with their plans to leave ❑ they have a saying in Arkansas which goes: Come and see us. We'll do so many nice things for you you're bound to like some of them. ❑ If your hospitality gets to runnin' mighty thin you can always use the old country hint, "I guess we'll get on to bed so you folks won't feel like you have to stay any longer."

HOT It was so hot, I saw a bird pulling a worm out of a hole and he was using pot holders ❑ it was so hot I saw a rattlesnake crawl into a campfire looking for shade under the coffee pot ❑ it was so hot the chickens were pluckin' themselves ❑ it got so hot the mercury in the thermometer evaporated ❑ it was so hot the centerfold in Playboy magazine took off her staples

HOT AS A bunkhouse cook stove ❑ a frog in a furnace ❑ as the devil's knee for a good person or as a preacher's knee to a sinful one

HOT ENOUGH To melt diamonds ❑ to melt the shoes off a horse ❑ to boil the water inside a watermelon while it's on the vine ❑ to melt dirt ❑ to bust open pea pods on the vine ❑ to pop corn in the shuck ❑ to sizzle spit on a sidewalk

HOUSEKEEPER, INEPT She waxed the carpet.

HOUSEKEEPER, GOOD She pushes a mean broom ❑ she's hell on dust and spider webs

HOUSTON (Use-ton)

HOW ARE YOU FEELING? How in the health are you?

HOW'S THAT AGAIN? Lick that calf again? ❑ Come again?

HUMANE She's so humane she washes everything on the gentle cycle.

HUMILITY When you say grace before eatin' crow

HUMOR A rich man's joke is always funny.

HUMOROUS That'd bring a grin to the face of a stuffed owl.

HUNGRY (hong-ree) He's so hungry he's become left-handed, which implies you are so hungry that your cerebral polarity has changed ❑ I'm so hungry my teeth itch ❑ my stomach is playin' a recital ❑ I'm so hungry my back bone is rubbin' a blister on my belly button from the inside ❑ I could take up the slack in my stomach and wipe the sweat off my brow ❑ hungry is something you don't get better at with practice ❑ a sign once seen in a ranch kitchen: "If you're hungry, grab a plate. You have my best wishes. But before you pull freight, be sure to wash the dishes."

HUNGRY AS A moth on a nylon sweater ❑ a woodpecker with a sore pecker

HUNGRY ENOUGH TO Play dead and try to attract a vulture ❑ to eat a full grown horse and it a buckin' ❑ to eat the stuffin' out of a rag doll ❑ to eat the tail off a dead skunk

HUNTER, AVID He'll trail a dog anywhere he can carry him ❑ he keeps a taxidermist on retainer

HUNTER, INEPT A bush shooter, which means he saw the bushes moving and fired away without really knowing what he was shooting at. Bush shooters have killed a lot more cattle than they have deer or antelope ❑ he won't shoot skeet 'cause he don't want to clean 'em *See also Bird Hunter, Dumb*

HUNTER, INEXPERIENCED He's nothing but a sign shooter. This comes from the practice of shooting at innocent signs along the highway. The theory is that anyone who would shoot at signs wouldn't be much of a real hunter. The most favorite targets for sign shooters are deer and cattle crossing signs.

HUNTER, POOR The only thing he shoots are pool, craps, and bull.

HUNTING DOG, GOOD braggin' dog ❑ he flushes a covey of quail, chases 'em down a prairie dog hole, and then let's 'em out one at a time for the shooter

HURRY You better hit the ground runnin' ❑ go to the whip ❑ get high behind (like an old hen in a hail storm)

HUSBAND Is like an egg, if he stays in hot water he gets hard boiled ❑ a wise man once observed that husbands are like state fairs, they get bigger and better every year ❑ some husbands are angels, the rest are still alive

HUSBAND, CUNNING He carries a doctor's prescription for panty hose in case his wife ever finds a strange pair in the glove compartment of his car.

HUSBAND, HENPECKED He's so henpecked he moults twice a year ❑ him and his wife will never join a nudist colony 'cause she wouldn't be wearing no skirt for him to hide behind ❑ he wears the pants in the family but he has 'em on under his apron ❑ the only time he gets to open his mouth is when he yawns ❑ he still takes orders from his first wife ❑ he gets his money the hard way, he asks his wife ❑ he washes dishes even if they are paper plates ❑ the only time he puts his foot down is on a spade in his wife's garden

HUSBAND, IDEAL An honest, loving, caring, good provider with a memory strong enough that he never forgets what he said at the alter ❑ a man who believes that woman's work is never done so he lends a hand

HUSBAND, INEPT His wife said she'd like to be seen in something long and flowing so he pushed her into the Mississippi River ❑ he put his wife on such a high pedestal that she can't get down to clean house so he has to do it

HUSBAND, LAZY He married his first wife's sister so he wouldn't have to break in a new mother-in-law ❑ his idea of helping out around the house is starting the lawn mower for his wife ❑ somebody who'd rather go thirsty than get up and get his own beer

HUSBAND, POOR He puts his wife under a pedestal.

HUSBAND, SMART He buys his wife the finest china so she won't throw any of it at him when she's angry and she won't ever trust him to wash it ❑ he tells his wife everything she might find out ❑ when he pulls the wool over his wife's eyes, he uses thick yarn ❑ if his wife gave him enough rope he'd claim he was tied up at the office

HUSBAND, UGLY Whenever his wife goes out drinkin' with the girls she always carries along his picture so that when he gets good lookin' she'll know it's time to stop drinking. Could also be reversed and used for ugly wife.

HUSBAND, UNFAITHFUL He ain't married but his wife is ☐ he's out doin' what he hopes his wife is home doin' without ☐ his wedding ring has worn a white circle on his watch pocket, which implies he takes off his ring when he goes out and tucks it in the watch pocket of his jeans. The fact that the ring has worn a white circle on the pocket means it has been in the pocket a lot of times.

HYPOCHONDRIAC He holds his breath when driving past a hospital ☐ a bed bug ☐ wants to be buried next to a doctor ☐ has an annual checkup once a month ☐ can tell you exactly how many chicken pox he had ☐ he takes so many vitamins and iron pills that when he dies his heirs will argue the mineral rights to his body

HYSTERECTOMY Where they get rid of the baby carriage and leave the playpen

This space is for your favorite sayings.

IN PAIN — I feel like a parakeet that got caught in a badminton game

I

I DON'T CARE I don't give a bed bug's behind about that □ that don't ruffle my feathers □ that don't mean any more to me than a hair on my backside

I'M READY My hair's set. After a hog is slaughtered, it is boiled in hot water which stands the hair on end — or sets it. When the hair is set, the hog is ready for scraping.

I'VE BEEN THERE I've been on the cow's side of the fence.

ICE, THIN Chicken foot ice, which is the first little layer of ice which forms on a stock pond when it freezes over. Normally, the first thin layer has small crack-like imperfections which are said to resemble chicken feet.

IDEA J. Frank Dobie once explained the difference between having an idea and thinking. He said, "Thought employs ideas, but having an idea is not the same thing as thinking. A rooster in a pen of hens has an idea."

IDIOT Lunk head □ his limits are limitless □ if the power failed, he could get trapped on an escalator □ he's about three fourths of a half wit □ he'd have to study up to be a crash dummy □ he's got the IQ of a dust mop □ sawdust head □ he ain't got a lick a sense □ he went to the tattoo parlor and asked for a pair of boxer shorts on his chest so he could have a chest of drawers □ he won't buy a dictionary 'cause he's waiting for the movie □ he almost froze to death at the drive-in movie waiting to see "closed for winter" □ he won't take a milk bath because he's afraid the cow will fall on him □ his mind is like a faulty parachute; it never opens when it should □ to drive him crazy, it'd just be a short trip *See also Dumb, Ignorant, Stupid*

IDLE He's about as busy as a pickpocket at a nudist colony □ he's no busier than a saddle maker at a dog show ❑ he's just standin' around like a big-eyed goose ❑ he's about as busy as a hibernating bear

IF I WAS YOU (Fize-you)

IF IT'S WORTH DOING, DO IT RIGHT If you're gonna trade horses, you might as well get the best of the deal ❑ the best stove-wood is always the stove-wood that is farthest away, which means if you're gonna get the best wood you gotta do it right and walk far

IGNORANCE Something that is a lot more expensive than an education

IGNORANT He cut down his only shade tree for firewood. The implication is that while the firewood might keep you warm for a little while, the entire summer will be mighty hot without that shade tree. ❑ he don't know chicken manure from chicken salad ❑ he don't know pine cones from pineapples ❑ he has a photo-graphic mind but nothing ever develops ❑ he'd play Russian roulette with a single shot derringer (or shotgun) ❑ he thinks Dairy Queen is a royal cow ❑ Joe Holsted said he knew some-one who was so ignorant he

couldn't get the same answer if he counted his nose twice ❑ took the screens off his windows so his fresh air wouldn't be shredded ❑ if he knew two languages he'd be bi-ignorant ❑ he don't know beans from rocks ❑ he's studying up to be a half wit ❑ he'd argue with a drunk liar *See also Dumb, Stupid*

IGNORANT, DANGEROUSLY SO He's so ignorant he don't even know he's ignorant, which makes him very dangerous.

IGNORE HIM Just play like his mother didn't have any children that lived ❑ don't give him a second thought and only half a first thought

IGNORE IT Turn a blind eye to it.

ILL He took down with miseries. Any specific illness such as the flu, gout, pneumonia, etc. can be substituted for miseries, which is an undiagnosed disease. ❑ he's feelin' mighty shy of bein' half well ❑ feelin' mighty puny *See also Sick*

Ill, NOT TOO SERIOUSLY The doctor told him not to pick up anything heavier than a biscuit or a nightgown for about two weeks ❑ he's fit as a fiddle but just a little bit out of tune

ILL, SERIOUSLY He's crippled sick ❏ he looks like about one more clean shirt is all he'll ever need ❏ if he was a building he'd be condemned

ILL EQUIPPED Working with sand, which means anything you do won't be permanent

ILLEGITIMATE He was born on the wrong side of the blanket.

ILLINOIS (Ill-a-noise)

ILLITERATE He's so stupid he signs his name with a holler 'cause he can't even make a mark ❏ he don't go to football games 'cause he can't read the words spelled out by the band at halftime

IMAGINATION What sets up with a wife when her husband is out late

IMMORAL A round heeled woman ❏ he don't have the morals of a yellow, suck-egg hound dog

IMPARTIAL He totes water on both shoulders ❏ a fence walker ❏ if a man sees both sides of a dispute, he don't have any money in the deal

IMPARTIAL AS A sad country song, which don't care whose heart it breaks

IMPOSSIBILITY You can't make butter from skimmed milk ❏ you're trying to hit a three-run homer with no one on base ❏ you're trying to measure water with a tea strainer ❏ you can't make a white-dress virgin out of a New Orleans hooker ❏ you can do that the day after a rooster lays an egg ❏ you're tryin' to lead a cow downstairs. For reasons best known only to cattle, you can lead a cow up all the stairs you want but you better have a different plan for getting her down 'cause no force on earth can make a cow walk down any stairs. Speaking as one who once lead a jersey milk cow up two flights of stairs to the top of the school building, you can trust me on this one — you cannot get them down by the same stairs.

IMPOSSIBLE You can't put a quill back in the goose ❏ you can't keep the dew off the grass ❏ you can't make a crab walk straight ❏ you can't shake hands with a clinched fist ❏ you can't unfry an egg ❏ you can't make a rose out of stink

123

weed ❑ you can't cook in cold grease ❑ you can't swim in a dry creek ❑ you can't make moonshine out of mare's milk ❑ James B. McSheehy once said, "You can't straddle the fence and keep your ear to the ground." ❑ Whoever said nothing was impossible never tried to slam a revolving door or flush a grapefruit down a toilet *See also Attempting the Impossible*

IMPOSSIBLE, ALMOST That'll take a heap a doin' but it can be done ❑ if you're gonna tree that coon you'll need all the dogs

IMPRACTICAL As giving a hug by mail ❑ as trying to carry water in a peach basket

IMPRACTICAL BEHAVIOR You're swatin' when you ought to be sqawkin.' This saying roughly means you're doing something that's not practical when you ought to be complaining to the boss.

IMPRESSED Showed 'em a thing or two

IMPRESSION, FALSE Just because his breath smells like bananas don't mean he's Tarzan ❑ just 'cause a hog has hair don't mean he can grow sideburns

IMPRESSIONABLE He has a head like a doorknob, anyone can turn it.

IN A DAZE His eyes are fogged over like frost on a windshield.

IN A HURRY He's in a sweeping trot ❑ he's in a two-forty trot, which is two minutes and forty seconds. When the stud book for trotting horses was started, a horse had to trot a mile in two minutes forty seconds or less to be included.

IN ALL DIRECTIONS Ever which a way

IN CONTENTION In the hunt

IN CONTROL He's holding all the trump cards (or all the count rocks in dominos) ❑ he owns the deer lease

IN DANGER You better circle the wagons ❑ you're fishing in troubled waters ❑ you're cussin' a range cook which, for a cowboy, was very dangerous. If the cook didn't simply whip the stuffin' out of the cowboy, he almost certainly saw to it the cowpuncher went hungry.

IN DANGER, BIG TIME You're passing a truck on a blind hill, at night, in a fog, without lights.

IN ERROR You're pulling the wrong pig's ears ❏ that's a bull you're tryin' to milk

IN HEAT In season. Jennifer Chariton didn't quite understand when told her pet dog was in heat. She changed it to the only thing she could understand, in steam.

IN PAIN I'm hurtin' worse than a parakeet that got caught in a badminton game. Since badminton is normally played with a little plastic birdie, if a real parakeet happened to fly into a game in progress, he would be hurtin' for certain by the time he flew out. Hummingbird can be substituted for parakeet.

IN TROUBLE You got your tit in a wringer and it's wash day at the orphanage ❏ you're up a creek in a wire boat ❏ you got your tail in a crack ❏ you're plowin' in a bad row of stumps ❏ the only light at the end of his tunnel is an oncoming train ❏ you got more problems than a mailman at a pit bull show ❏ you got grasshoppers in your axle grease ❏ the hog is dead and you ain't got no wood for a fire, which is a reference to scalding slaughtered hogs ❏ you struck oil in your water

well. There was a time when water was a lot more important than oil. In parts of West Texas, ranchers often struck oil when what they needed was water for the stock. Burk Burnett is supposed to have struck oil in three successive wells and exclaimed "Damn, cattle won't drink that stuff." All's well that ends well, however, because Burnett eventually found enough Texas Tea to make him one of the richest ranchers in the world. Someone later pointed out to him that he had made enough money from oil to buy enough water to fill the Indian Ocean.

IN TROUBLE, BIG TIME A Gypsy fortune teller offered to refund my money ❏ don't worry about biting the bullet, just go on and swallow it ❏ I got so many problems, if something else happens it'll be two weeks before I can worry ❏ you're up to your armpits in manure and somebody is still shoveling ❏ you got your foot caught in the stirrup of a runaway horse, which was a leading cause of death among cowboys ❏ you're itchin' for a good lickin'

INCLINED TO I got a good notion to, as in "I got a good notion to drink that six pack of beer all by myself."

INCOME TAX The government's name for outgo tax ❑ has made more liars out of people than golf and fishing combined

INCOMPETENT He's so incompetent that he couldn't be crew chief on a sunken submarine, which is how Billy Martin once described a baseball umpire.

INCOMPLETE A kiss without a squeeze is like a biscuit without syrup (or chocolate pie without the meringue) ❑ not fully baked ❑ that deer's only half skint

INCONSEQUENTIAL As a bee sting to a honey lovin' bear ❑ as one more pebble on the beach ❑ as one more wart on a frog

INDEBTED TO Beholden to, as in "I'm beholden to you for helpin' pull my pickup out of that bar ditch."

INDECISIVE He has a four-year-old son who ain't been named ❑ he's just a fly-up-the-creek, which means he changes his mind and probably never will make a decision

INDEPENDENT He'd rather leave some hide on a fence than stay corralled ❑ as a hog on a dance floor ❑ enough to pull his own teeth ❑ he sits on the back row and sings bass ❑ he don't march to any drum beat

INDICATIVE A man in a silk shirt probably never picked much cotton ❑ it ain't the size of the dog in the fight, it's the size of the fight in the dog ❑ the cleaner the cafe, the worse the food

INDIFFERENT I don't care no more about it than I do about spit on a sidewalk.

INDIVIDUALISM You gotta pick your own nose ❑ every pot has to stand on its own bottom ❑ some people follow old wagon tracks, others blaze their own trail

INDIVIDUALIST She's one duck you won't ever get in a row.

INDUSTRIOUS Her kindling box is always full.

INEFFECTIVE "It had no more effect than a pint of whiskey split five ways," said *Houston Chronicle* columnist Leon Hale. A fifth of a pint wouldn't be enough whiskey to affect anyone very much. Now a whole pint, that's a different story. ❑ ineffective as a scarecrow covered with bird droppings. The implication here is that the scarecrow not only did not scare the crows away but the birds actually used it as a perch to decide which row of your corn they'd eat first. For the opposite side of the story, see *Scarecrow, Good*.

INEFFICIENT We got too many colonels and not enough cavalry ❑ too many chiefs and not enough Indians ❑ too many cooks and not enough chili meat

INEPT If he had a goose that was laying golden eggs, he'd eat the thing for Thanksgiving dinner ❑ he couldn't even organize a piss off at a brewery ❑ he couldn't get a hooker a date on a troop train ❑ he'd pay extra for an air conditioner on a motorcycle ❑ he'd put a bucket under a natural gas leak ❑ he could get splinters from wrestling timber wolves

INEVITABLE A man who was born to drown would drown in a desert ❑ every turkey has his Thanksgiving ❑ if you fool with a bull, you'll get to see his horns ❑ the more expensive the syrup, the drier the biscuits ❑ there is always someone to

take the slack out of a trouble maker's rope ❑ chips happen ❑ if the stable (or barn) is gonna get clean, somebody is gonna get dirty ❑ if you drill enough oil wells you will learn the sound of suckin' air that you hear from a dry hole ❑ if you sit down in a cactus patch, you can count on pullin' stickers out of your butt ❑ no matter how hard the winter, spring always comes ❑ the only way to keep from growing old is to die young *See also Accept the Inevitable*

INFATUATED He took to that like a hog takes to slop.

INFLATION When the buck doesn't stop anywhere

INGENIOUS He could split something down the middle and still get the biggest half.

INHERITED He fell into a clover patch.

INITIATIVE, POOR He has the initiative of an echo.

INNOCENT As a fresh laid egg

INSIGNIFICANT As dirt under a gnat's fingernail ❑ as gas passed in a whirlwind (it'll be long gone before anyone notices) ❑ as ice to a polar bear ❑ wouldn't even be a pimple on a frog

INSIGNIFICANT PERSON He's just an empty whiskey bottle in life's honky tonk ❑ he's just one bubble in the beer foam of life ❑ he's just a cancelled stamp in the post office of life

INSINCERITY If you ever need an artificial heart, take his.

INSOMNIA Mind over mattress

INSOMNIAC He gets less sleep than a man with three daughters and two back doors ❑ he suffers from the big-eyes

INSOMNIAC, SEVERE When he does go to sleep he dreams about being awake.

INSTALLMENT BUYING By the time you're sick and tired of the thing, you own it.

INSTANTLY Sudden like

INSTEAD OF (Sted-uf)

INSTRUCTIONS, LACKING I can't do what I ain't been told any more than I can go back to where I ain't been. Sam Rayburn once said, "To know where we are going it is important to know where we have been."

INSUBORDINATION Saddle your hoss before you sass the boss.

INSURANCE (IN-sure-unce) Where you come into a lot of money three weeks after you die

INTELLIGENCE Is like a river, the deeper it is the less noise it makes

INTELLIGENCE, AVERAGE He don't know much but he does know not to slap a man in the face when he's chewing tobacco ❑ he wasn't in the top half of his class but he was one that made the top half possible.

INTELLIGENT, VERY He has a total lack of ignorance ❑ he's smarter than a tree full of wise old owls

INTENDS TO STAY He's pitched out his anchor.

INTERNAL COMBUSTION When mortgage papers and insurance policies are in the same drawer and they rub together.

INTEROFFICE ROMANCE Don't cut your heifers out of the company corral ❑ don't dip your quill in the company ink well ❑ don't work the breedin' stock and don't breed the workin' stock

INTERRUPTING Who's robbing this train, me or

you? ❏ Who mashed your button? ❏ Who rattled your cage?

INTOXICATED *See Alcoholic; Drunk*

INTUITION A guess that made good

IRON Smoothin' iron

IRRATIONAL BEHAVIOR He's plowin' blindfolded which, for a farmer, would be very irrational behavior.

IRRESISTIBLE As a can on a sidewalk; you just can't resist kicking it

IRRETRIEVABLE You can't get words back once you've spit 'em out ❏ you can't get the cigar back once you've smoked it ❏ you can't get back spit from the ocean

IRRITATED Something gored his ox.

IS THAT RIGHT? (Zat-right?)

ISN'T IT (Idinit)

ITALIAN (EYE-tal-yun)

ITCHING Like I spent the night in a bed of chiggers

IT'S OVER You can pull down the shades 'cause there ain't nuthin' left for the neighbors to see ❏ Elvis has left the building

This space is for your favorite sayings.

J-K

JEANS, TIGHT — her jeans were so tight I could hardly breathe

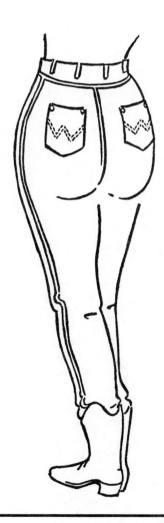

J

JAIL The cross bar hotel

JALAPENO PEPPER (hal-a-peen-ya) Mexican bullet ❑ napalm seeds ❑ the devil's strawberries

JANITOR Floor flusher

JEALOUS MAN His wife has to bring home a note from the preacher to prove she went to church alone ❑ the only time he trusts his wife to go out with the girls is when she takes a Girl Scout troop camping ❑ he trusts his wife about as far as he could throw a baby grand piano ❑ he's been bit by the green-eyed monster, which is a term Shakespeare used to describe jealousy that became a favorite among country folks for some reason

JEALOUS WOMAN If you went home to her with a hair on your coat, you better have a horse to match ❑ someone who sits up with her imagination when her husband is out on the town ❑ she wouldn't trust her

husband if he was in solitary confinement in a Mexican jail

JEANS, TIGHT Her jeans were so tight, I could hardly breathe ❑ if she gets goose bumps she'll bust some seams ❑ her jeans are so tight they look like they were put on with an airbrush. The preceding can also be used for tight dresses, tight shorts, or tight sweaters. Also, her jeans were so tight she had to carry her handkerchief in her mouth ❑ she wears jeans so tight that if she ever drops her purse, she has to walk off and leave it 'cause she can't bend over to pick it up

JEOPARDY *See Double Jeopardy*

JILTED *See Female, Jilted or Male, Jilted*

JIMSON WEED Cow-lily

JOB, BIG I lacked one hand of being able to do it, which means it was more than a two-hand job.

JOB, UNFINISHED All I got out of him was an inch of cordwood and an ounce of cornshucks, which means he didn't finish chopin' the wood and he didn't shuck all the corn.

JOIN IN A dog enjoys the hunt a lot more if he does some of the barkin' ❏ take a seat on the bus and go along for the trip ❏ grab a knife and do some skinning ❏ bait a hook and drop your line in

JOKE, FUNNY A real knee slapper ❏ a real hooter ❏ I ain't laughed that much since grandma got her hair caught in the wringer

JOKE, OLD The first time I heard that I laughed so hard I kicked a slat out of my crib.

JUDGE, POOR He let's 'em go faster than the law can catch 'em.

JUDGEMENT Don't judge a man by his arrows but by how he shoots them ❏ don't judge a woman by the size of her biscuits but by how they taste ❏ you can't judge a man or a car by the sound of the horn

JUDGEMENT, DELAYED Don't judge the cook till you see how he handles the heat in the kitchen.

JUDGEMENT, POOR You're swinging at a wasp nest with a real short stick ❏ he's only got hog sense, which is several shades worse than horse sense

JUKEBOX A no-armed bandit. A slot machine is a one-armed bandit but at least you have a slim chance of winning something when you drop your money into the slot. With a jukebox, you might get a dance but you have no chance to get your money back if you don't.

JUMPS Like a cockroach on a hot griddle ❏ like a downed high line wire ❏ like an armadillo. When an armadillo is frightened his natural instinct is to jump first and then start running. When crossing the road, if an armadillo is scared by a car, he jumps straight up, which is why most are killed by a bumper or grill rather than by being run over.

JUMPED ON ME A friend said he was once in a honky tonk in South Texas when he noticed an attractive young lady walk in the door. He made some comment about the lady to the ol' boy sittin' on the next stool who turned out to be the lady's husband. "That ol' country boy," said my friend, "jumped on me so quick I thought I was under a bridge that had collapsed."

JURY Twelve people who decide who had the best lawyer ❑ one thing that don't work right when fixed

JUST REWARD He got what was comin' to him.

JUSTICE If you're gonna put a goose on trial don't put coyotes on the jury.

K

KEEP ACTIVE If your pot's boiling the flies won't come around ❑ keep your plow moving ❑ it's better to wear out than to rust out

KEEP ALERT Never approach a bull from the front, a horse from the rear, or a fool from any direction ❑ keep a weather eye peeled

KEEP QUIET The only time a whale gets harpooned is when he's spouting off ❑ it ain't the whistle that pulls the train so don't blow or brag

KEEP STILL Pretend you're in a coma.

KEEP THE FAITH Keep your dauber up and your dander down.

KEEP TRYING Another try is better than an alibi ❑ you

gotta start from scratch and keep on scratching ❑ it's OK to give out but don't never give in ❑ a steam kettle keeps singing even though it is up to its neck in hot water

KEEP UP Pack your backside with powder and fire yourself on up here with the rest of us.

KEEP YOUR COMPOSURE Whatever you do, never let 'em see you sweat.

KEEP YOUR MOUTH SHUT Every time the cow bawls, she loses a mouthful of hay.

KEEPSAKE Something you never earmark for a garage sale

KEROSENE Coal oil

KIDDED, BIG TIME He pulled my leg plumb out of the socket.

KILLER He don't believe in life after birth ❑ he has a gunfighter's mentality ❑ funeral maker

KILLING TIME Just grazing

KIND, BUT DUMB He's whole hearted but half witted.

KIND HEARTED She'd buy crutches for a lame duck ❑ she has a heart as soft as summer butter

KINDLING Lighter wood

KINDNESS The milk of human kindness never curdles.

KISS Swap spit or slobber as in "Quick, get me the mouthwash 'cause the dog just swapped slobber with me" ❑ mouth full of nothing that tastes good and sounds like an old milk cow pulling her foot out of a mud bog *See also Incomplete*

KISS, LONG It was wet enough to water a Shetland pony.

KISS, QUICK A Yankee dime, which is about all a Yankee girl's kiss would be worth to most southern boys.

KISSING Is like getting pickles out of a new jar; once you get the first one the rest are easy ❑ remember, kissing don't last but cooking does

KLEPTOMANIAC He helps himself because he can't help himself ❑ he'd steal the gold out of his own teeth

KNICK KNACK A feather duster target ❑ dofunnies ❑ dohickies

KNIFE FIGHT VICTIM A coroner was once asked how many times a man had been stabbed. He replied, "I haven't counted them yet but I'll tell you this. He's got so many holes in him that you could stick a garden hose down his throat and use him for a lawn sprinkler." *See also Bloody*

KNIFE, DULL If the blade was big enough, your kids could use it for a stick horse and not get cut.

KNIFE, LARGE An Arkansas toothpick

KNIFE, SHARP You could use the shadow of the blade to shave with ❑ it's so sharp when I took it out of the sheath the shadow of the blade cut a leg off the kitchen table

KNIFE, SMALL Apple peeler ❑ a bubble gum knife, which is a reference to the small toy knives that were once prizes in bubble gum machines in general stores

KNIFE, SWITCHBLADE A Mexican express card. This saying probably originated because, although switchblade knives have been outlawed in most of the United States, they can still be purchased in Mexican border towns south of California and Texas.

KNOCKED DOWN He went down like a power line in a hurricane or a scarecrow in a whirlwind.

KNOW SOMEONE The best way to know someone is to find out what makes him mad.

KNOW YOUR WORTH Every ol' sausage knows if he was made from a hog or a dog.

KNOWING WITHOUT DOING Is like plowing without sowing

KNOWLEDGEABLE He knows enough to keep his mouth shut when he's up to his chin in a pile of manure ❑ he knows more about that than he does about the back of his hand ❑ he's pig smart, which means he knows a lot about how pigs work. You can substitute horse, cow, sheep, ostrich, or just about anything for pig. Do not, however, substitute woman 'cause there isn't any such thing as a man who knows a lot about how a woman works. *See also Common Knowledge*

This space is for your favorite sayings.

LOVE — is like lightning, it's as apt to strike an outhouse as it is a mansion

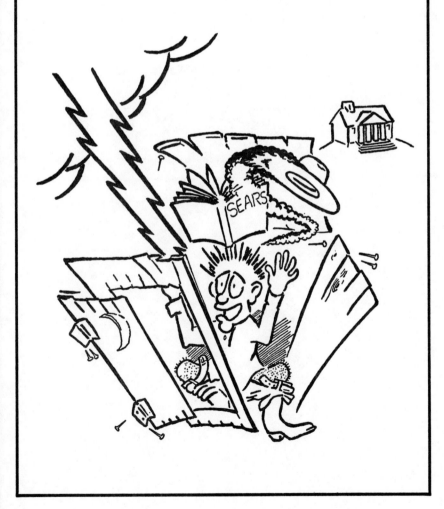

L

L.A. Los Angeles to some, Lower Alabama to many country boys

LADIES MAN, SUCCESSFUL Some ball team ought to sign him 'cause he never strikes out ❑ he could pick up a girl even if he was in a body cast ❑ he's sown more wild oats than all the farmers in Kansas combined

LAKE A fisherman's farm

LAMB FRIES *See Calf Fries and Brave As*

LAND, DRY So dry we had to buy dehydrated water at the 7-Eleven ❑ had to put on postage stamps with paper clips ❑ it takes twenty years for a nail to rust ❑ it's so dry the only time we see rain is when they show pictures of it on television ❑ a man in West Texas swears that one year it was so dry that when it finally did rain he had three and a half inches of mud in his rain gauge *See also Drought*

LAND, FERTILE You could plant a beer can and grow a Japanese car ❑ you could plant cow chips and grow a herd of longhorn cattle ❑ you could plant a whisper and grow a rumor ❑ chickens have to catch the corn on the fly or wait and eat it off the stalk in a day or two

LAND, FLAT You could stand on a tuna fish can and see another 100 miles away. There are some places in West Texas where they claim they can stand on a tomato can and see another one in Kansas.

LAND, POOR You'd have to put fertilizer around the bottom of a pole to raise a flag ❑ so bad it couldn't start a good cuss fight ❑ two red-headed women wouldn't even fight over it ❑ you couldn't raise your voice on it ❑ that piece of ground is so sorry the only thing that ever gets raised on it is taxes, implying that taxes are raised on worthless land as well as good land

LAND, RICH This land is so rich we can't ship anything to another county 'cause the seeds refuse to leave.

LAND, STEEP Our land was so steep we could look up the chimney and watch the cows come home.

LARD Pig salve

LARGE PERSON *See Female, Large; Male, Large*

LAS VEGAS You get better odds by putting your money in a toilet, flushing it, and hoping the plumbing is stopped up.

LASTS FOREVER That lasts as long as an ex-husband. A husband lasts as long as the marriage but an ex-husband lasts forever. (Also holds true for an ex-wife.)

LAUGH HARD Enough to bust a gut ❑ hard enough to shake a tonsil loose from the roots

LAWSUIT Something you go into as a pig and come out of as sausage ❑ a poor country boy caught between two city attorneys in a lawsuit is like a fish caught between two hungry cats

LAWYER A two-legged shark ❑ a professional liar ❑

the only difference between a dead lawyer laying on the road and a dead possum laying on the road is skid marks in front of the possum ❑ his bread and butter is your misery ❑ he climbs the ladder of success wrong by wrong ❑ a lawyer is someone who takes six months to get something started that might take you 10 years to life to finish ❑ the more lawyers involved, the longer the case ❑ is like a wagon wheel, he has to be greased to work ❑ is like a frog, what ain't belly is mouth ❑ something you can't live or die without ❑ one of life's mysteries is what happens to lawyers when they die? They can't get into heaven and the devil won't take 'em 'cause he knows they'd take over. Maybe that's why you see so many old lawyers around.

LAWYER, DEDICATED He's willing to spend every dollar you can beg, borrow, or steal to prove you have a case.

LAWYER, EXPERIENCED He's been through more briefs than a BVD inspector ❑ he could find a loophole in the ten commandments

LAWYER, GOOD If I ordered a trainload of

lawyers and he was the only one that got off I'd be satisfied ❑ good lawyers are like knees on a bowlegged cowboy, they're few and far between

LAWYER, POOR He can have your speeding ticket reduced to a charge of manslaughter ❑ thinks he's dressed up when he gets a paternity suit

LAWYER, PROMISCUOUS He spends more time taking off his briefs than he does writing them.

LAWYER RELATIONS The only time you should call a lawyer is into a burning building.

LAZY AND CAUTIOUS He knows hard work never killed anyone but he don't want to risk being the first victim.

LAZY BUT LIKEABLE He's a good old dog but he won't hunt a lick.

LAZY MAN He's so lazy, if his house caught on fire he'd go outside and pray for rain instead of trying to put it out ❑ he wouldn't move if the hogs were eatin' his boots and he was wearing 'em ❑ he won't even shoo flies off

watermelon ❑ he'd try to pick up a girl on another man's whistle ❑ he's so lazy, his self-winding watch stopped ❑ the only time he lifts weight is when he stands up ❑ he hired someone else to court his girl ❑ he only goes through a revolving door if someone else pushes ❑ if his ship came in he wouldn't bother to unload it ❑ the only thing he does fast is get tired ❑ his feet can go to sleep running for the bus ❑ if hard work is the key to success, he'd rather pick the lock ❑ the bright spot in his life is on the seat of his pants ❑ he wouldn't hit a lick at a snake at a women's garden party ❑ he's a shade follower, which means when he's sitting in his rocking chair out on the porch, as the movement of the sun changes the position of the shade, he moves his chair so he is always in the shade ❑ he's sat in the rocking chair so long the shadow of his arm has worn a hole in the carpet ❑ the only time he works his fingers to the bone is when he's eatin' pork chops ❑ an electric chair couldn't jump start him

LAZY WOMAN She's so lazy she don't even shave her

legs. She just spreads ice cream on 'em and lets the cats lick it off ❑ she's so lazy she keeps hittin' the snooze alarm on her biological clock ❑ she even washes dishes in bed ❑ she won't even exercise discretion ❑ the only exercise she gets is jumping to conclusions ❑ she'll never die 'cause it would take too much energy to draw her last breath ❑ she's so lazy, she wouldn't say shoo if the goats got into the living room and started eatin' the carpet ❑ she thinks she's in a hen house 'cause all she does is lay around

LEADER Big duck in the puddle ❑ big buzzard on the carcass

LEAKS That holds water like a crocheted handkerchief holds snot.

LEAVE Why don't you lay down tracks in the direction of out a here? ❑ run around the barn three times and come back twice ❑ cut a hole in the wind

LEAVE HIM ALONE Don't cross swords with him ❑ don't lock horns with him

LEAVE IT ALONE Leave it be ❑ don't ever try to fix a clock that's keepin' good time, which is a variation of

the popular "Don't fix it if it ain't broke."

LEAVE ME ALONE Don't crank my motor unless you want to see it runnin' ❑ why don't you go run up a stump?

LEAVING I'm out a here ❑ I'm off like a dirty shirt (or prom dress)

LEFT HOME He jumped out of the nest.

LEFT FAST He took off like a goose in a hailstorm ❑ he headed for the tall timbers in a short time

LEGS, THIN You ought to sue those legs for nonsupport, which is what Denver coach Dan Reeves once said to teammate Don Meredith ❑ looks like he traded legs with a killdee (or stork) and got the short end of the deal

LEMONADE, SOUR That would even make the pitcher pucker

LET EVERYONE KNOW Put it right out on the front porch. In the country, houses are often few and far between so when you pass a house, you almost always glance at the front porch. Anything on that front porch would be seen by everyone who passes.

LET SOMEONE ELSE DO IT Let somebody else catch the snakes.

LET'S DISCUSS IT Let's hoe that row ❑ I got a crow to pick with you

LEVEL HEADED He's so level headed he has tobacco juice runnin' out of both sides of his mouth.

LIAR, FEMALE She has to send the dogs to bring the kids home 'cause they don't believe her when she calls 'em ❑ she thinks truth is like a girdle, made to be stretched ❑ she tells such big lies she has stretch marks around her mouth ❑ all her blankets are stretched plumb out of shape, which is derived from the saying that to lie is to "stretch the blanket" *See also Female, Lying*

LIAR, MALE He believes that truth is scarce so he don't want to use it up ❑ he never lets the truth stand in the way of a good story ❑ he tells the truth about as often as an Arizona prospector ❑ he's a point blank tale teller, which means he'll lie right to your face ❑ he'd tell a lie even if the truth sounded better ❑ he'd rather climb a tall tree and tell a lie in the sunshine than to sit in the shade and tell the truth ❑ the only time he tells the truth is when he admits he's a liar ❑ you can tell if he's lying if his lips are moving ❑ he's such a big liar he would have been right at home in law school ❑ if he ever told the truth his tonsils would be so shocked they'd slap the tongue right out of his mouth ❑ he can talk out of both sides of his mouth and tell lies from each side, which is how Harry Truman once described Richard Nixon ❑ the biggest liar ever recorded was the golf playing fisherman who gave up his law practice to go to congress and later retired to become a used car salesman

LIE, BIG I once met an honest fisherman. Note: politician, lawyer, or jogger may be substituted for fisherman. In actual practice, joggers may be the biggest liar's of all time, especially when someone asks them how far they ran.

LIES There are three kinds of lies: lies, damn lies, and Chamber of Commerce statistics.

LIFE Is like a suitcase, if you cram enough into it something has to give ❑ is like square dancing; about the time you get into the swing of things, someone changes directions on you ❑ is like a poker game; if you don't put anything into the pot, there won't be anything to take out ❑ is like riding a bicycle; you either go or you get off ❑ is something that is too short and too full of blisters

LIFE, BORING If it wasn't for Gamblers Anonymous, Alcoholic Anonymous, and Weight Watchers, he wouldn't have nothing to do.

LIGHT (WEIGHT) As a mother-in-law's baggage when she's moving out

LIGHT A MATCH Strike a match ❑ scratch a match *See also Zipper*

LIKE FATHER, LIKE SON Fruit don't fall far from the tree.

LIKELY TO Libel to, as in "If your wife catches you drinkin' any more beer she's libel to snatch you bald headed."

LIMITED CAPABILITIES His pony only knows one trick.

LIMP As a neck-wrung turkey

LIPS, ATTRACTIVE *See Mouth, Female*

LIPSTICK Pucker paint

LIPSTICK SMEARS A leading cause of powder burns

LIQUOR Bottled courage ❑ gut warmer ❑ snake oil ❑ wild mare's milk ❑ stomach varnish *See also Whiskey*

LIQUOR, JUST RIGHT If it was any better you wouldn't a given it to me and if it was any worse I wouldn't a drunk it.

LIQUOR, STRONG That stuff would make an earthworm bite a catfish. *See also Whiskey, Strong and Fisherman, Clever*

LIQUOR, WEAK It's got the kick of a 75-year-old pregnant chorus girl.

LITTER There's a town in Kansas that is so strict about litter that you can get a $50 fine for telling a dirty joke.

LIVES CLOSE They just live a howdy and a half away down the road ❑ just a hop, skip, and a jump from here ❑ just a hoot and a holler away

LIVESTOCK, LACKING I ain't even got a scapegoat.

LIVING WITHOUT FAITH Is like driving in a fog all the time

LOAFER He gets his exercise watching others do the work ☐ the man who looks for easy work goes to bed all tired from looking ☐ an expert loafer is one who does nothing better than anyone else *See also Lazy*

LOBBYIST, GOOD He can make you believe you left five minutes ago and were never there in the first place.

LOCATION, GOOD Jerry Glanville, head coach of the Falcons, once said of Atlanta, "This ain't heaven but you can see heaven from here." Folks in places like Texas, Colorado, California, etc. might be compelled to point out that they have just as good a view of heaven as Glanville does in Atlanta.

LOGGERS Flatheads

LONELINESS Makes friends out of strangers

LONESOME As an homely girl under mistletoe

LONG As a Georgia well rope.

LONG LASTING Lasts as long as a necktie you don't like ☐ as a scar from a vacination

LONG WINDED *See Speaker, Long Winded*

LONG TIME In a coon's age, as in "I ain't been to the Grand ol' Opry in a coon's age" ☐ longer than a wet week. Nothing seems longer than when it rains constantly for an entire week, especially to the mother of five.

LONG TIME BETWEEN KISSES The great Minnie Pearl may have said it best with, "I haven't been kissed in so long I don't remember if you suck your breath in or let it out."

LONG JOHN UNDERWEAR Longhandles

LOOK, MEAN She looked at me like I had just tracked horse manure (or fish guts) across her clean floor.

LOOK, SWEET You could pour it on a biscuit

LOOK EVERYWHERE Look all over hell and half of Georgia.

LOOKS *See Appearance*

LOOKING FOR TROUBLE He's campaigning for a butt kicking.

LOOSE As the hide on a Brahma bull. In a rodeo, Brahmas are usually hard to ride, not only because they are mean but because their skin is so loose it is hard to hold onto in an emergency. One ol' rodeo rider sought to solve the problem when he walked into the arena carryin' a hammer and some shingle nails. When asked what he intended to do, the cowboy replied, "I'm nailing that critter's hide in place so I'll know if I'm sittin' on his back or hangin' onto his belly."

LOSER He's like the cow that went dry, an udder failure ❑ he got the small end of the horn which is a reference to there being very little in the small end of the Horn of Plenty ❑ he came up empty handed ❑ he got left holdin' the empty sack ❑ he started slow and tapered off ❑ he was in the outhouse when opportunity knocked on the front door of his house ❑ when opportunity knocked he was out hunting for a four leaf clover ❑ he had Las Vegas surgery and he's got the scars on his bank account to prove it ❑ he struck out before he even came up to bat ❑ he got

throwed before the horse started bucking.

LOSING PROPOSITION You're feeding a lost dog, which means you'll lose the feed and the dog when his owner shows up.

LOSING GROUND The faster I go, the behinder I get.

LOSING WEIGHT He looks like he's evaporating ❑ she's fallin' away to nuthin'

LOST Joe Holsted of WBAP radio in Fort Worth, Texas said it best when he explained he was "lost as an outhouse in the fog" ❑ as a turtle at the bottom of a barrel of molasses ❑ as a goose in a snowstorm ❑ as an Easter egg ❑ as a nickel down a Georgia well

LOST CAUSE You can't get blood out of the heart of a watermelon.

LOST CONTROL He come apart like the seams in a fat man's pants.

LOST HIS TEMPER Flew off the handle, which is a country equivalent to "went ballistic."

LOUISIANA (Luzy-ann-ah) Coonass state

LOVE Is like measles, the later it comes the worse it is

❏ is like lightning, it's as apt to strike an outhouse as a mansion ❏ is like the morning dew, it's just as apt to be on a cow patty as on a cactus rose ❏ conquers all things except poverty and a real bad toothache

LOVE, DEVOUT Grade A pasteurized passion

LOVE, TRUE Is like a circle, it has no end

LOVERS ADVICE Never make love by the garden gate; love is blind but the neighbors ain't.

LOW As a snake's navel in a deep wagon track ❏ as a mole's navel on diggin' day

LOW DOWN PERSON He could wear a ten-gallon hat and walk under an armadillo.

LUCK, TURNING Everything was going good but they're gettin' back to normal.

LUCKY He could sit on a fence and the birds would feed him ❏ if he fell face down in a fresh cow patty he'd find a diamond ring when he washed his face ❏ he relies on a rabbit's foot instead of horse sense ❏ if you've got enough luck you can get by with barbed wire for brains ❏ he's got all his squirrels up one tree ❏ he could throw marbles into a swinging jug

LUCKY, EXTREMELY He could fall into the squat hole in an outhouse and come out smelling like a Beaumont whore ❏ he could skinny dip in a septic tank and end up smelling sweeter than fresh mowed grass ❏ there are many variations of this theme and one of the best was in *Handy as Hip Pockets on a Hog* by Donald Chain Black. Under fortunate, which is the same as lucky to a country boy, Mr. Black wrote, "He could fall through a toilet hole and come out smelling like Evening in Paris."

This space is for your favorite sayings.

M

MALE, LARGE — his overcoat could be a pup tent for a boy scout troop

M

MAD He's so mad he can't spit straight ❑ enough to kick the cat *See also Angry; Male, Angry; Female, Angry*

MADE LOVE They went to the pea patch. *See also Related, Sort Of*

MADE MONEY Got well, as in "He got well in the hog business."

MAKE A CHOICE You can't sell your cow and have the milk too ❑ pick one out of the herd

MAKE IT EASIER Sugar the pill.

MAKE IT QUICK Short stroke it ❑ take the slack out of it

MAKE PEACE Don't stir the fire with a sword.

MAKE ROOM Scootch over a little bit.

MAKE THE JOB EASIER Put the hay down closer to the ground so the goats can get at it.

MAKE UP YOUR MIND Don't pray for rain if you're gonna complain about the mud ❑ fish, cut bait, or swim to shore

MALE Old hairy legs ❑ a man is like a watermelon, you can't tell how good he is till you thump him ❑ a man is seldom as smart as his mother thinks or as dumb as his mother-in-law thinks

MALE, ACTIVE He's got tumbleweeds in his blood, which basically means he just can't sit still.

MALE, ANGRY He's fightin' with his hat. A lot of country boys will occasionally get so angry that they'll take off their hat and wave it in all sorts of motions. They might hit the ground, their knee, a fence, or even whoever they're talkin' to with the hat. In any event, when a country boy starts fightin' with his hat, he's gettin' real angry and about ready to start fightin' with fists or firearms. ❑ he'd make an untipped New York cab driver look like a Baptist choir boy ❑ he had a fit and fell in it ❑ he was fit to be tied ❑ he's bent plumb out of shape ❑ he came on like a mad father with a loaded shotgun ❑ something got him cross-legged

MALE, EFFEMINATE He's got a little sugar in his blood.

MALE, EVIL He prefers vice to advice ❑ he would chase off a widow woman's ducks ❑ he's the one your mamma warned you about ❑ he'd steal the air out of a widow woman's tires ❑ when he's alone he's in bad company ❑ he's a trigger looking for a finger ❑ nothing wrong with him that reincarnation (or cremation) wouldn't cure ❑ when he dies, they'll print his obituary under Public Improvements ❑ he'd make Clyde Barrow look like a Baptist choir boy *See Female, Evil*

MALE, FAT He's a member of the sprawl of fame ❑ he's well watered ❑ his overcoat could be a tent for a boy scout troop *See also Fat Man*

MALE, HARD HEARTED If he ate his heart out he'd break a tooth.

MALE, JEALOUS *See Jealous Man*

MALE, JILTED When she took him by the hand he thought she was takin' him by the heart but she was only takin' him for a fool (which surely ought to be the name of country song).

MALE, LARGE He's large enough to be a quartet ❑ he's so big it takes a committee of five to look him over ❑ the question most people ask him is "Where did you put Fay Ray?" ❑ he's as big as a John Deere gang plow ❑ he's big enough to hunt a bear with a stick ❑ the last time I saw anything that big it had a bulldog on the hood. In case you don't know, Mack trucks use a bulldog hood ornament on all their trucks.

MALE, LARGE AND MEAN He could be the bouncer in the devil's saloon.

MALE, LIAR *See Liar, Male*

MALE, LAZY *See Lazy Man*

MALE, MEAN *See Mean Man*

MALE, PROMISCUOUS He's like a real estate investor, he believes in gettin' lots while you're young ❑ when the wages of sin are paid, he'll have to pay time and a half ❏ the only people who know he's married are the ones who were at the wedding ❏ you can find him in the yellow pages under recreational facilities ❏ he has all the resistance of a willow tree in a hurricane

MALE, ROWDY He'd rather talk some trash than carry out the trash.

MALE, SHORT When he stands up he looks like he's standing in a hole.

MALE, SKINNY He's so thin you can hear his bones rattle when he walks ❏ he could take a shower in a fountain pen ❏ he's so thin, his muscles look like flea bites on a cane pole ❏ you could use him for a dipstick

MALE, SORRY He's a man without principle so he don't draw much interest.

MALE, STUPID The only time you'll find him in an institution of higher learning is if he shows up as a test body in an anatomy class ❏ some of the lights in his string are burnt out ❏ his brain on the edge of a razor blade would look like a BB on an interstate highway ❏ if brains were gasoline, he couldn't run an ant's motor-

cycle around a cherry pit ❏ could mess up a two-car funeral ❏ he's a forthright person — he's right about a fourth of the time ❏ he don't know the difference between working up steam and generating fog ❏ he could teach a rock to be dumb ❏ used his food stamps to mail a letter ❏ food for thought gives him indigestion ❏ he forgot his twin sister's birthday *See also Stupid Man*

MALE, UGLY He's so ugly he couldn't get a date if he was shipwrecked on a island full of lonely women ❏ he's so ugly only his mother could love him and then only on payday ❏ could scare night into day ❏ he could sour milk in the carton ❏ if he broke his leg, we'd have to shoot him ❏ if ugly was a crime, he'd being doing life without parole ❏ he could kill waist high cotton *See also Ugly Man*

MALE, AGE A man is as young as the woman he feels.

MANIPULATIVE He can play you like a $50 fiddle.

MANNERS, GOOD He can yawn with his mouth closed.

MANNERS, POOR He'd pass gas when he was playing the front end inside a horse costume.

MANURE Something that makes crops and the government grow ❑ something you find under the outhouse and in the White House

MARITAL ADVICE FOR HER When she said "I do" she said too much ❑ it is better to buy a good horse than to marry a man 'cause at least you know the horse won't turn into a jackass ❑ a husband is like a fire in a cook stove, he goes out if unattended ❑ wear shows where the wife stands and the husband sits ❑ marry an ugly man. He won't leave you 'cause he can't do any better.

MARITAL ADVICE FOR HIM Marry an ugly woman. She'll leave you but you won't mind much ❑ marry a woman with brains enough for two and you'll come out about even ❑ never try to drown your troubles if she can swim ❑ the husband who treats his wife like a thoroughbred will find she don't turn into a nag ❑ a wife is like a baseball umpire, she don't think you're safe when you're out ❑ a husband controls his wife like a barometer controls the weather ❑ a poor man who marries a rich woman gets a boss

instead of a wife *See also Three R's*

MARITAL RELATIONS It's a big problem that can't be solved in a double bed ❑ a successful marriage is like eating with chop sticks, it looks easy till you try it

MARKSMAN An expert at triggernometry

MARRIAGE For better or worse means for good ❑ stops your circulation faster than a tourniquet on a snake bite ❑ a life sentence that can be suspended by bad behavior ❑ like taking a hot bath, once you get used to it, it ain't so hot ❑ they were married by a judge but should have held out for a jury ❑ is like farming, you have to start over again every morning if you want to be successful ❑ marriage is the leading cause of divorce ❑ marriage is the difference between painting the town and the back porch

MARRIAGE, PERFECT A deaf man and a blind woman

MARRIED, OFTEN She's been married so many times she has rice scars.

MARRIED MAN He may not be the best informed, but he is the most informed.

MASS CONFUSION The blind leading the blind ❏ like a herd of mules in a hailstorm ❏ three lawyers and one case ❏ like a sudden shower on an eat-off-the-ground church social, no one knows whether to stay dry or save the food

MATCH, POOR They go together like mustard and pancakes ❏ they go together like scotch and Dr Pepper

MATERNITY BLOUSE Hatching jacket ❏ a slip cover

MATHEMATICIAN, POOR To him, it's four of one and half a dozen of the other ❏ he counts real good till he runs out of fingers and toes

MEAN AS A bitin' mule ❏ as an Alabama wildcat ❏ as a two-stingered yellow jacket ❏ as a rattlesnake with a headache ❏ as a Louisiana alligator with a gum boil

MEAN MAN He's mean enough to pitch his bath water on a widow woman's kindling ❏ he can raise more hell than an alligator in a drained swamp ❏ if he went deaf he wouldn't tell his barber ❏ he was baptized in vinegar ❏ given the chance he would a rooted for Goliath ❏ he'd put a rattlesnake in your pocket and then ask you for a match ❏ he'd steal the light bulb from the porch lamp at an orphanage ❏ Jerry Brooks' favorite is "He'd take the manure away from a tumble bug and send him on the wrong road home."

He'd flush the toilet when you're in the shower. If your shower and your toilet operate off the same feeder pipes as most facilities do, then you have only one hot water pipe and one cold water pipe supplying your entire bathroom. If you are in the shower enjoying water that is balanced just right between hot and cold and some dastardly person flushes the toilet, you are in big trouble and left singing in water that's become scalding hot.

Also, if he was baptized all the fish in the creek would die. When Sam Houston, former governor of Tennessee and Texas, was baptized he was told that all his sins had been washed away. He replied, "Lord help the fishes down below."

MEAN WOMAN If she died, everyone would rest in peace ❏ she makes a Georgia junkyard dog look like a miniature French poodle in a

New York dog show ❑ a hurricane with two eyes ❑ she even whips her husband while he's doing the dishes ❑ she'd send a get well card to a hypochondriac ❑ the cake she baked to leave for Santa Claus was made with Ex-Lax

MEAN, BUT STUPID He'd take a knife to a gun fight.

MEANINGLESS That and a half a buck will get you a cup of coffee ❑ as warts on a hog's belly ❑ as a striptease to a blind man ❑ that don't amount to any more than what the little bird left on top of the flag pole

MEASUREMENT, DOUBTFUL I believe that was measured by a pelt with the tail still on. When purchasing pelts by the pound, the tails are normally removed before the skins are weighed. If the tails are left on, the measurement is not anywhere near true.

MEAT, RARE *See Rare Meat*

MECHANIC, POOR He treats your car with sunshine, which means he basically leaves it parked outside for several hours hoping the problem will go away.

MECHANICAL APTITUDE, POOR He has to avoid a wheelbarrow 'cause he don't know nothing about machinery.

MEETING A dog and pony show

MEETING, DISASTROUS We had a dog and pony show but the dog wet everywhere and the pony didn't know any tricks.

MELTS Like a chocolate Easter bunny on a pickup dash board ❑ like a snowball on the devil's prong

MEMORIAL SERVICE A going away party for someone who has already gone

MEMORY, POOR He could hide his own Easter eggs ❑ he can't remember names but he always forgets faces ❑ he can't even remember the Alamo ❑ he can't even remember the first girl he kissed ❑ his memory is shorter than a chigger's eyebrow

MEN Most men are like barbed wire; they have their good points. *See also Male*

MERCY *See At His Mercy*

MIDDLE AGE The age when you'd rather skip a night at the honky tonk than have to get over it the next day ❑ when a narrow waist and a broad mind swap places ❑ when you lose more hair in the shower than you do in the barber's chair ❑ when your actions creak louder than words ❑ when your favorite night spot is on the couch in front of the TV ❑ when you only chase girls who are going downhill ❑ for a woman, middle age is when men stop pinching and the girdle starts

MILK, CANNED A favorite among cowboys was once Carnation milk that came in a can and thus would not sour quickly like fresh milk. Some unknown poet summed up the feelings of many cowboys about canned milk with this little poem: Carnation Milk, best in the land; comes to you in a little red can. No tits to pull, no hay to pitch; just punch a hole in the son of a . . . gun.

MILKING Burglarizing a cow ❑ draining the spigots ❑ flushin' a cow

MIND Is like a parachute, it only works when open

MIND YOUR OWN BUSINESS Burn your tongue in your own coffee ❑ if it don't bother you, don't

bother it ❑ never get between a dog and his bone ❑ tend to your own bees

MISCONCEPTION A rustler who's never been chased by a posse thinks it's his right to steal ❑ he thought she was his but he was hers

MISER If he spent two weeks in the mountains of Colorado, he'd send you a post card with a picture of the motel swimming pool because it was free ❑ he's such a miser, when company pulls into the driveway, he makes everyone in the family grab a toothpick so it'll look like they just finished dinner ❑ he's mighty tough to live with but he's gonna make a great ancestor *See also Cheapskate; Frugal*

MISERABLE I'm in a world of manure.

MISGUIDED You're in the up elevator but it's on the Titanic.

MISSISSIPPI (Mis-sippe)

MISSISSIPPI RIVER The Big Muddy

MISSOURI (Ma-zur-ah)

MISTAKE Anyone can make a mistake but it is always

someone else who makes the damn fool mistakes.

MISTAKE, COSTLY You shot your best hunting dog.

MISTAKEN Your calf ain't sucking the right cow ❑ you're doin' a two step and the band's playing a waltz

MIXED EMOTIONS Dwight "Paddlefoot" Sloan, a star football player with the University of Arkansas in the 1930s, may have said it best. When Arkansas decided to leave the Southwest Conference and join the Southeast Conference, Sloan, like a lot of Arkansas fans, had mixed emotions. "It's like your mother-in-law driving off a cliff," he said, "in your Cadillac."

MODEST She makes her husband wear a blindfold when they shower together ❑ she can't even tell the naked truth ❑ she won't walk over grates in the sidewalk 'cause she don't know who might be down there ❑ she wouldn't wear patent leather shoes 'cause she's afraid of what might be seen in the reflection ❑ she won't even look at things with a naked eye

MONEY Is like a drunk, the tighter it gets, the more it talks ❑ isn't everything but take it away from some people and there ain't much left ❑ the only known cure for poverty ❑ what goes down the drain when Santa comes down the chimney

MONOGAMY *See Bigamy*

MOOCHER You'll always find him on the dock when someone else's ship comes in.

MOONSHINE Swamp dew ❑ homemade lightning ❑ bottled lightning ❑ Tennessee tea ❑ quart juice

MOONSHINE, GOOD You can taste the feet of the farm hand that hoed the corn it was made from ❑ If you ask a country boy about the qualities of moonshine, he'll probably tell you to try this test: get two glasses and fill one with water and one with moonshine. Then drop a live worm into each glass — the worm in the water lives and the worm in the moonshine dies. The moral? Drink moonshine and you'll never have worms.

MOONSHINE, POOR Panther spit

MORALS, POOR His morals are about as loose as the bowels of a Mexican tourist.

MOSQUITOS, LARGE The mosquitos around here are so big we catch 'em in mouse-traps ❑ it's got an ice pick for a nose that can drill through a rawhide boot ❑ the mosqui-tos are so large in Texas that a fisherman swears he killed one and found three wood ticks on the body ❑ we don't shoot skeet we shoot skeeters *See also Get To Work*

MOTHER If mamma ain't happy, ain't nobody happy ❑ the hand that rocks the cradle will also slap hell fire out of you if you get on her bad side

MOTHER, GOOD She's like an old quilt, keeps the kids warm but doesn't smother them.

MOTHER, PROTECTIVE She sewed nametags in the clothes her son wore when he left for the army ❑ she has the longest apron strings in the county, which implies that her kids have have trouble gettin' untied

MOTHER-IN-LAW, EVIL She has to add antifreeze to her pacemaker.

MOTHER-IN-LAW, LAZY If it wasn't for giving directions she wouldn't get any exercise.

MOTHER-IN-LAW SANDWICH Warm tongue, cold shoulder

MOTHERLY PATIENCE Is like toothpaste in a tube, it is never quite all gone

MOUNTAIN LAUREL Calico bush

MOUTH A hole under your nose where the firewater goes in and the cuss words come out

MOUTH, FEMALE A famous Texan named Big Foot Wallace once said that a certain young lady had a mouth that looked "like a gash cut in a juicy ripe peach."

MOUTH, LARGE His mouth is so large, if it wasn't for his ears the top of his head would look like an island ❑ he can sing a duet by himself ❑ looks like a torn pocket ❑ her mouth is so large she gets lipstick on her ears when she smiles ❑ the bigger the mouth, the better it looks closed

MOUTHFUL Dipper full

MOVES A LOT We moved so much when I was a kid that every time we started packing, the chickens would lay down and stick up their feet to be tied. This came from the depression days when families moved often. Usually, country folks had chickens and they would load them on the truck with their feet tied.

MOVES SLOW Like a woman entering her thirties ❏ about as fast as the Great Northern glacier ❏ as a deadbeat father writin' out a child support check ❏ he moves so slow pigeons could roost on his hat

MOVIE, FRIGHTENING Would make the hair on a mink stole stand on end

MOVIE, SAD *See Sad Movie*

MOVING FAST Ginnin', as in "He was really ginnin when the sheriff got after him."

MUCH LESS Let alone, as in "I can't afford the horse, let alone the feed."

MUDDY ENOUGH To bog a kitten

MUD HOLE Loblolly

MULE, FAST You have to yell whoa before you yell giddy up.

MULE SENSE Approach a mule the way a porcupine

makes loves, slow and careful.

MUSIC To a woman, the sweetest music is another woman playing second fiddle.

MUSIC, GOOD Foot stompin' music, which means it is so good it makes you want to dance even if you'd have to use a wooden chair for a partner.

MUSIC, SLOW Buckle polishing music

MUSIC LOVER If he hears a pretty girl singing in the bathtub he puts his ear to the keyhole ❏ she applauds when her husband comes home singing at 4:00 a.m.

MUSICIAN, GOOD He can play both kinds of music, country and western.

MUSICIAN, POOR Shade tree musician ❏ the proper pitch for his guitar would be out the window

MY TURF My stompin' ground

MYSTERIOUS AS A neighbor who keeps the shades drawn shut all the time

N

NERVY — as a 300-pound jockey

NAIVE He could be held up through the mail ❑ she's just a babe in a woods full of wolves ❑ he believes everything he reads in the newspaper

NAKED (Nekkid)

NARROW ESCAPE *See Close Call*

NARROW MINDED He's so narrow minded his ears rub together ❑ narrow minded people are like long neck beer bottles, the less they have in them the more noise it makes coming out

NATURAL ABILITY *See Ability, Natural*

NATURE CALLING If I don't find a sand box soon I ain't gonna have a single dry pocket ❑ my back teeth are floating ❑ I'm beginning to see yellow

NAVY MAN Anchor cranker. A lot of country boys eventually find themselves in the navy, perhaps because many of them grow up without ever seeing much water at any one time. *See also Submarine Crewman*

NEARBY *See Lives Close*

NEARSIGHTED He could lose a bass fiddle in a phone booth ❑ he mistook the shampoo for the mouthwash and almost gargled to death

NECK, LARGE If you put him into a guillotine it'd take three chops to cut off his head.

NEIGHBORHOOD, POOR If Diogenes ever went through that neighborhood with his lamp looking for an honest man, they'd steal his lamp. (Said of any neighborhood in New York City.)

NEIGHBORLY Good fences make good neighbors. If you ever live in the country next door to someone who doesn't keep his fences mended, about the third time you have to chase that neighbor's livestock out of your garden, you will understand what this saying means.

NERVOUS He wants to know how many calories in fingernails ❏ wound tighter than an eight-day clock on Sunday morning, which is a reference to the old country practice of winding the clock on Sunday morning before going to church ❏ she's as jumpy as a bushel basket full of Louisiana hoppin' frogs ❏ she's about as calm as a cyclone

NERVOUS AS A tongue-tied lawyer ❏ as a de-clawed cat ❏ as a fly around a glue pot ❏ as a leap frog with a broken leaper ❏ as a porcupine in a balloon factory ❏ as a worm on a hook ❏ as a cat in a tennis racket factory ❏ as hungry tick on a skinny dog ❏ as a pregnant mule in a traffic jam ❏ as a horse on a high wire ❏ as a tree outside a dog show ❏ as a boy waiting to be spanked ❏ as an old hog on a cold morning (see *Cold Weather*) ❏ as a small kitten up a big tree ❏ as a hooker in a confessional

NERVY He's got more nerve than a three-hundred-pound jockey.

NEVER When cows give beer ❏ when hell turns into a popsicle ❏ that'll happen about the time Sunday comes after Wednesday

NEVER DO IT Never learn to iron, someone will expect you to do it ❏ never pet a polar bear until he's a rug ❏ never put a broom on a bed unless you want bad luck ❏ never put the cart before the horse unless you are backing up

NEVER ENDING About the time you finish hoeing weeds in the cotton field, new ones have already sprouted.

NEW INFORMATION Now that's a new wrinkle (or ring) on my horn.

NEW ORLEANS (Nawlins or New Are Leans), pronounced as three words.

NEW YORK CITY Like marriage, everyone ought to try it once

NEWS There is an old saying that a dog biting a man is not news but a man biting a dog is. A modern version is a senator throwing bull is not news but a bull throwing a senator would be news.

NEWSPAPER Something you read to find out what people really do, after reading the Bible to find out what they ought to do.

NEWSPAPER, POOR Prints enough manure to fertilize the San Fernando Valley

NIGHT, DARK *See Dark Night*

NO INTENTION Not about to, as in "I'm not about to loan you my pickup."

NO SIMILARITIES They're about as similar as a French negligee and a flannel nightgown ❑ they're about as similar as a rat and a reindeer ❑ they're no more similar than nylon hose and a garden hose

NO SUCH THING There ain't no such thing as betting enough on a winning horse.

NOBODY CAN HELP YOU You got to chew your own tobacco ❑ tote your own skillet

NOISE, OMINOUS *See Sound, Ominous*

NOISY As a scrub calf in a briar patch ❑ as wind blowing over a bung hole in an empty barrel ❑ as a longhorn steer in a dry thicket ❑ as a restless mule in a tin barn ❑ as a kid playin' with a coffee can that has one rock inside ❑ as hailstones on a tin roof ❑ as a hungry calf

NOISY, SOMEWHAT There was about as much noise as a harelip cowboy tryin' to whistle Dixie.

NONCHALANT Ability to look like a thoroughbred when you just acted like a jackass

NONCOMMITTAL He won't stay hitched ❑ he's a fence rider (or straddler)

NONEXISTENT As a nose on a football ❑ as a jackalope. According to country legend, the world's fastest animal is a cross between a jackrabbit and an antelope. Unfortunately, no one has ever seen a real jackalope.

NONSENSE Rooster eggs ❑ horse hockey ❑ that's just a load of chicken teeth

NOSE, BROKEN His nose has been broke so many times he has to breathe through his ears.

NOSE, LONG His nose is so long he could suck the guts out of a pumpkin through a keyhole.

NOSE, LARGE You could store a small dog in that hole.

NOT FUNNY That's about as funny as a crutch.

NOT IMPORTANT Ain't no great shakes

NOT INVOLVED "I don't have a dog in that fight," said Texas Speaker of the House Gib Lewis.

NOT WORKING The ox ain't plowin.'

NOT WORTH THE EFFORT You can bail all day with a thimble but the boat is still gonna sink.

NOTHING IS IMPOSSIBLE You can carry water in a tea strainer if it's in the form of ice cubes.

NOTHING Just a tap hole without a beer keg around it ❏ what most politicians are good for

NOTHING TO DO He's got about as much to do as the vice president. Will Rogers once said the vice president had the best job in the country because all he had to do was get up each morning and say, "How's the President?"

NOW I UNDERSTAND The nickel finally dropped. This is a reference to the old days when pay telephones were first perfected, sort of. The cost of a call was a nickel but frequently the coin would hang up in the mechanism requiring several "whomps" on the phone to get it to drop and complete the connection. Of course, to modernize the saying you'd have to use quarter instead of nickel.

NUDIST Someone who grins and bares it

NUMEROUS More than Quaker has oats ❏ more than you can shake a stick at

NURSE A pan handler

NUTRITIONIST, POOR He thinks a balanced diet is a cheeseburger in each hand.

NYMPHOMANIAC Mattress tester

O

OUT OF PLACE — as an udder on a bull

O

OAF He could make an anvil complicated.

OATH Well cut off one of my legs and call me "I" lean ☐ well I'll be a suck-egg mule ☐ well I'll be dipped in snuff ☐ well don't that twirl your spurs ☐ that beats anything I ever saw or heard tell of ☐ I'll be dipped in shellac ☐ well shoot me a runnin' ☐ well I'll be switched ☐ well that tears a plank off the wall ☐ well shoot me for a billy goat ☐ well slap me naked and sell (or hide) my clothes ☐ well flip my garters

OBITUARY Only known form of bad publicity

OBNOXIOUS If she asked for a ride, she'd want to drive ☐ he's a goat-gitter

OBSERVANT He can spot rat droppings in a raisin pie. Note, dead house fly can be substituted for rat and any number of words can be substituted for droppings.

OBSOLETE As a horse drawn combine

OBSTACLE, SMALL That grass ain't tall for a high stepper.

OBSTINATE She's so obstinate she won't even listen to both sides of a record album.

OBVIOUS As plain as the hand on the end of your arm ☐ plain as a glass eye on a goat ☐ plain as the nose on your face

OBVIOUS, SOMEWHAT Clear as looking through lace curtains.

OCCURRENCE, RARE That happens every once in a blue moon.

ODD BEHAVIOR That's a strange way to run a railroad

ODD PERSON His cross hairs ain't lined up ☐ there's a few pieces missing out of his puzzle *See also Strange Person*

ODDS, POOR About the same as those of a turtle tryin' to cross a six-lane highway in rush hour ☐ the chances of that happening are about the same as those of you diving into an empty swimming pool and stopping before you hit bottom *See also Chances, Slim and Las Vegas*

OFFICE, LARGE You could hang a stuffed whale on the wall, which is a reference to fishermen liking to hang their trophy catches on the wall ❏ it's big enough for a putting green instead of just a putting machine

OFFICE, SMALL If it was twice as big, it might qualify as a broom closet ❏ if you hung a fish on the wall it would have to be a minnow

OFFSPRING, POOR She needs a large apron to cover her children's faults.

OIL FIELD WORKER Roughneck. According to Donnis Baggett, a roughneck is either an oil field worker or what an unemployed oil field worker feels after shaving too long with an old blade.

OLD As black pepper, dirt, rocks, sunshine, or sin

OLD AGE When most of the names in your black book are followed by the initials M.D.

OLD AND FAT He ain't seen his feet since a Roosevelt was in the White House. The name of the president can be changed to adjust the age.

OLD LOOKING She looks like she aged in dog years.

OLD PERSON When he was born the sun was just a match-head and there weren't no moon atall ❏ he was a stowaway on the ark ❏ he's three years older than dirt ❏ Jesus was still in high school when he was born or he went to high school with Moses ❏ he used to bang the gong to release the lions in the Roman coliseum ❏ when he was born Moby Dick was just a minnow

OLD-TIMER His back goes out more than he does ❏ the only exercise he gets is acting as a pallbearer for his friends ❏ he's so old he don't buy green bananas ❏ tells it like it used to be ❏ can remember when a woman looked the same before and after washing her face

OLD-TIMER, COUNTRY BOY He's been scrapin' manure off his boots for more years than you could count or he's scraped enough manure off his boots to fertilize the Rio Grande valley. Either expression means he's been working around farm animals and manure for a long time.

OMEN Invisible handwriting on the wall

ONCE IN AWHILE (wunsinawhall) Usually pronounced as one word ❏ ever now and again

ONE OR THE OTHER When an old hen cackles, she's either layin' or lyin.'

ONE SIDED As a turkey shoot

ONLY ONE Ownliest one, as in "I have to find my hat 'cause it's the ownliest one I got."

OPEN MINDED, EXTREMELY His mind is so open it could double as a vacant lot.

OPERATION, MINOR One performed on somebody else

OPINION, CASUAL Horseback, back porch, or back fence opinion

OPINIONATED Jim Hightower said, "The only things in the middle of the road are yellow stripes and dead armadillos."

OPPORTUNITIES, PLENTIFUL There are still fish in the lake as big as any that have been caught, maybe bigger ❏ everything is fair game ❏ the field is wide open

OPPORTUNITY MISSED He was asleep at the switch ❏ is like fallin' off a wagon; you have to walk home when you could have rode ❏ you can't get back water once it's gone under the bridge

OPTIMIST Starts putting on his shoes when the preacher says, "Now, in conclusion" ❏ you wouldn't want to borrow money from him 'cause he would expect you to pay it back ❏ he only takes one ball to the golf course ❏ he only takes one match to light the BBQ fire

OPTIMISTIC As a fisherman (or deer hunter) who takes along a camera

OPTIMISTIC, OVERLY He don't count his chickens before they hatch, he counts 'em before the eggs are laid ❏ he'd expect to bring home a bird from a wild goose chase

ORGANIZATION, POOR A Chinese fire drill is better organized than that place. This term is often used to describe almost any government agency.

ORIGINAL SOURCE Straight from the horse's mouth

ORNERY As a snappin' sow

OUT DID ME He stole my thunder and my lightning and all he left behind was a lot of hail.

OUT IN THE OPEN Out in the broad daylight ☐ out of the closet

OUT OF CONTROL He's a loose fire hose (or cannon).

OUT OF DATE As a drive-in movie ☐ as a magazine in a doctor's office

OUT OF PLACE As a Methodist bell choir in a honky tonk ☐ as a whale in a washtub ☐ as a white dress on a witch ☐ as overalls on a rooster ☐ as a hickey on a nun ☐ as a cow patty in a whirlpool ☐ as a snowstorm in July ☐ as a bow tie on a black snake ☐ as a dog in a cat fight ☐ as dirt under a beauty queen's fingernails

OUT OF SHAPE The only things he lifts are a fork and knife ☐ it's hard to be fit as a fiddle when you're built like a cello ☐ you can lie about being in shape but you can't fool a flight of stairs

OUT OF TOUCH As the ends of a fat man's belt

OUT OF TROUBLE, ALMOST He's finally got his ends meeting but he ain't quite got 'em tied.

OUT OF WORK As a flat-chested stripper

OUT OF YOUR LEAGUE You're a Dachshund runnin' with a pack of Great Danes ☐ you're a parakeet tryin' to fly with eagles

OUT RAN ME He went by me like I was parked (or up on blocks in the garage).

OUTDOORSMAN, POOR His idea of roughing it is having to watch black and white television in a motel that doesn't have room service.

OVER DID IT You wound your watch a little too tight ☐ you picked up more than you can carry

OVERALLS Redneck tuxedo

OVERANXIOUS You're runnin ahead of the dogs ☐ you're tossin' the rope before you build a loop ☐ you're shopping for maternity dresses before the rabbit died

OVERATE I'm as full as an egg ❏ stuffed to the gills

OVERCOME WITH EMOTION His words stuck in his throat like a lure in a fish's mouth.

OVEREATER You're gonna dig your grave with them teeth ❏ if you keep eatin' your knees are gonna buckle but your belt won't

OVEREATING The destiny that shapes your ends

OVEREXTENDED She hung the ivy basket higher than she can reach, which means she won't be able to water the plants ❏ you're weeding a mighty wide row ❏ you got six pots on a four-burner stove ❏ this camper has too much gear to haul around ❏ you got twenty pounds of fish on a ten-pound stringer ❏ I feel like a country dog trying to wet on all the fire plugs in town ❏ I got a big cotton sack to tote ❏ my dam is overflowing with opportunity ❏ I got more on my plate than a television evangelist could say grace over

OVERNIGHT GUEST Suitcase company, which means they brought along a change of clothes and toothbrushes in case you invite them to spend the night.

OVERPOWERED They took it like Grant took Richmond.

OVERREACTING You're using dynamite for a fly swatter ❏ you're using a sledge hammer to drive thumb tacks into paper-mache

OVERSEXED There ain't no neutral in her transmission ❏ whoever turned her on forgot to turn her off

This space is for your favorite sayings.

P-Q

PATIENT — as a cat camped out under a bird bath

P

PACEMAKER, POOR Every time a pretty girl walks by, his garage door goes up.

PAINFUL As a hiccup (or sneeze) with a broken rib *See also In Pain*

PALE Peak'd as in "Ever since he got that letter from the IRS he's been lookin' mighty peak'd."

PANTS, TORN IN THE REAR Looks like he ate a wildcat

PAPAWS Arkansas bananas. For non-country folks, papaws are the yellow, edible fruit of the papaw (papaya) tree which is common in Arkansas.

PARANOID He puts a safety pin on his back pocket ❑ Pete Gent the former Dallas cowboy and author of *North Dallas Forty*, said, "A paranoid is someone with all the facts."

PARENT, POOR He's more worried about his golf swing than his offspring.

PARENTING If you want to keep your teenage daughter out of hot water, put some dirty dishes in it.

PARTED Like the Red Sea

PARTICIPATION Abraham Lincoln said, "Anybody not doing the skinning can hold a leg."

PARTY, DULL It was dull as a graveyard cleaning. Many country churches have an annual picnic at their local graveyard. After eating, everyone turns out to cut the grass, pull the weeds, and right the leaning tombstones. All in all, a graveyard cleaning is a rather dull affair.

PARTY, WILD It was a tooth kickin' party.

PARTY CONSEQUENCES "The less I behave like Whistler's mother the night before, the more I look like her the morning after," said Tallulah Bankhead.

PASSES GAS, A LOT They call him "thunder pants" ❑ he can pass more gas in a weekend than a pipeline could carry in a month ❑ if they ever perfect a car that'll run on natural gas, he can hook up his rear end to his carburetor and drive around the world

PATIENCE What you have to have when your wife is on a diet *See also Be Patient*

PATIENT As a cat camped out under a bird bath

PAY ATTENTION Cinch your mind to it.

PAY YOUR DUES If you're gonna rock you gotta have a big roll.

PEACEFUL, MOSTLY He loves his enemies but he keeps his gun well oiled.

PEACEFUL PERSON He believes in evolution not revolution.

PECANS (Pee-cans), which are not portable toilets

PENCIL WITH AN ERASER A golfer's best friend

PENICILLIN A wonder drug. Anytime the doctor wonders what you have, you get it ❑ what you give the man who has everything

PEOPLE There are two kinds of people, those that make good and those that

make excuses (or those willing to work and those willing to let 'em).

PERFECTION If you go looking for the perfect horse you'll be walking for a long time ❑ if you go looking for the perfect husband, you'll be sleeping alone

PERFECTIONIST One who believes you either make good or make tracks

PERFUME Chemical warfare

PERMANENT As a temporary tax ❑ as an autopsy

PERSEVERE Stick to your guns ❑ you can teach an old dog new tricks but it takes more time ❑ if she says no, you didn't ask the right question, you didn't ask the question right, or you didn't ask the right person ❑ Spike Dykes, the West Texas sage who also doubles as the head football coach at Texas Tech, was asked to comment after his team beat the University of Texas in Austin for the first time in 22 years. "If you keep scratchin," he said, "sooner or later you dig up a worm."

PERSEVERING Hanging in like a hair in a biscuit.

PERSIMMONS Ozark dates

PERSISTENT As a sick kitten sticking to a warm brick

PERSON, COLD You couldn't warm up to him if ya'll were cremated together.

PERSON, CONTROVERSIAL Billy Martin was perhaps the essence of controversy. After his accidental death, Randy Galloway of the *Dallas Morning News* wrote: "Billy Martin was one of a kind. He came, he went, he left a long skid mark." Martin himself may have explained why he was so controversial when he said, "I don't throw the first punch. I throw the second four."

PERSON, EDUCATED He's got more degrees than a thermometer.

PERSON, MEAN He's the kind of ol' boy that'll cut your trot line or run your trot line for you and forget to give you the fish. *See also Mean Man*

PERSON, STRANGE They ought to make him ambassador to the Bermuda Triangle.

PERSONAL LIFE, BORING His life would bore the shell off a turtle. *See also Boring*

PERSONAL RESPONSIBILITY Every cat has to lick his own backside.

PERSUASIVE He can convince his wife to be sorry for the girl that left her bra in his glove compartment ❏ she could convince her husband to be sorry for the man who left a cigar butt in the ashtray 'cause he's a smoker ❏ the most persuasive of all is the lady who can talk her way out of a traffic ticket when she's stopped by a female cop

PESSIMIST The only thing he'd expect to find on a silver platter is tarnish ❏ he never puts anything away for a rainy day 'cause he's always expecting a drought ❏ always try to borrow money from a pessimist 'cause he won't expect to ever get it back

PHILANTHROPIST Somebody who is giving away what he ought to be giving back

PHILOSOPHY Horse sense in a dress suit

PHILOSOPHY, SIMPLE Alice Roosevelt Longworth described it best with: "Fill what's empty. Empty what's full. Scratch where it itches."

PHONY He talks the talk but he don't walk the walk. This is a fairly modern saying that originated in honor of the late, great John Wayne. A lot of people can imitate his voice but not many can walk like he did.

PICK YOUR SPOT An orchid is a weed in a corn field ❑ you never want the spot in the parade that's just behind the sheriff's mounted patrol (cause you'll be dodging horse manure while you march)

PINE RESIN Rozzum

PIG FRIES *See Calf Fries and Brave As*

PLAGIARISM The art of concealing your sources. If you steal from one person it's plagiarism, if you steal from two or more it's research.

PLAIN Without frills, bells, or whistles ❑ stripped down model ❑ with the bark off ❑ unwrapped version ❑ as day, as in "I saw him kiss her on the mouth plain as day"

PLAN Aim, as in "I aim to get that bill paid one of these days."

PLAN AHEAD Don't build the gate till you've built the fence ❑ don't buy the saddle till you've got a horse ❑ don't start choppin' till you've treed the coon

PLANNING No amount of planning will replace dumb luck.

PLANNING TO STAY He's wearin' his sittin' britches.

PLASTIC SURGEON Somebody who increases your face value

PLASTIC SURGERY Cutting up the credit cards

PLAY DEAD Play possum

PLEASED As a kitten that lapped up milk from a contented cow ❑ he was overcome with the gratefuls

PLEASING That really melts my butter ❑ pleases me to no end

PLEASURABLE Ain't never had this much fun with my clothes on ❑ had as much fun as two hogs in a wallow

PLEASURE TRIP Takin' your mother-in-law to the airport

PLUMBER, GOOD He could plug Niagara Falls in half an hour ❑ he could repair a hole in the ozone layer

PLUMBER, POOR He don't make house calls.

POINT OF VIEW The ugliest pig is pretty to another pig.

POINTED As the devil's tail

POINTLESS As painting manure ❑ as a june bug arguing with a duck

POISE The ability to not look conspicuous when you have to sit on the front row in church ❑ the ability to raise an eyebrow instead of the roof

POKER Chips passing in the night ❑ the key to poker is not in holding a good hand but in playing a bad hand well

POKER GAME, SMALL TIME It ain't worth the cost of keepin' the lights on, which means the amount of money that changes hands wouldn't cover the bill from the electric company for running the lights. In the old days, a small-time poker game wouldn't cover the cost of the coal oil for the lamp or the candles that would be used up.

POKER HAND, WORTHLESS An Arkansas or hillbilly straight. In normal poker, a straight consists of five cards in any suit in numerical order, such as 3, 4, 5, 6, 7. An Arkansas straight, however, skips one card between the others such as 3, 5, 7, 9, Jack. Such a hand is absolutely worthless, which means if you bet the ranch on it you'd probably be out of the ranchin' business pretty quick. It follows, then, that an inept gambler would, indeed, bet the ranch on an Arkansas straight.

POKER RAISE, LARGE Clearing the top water. In poker, to get rid of those players barely hangin' on, you make a large raise which clears the top water.

POKER RAISE, SMALL You sent a boy to do a man's job. This expression is generally used by someone who raises your bet considerably to separate the men from the boys.

POLITE As an insurance salesman (or cemetery lot salesman) ❑ he says thank you when an automatic door opens

POLITICAL AUDIENCE, GOOD Mark Twain said the perfect political audience would be "intelligent, witty, capable, inquisitive . . . and drunk."

POLITICAL CANDIDATE A fool runnin' for election to get your money

POLITICAL INEFFICIENCY Don

Bowman wrote, "Politicians are like cockroaches. It's not what they carry off, but what they fall into and mess up."

POLITICAL INCOMPETENCE He don't ever lie knowingly but then he rarely does anything knowingly.

POLITICAL ISSUES No two issues are so far apart that a politician can't straddle 'em.

POLITICAL PHILOSOPHY "He never met a tax he didn't hike," which is how Donnis Baggett defines Texas political philosophy.

POLITICAL PLATFORM Is like the second stanza of the national anthem, everyone knows there is a second stanza but no one knows the words.

POLITICAL POLICY, POOR Let them who don't want none have memories of not getting any.

POLITICAL RUMORS He's runnin' a whispering campaign, which means he's planting rumors and letting them take their course. Any good politician knows that very few things travel faster than rumors around election time.

POLITICAL TRUISM You can lead a man to congress but you can't make him think ❏ Former Texas Lt. Governor Ben Ramsey came up with another political truism when he said, "Politicians love taxes like a hog loves slop."

POLITICIAN A promise merchant ❏ a man who thinks twice before saying nothing ❏ somebody who stands for what he hopes most people will fall for ❏ repairs his fences by hedging ❏ give him a free hand and it'll wind up in your pocket ❏ he'll promise to build bridges where there ain't no rivers ❏ he's got what it takes to get what you got ❏ has to get money from the taxpayer without disturbing the voter ❏ he promises equal rainfall

POLITICIAN, CHEAP When he gives a thousand-dollar-a-plate barbecue, he serves it on paper plates. Such a politician usually gets elected because he has a good memory and voters have a bad one. Then when he is elected, people will admit "Sure he's a crook, but he's our crook."

POLITICIAN, CUNNING He'll stand up and rock the boat, then try to convince you he's the only one that can save you from the storm.

POLITICIAN, DEVIOUS
Donnis Baggett defines it as "He's so slick his socks won't stay up."

POLITICIAN, DISHONEST He didn't even run an honest race when he was on the track team in high school ❑ the only time he ran an honest race was when he outran the sheriff to the county line ❑ he's so crooked he couldn't even vote a straight ticket

POLITICIAN, EXPERIENCED He's like a football coach, smart enough to know the rules and dumb enough to think the game is important.

POLITICIAN, EXPERT He can borrow $20 from you, keep it six months, pay you back only $10, and then convince you that you're even because you both lost $10 ❑ if he was being chased naked down Main Street by an angry, armed lynch mob, he could make you believe he was leading a Memorial Day parade ❑ he can stand firmly in midair

POLITICIAN, GOOD One that will stay bought ❑ good

politicians are like eclipses, they're few and far between

POLITICIAN, HONEST Something money can't buy ❑ stands out like a do-it-yourself haircut

POLITICIAN, LIAR Any resemblance between his campaign speeches (or television ads) and the truth is purely coincidental.

POLITICIAN, POOR He's a coattail politician, which means his fortunes turn on the fortunes of some other higher up politician ❑ his credibility has stretch marks ❑ they thought he was presidential timber but he turned out to be just bark ❑ he couldn't get elected if the national guard stuffed the ballot boxes

POLITICIAN, SMART He understands the best position is the one in front of the camera.

POLITICIAN, UGLY You could use his campaign posters to wean calves off their mothers. There is an old story about a politician being so ugly that some farmers would tie his campaign posters on their cows and the calves would be so scared they would stop sucking and start eating grass. Being a consummate professional, the ugly politician, when told of the use for his signs, simply replied, "I am glad I could be of service to our valuable farmers."

POLITICIAN, UNPOPULAR If buzzards could vote he'd be a shoo-in.

POLITICIAN, VERSATILE He has a mind open at both ends ❑ he takes a firm stand on all sides of the issues ❑ once he makes up his mind he's full of indecision

POLITICIAN, WINDY He can give mouth to mouth resuscitation over the phone ❑ listening to him is like shooting at a moving target, you have to allow for the wind

POLITICS The art of promising ❑ the public goldfish bowl ❑ the only thing harder to clean up after than a small boy ❑ the only thing that makes a man faster on his feet than politics is bigamy

POLLUTION That place is so polluted you get dirty echos.

POOR He was so poor he had to stand on a bag of fertilizer to raise an umbrella ❑ we ate so many rabbits when we were young that we'd hide under the porch every time the dogs barked ❑ if an elephant overcoat cost a dollar, I couldn't buy a jacket of a gnat ❑ our cockroaches starved to death ❑ the only time we had ice was right after a good hail storm ❑ he couldn't buy hay for a nightmare ❑ I have to stay alive 'cause I can't afford to be buried ❑ if he had a $100 bill in his pocket he'd be wearing somebody else's pants ❑ the only time he carries any money is when he's an usher in church ❑ poor as Job's turkey ❑ we were so poor the wolf wouldn't come to our door 'cause he knew he would have ended up on the dinner table ❑ if it cost a dollar to send a ton of manure around the world, I couldn't send ten ounces worth to my next door neighbor ❑ Ed Wilkes of Lubbock, Texas said when he was young they were so poor that, "We ate so many collard greens that we had to wear coal oil rags around our feet to keep the cut worms off." Lee Trevino once said, "When we were young, if mom threw the dog a bone, he'd have to call for a fair catch."

One of the best descriptions came from Paul Peterman of Celina, Texas. He said that when he was young they were so poor that they'd eat dried apples for breakfast and dried apples for dinner. Then at supper time they'd drink water and the apples would swell up so much that they'd go to bed thinking they were full.

Regardless of how poor someone might be, another old country saying is important to remember: A hard working, God-fearing plow hand on his knees stands taller than a lazy rich man standin' on his feet. *See also Broke; Destitute*

PORK (FATTY) Fatback

POSITIVE If it ain't true there ain't an Indian in Oklahoma, a pine tree in Georgia, a pretty girl in Texas, or a white tooth in Hollywood.

POSITIVE, ALMOST I'm purt-near positive ❑ purdy-nigh sure

POURED OUT Like hens through a hole in the fence. Anytime you keep hens in a fence they become convinced the pecking is better on the other side, so if even a little hole gets punched in the fence the hens pour out.

POVERTY What you have left when all your friends saddle up and leave ❑ the only time it's good to be poor is when the tax man comes knocking *See also Poor*

PRACTICE Everything gets easier with practice except getting up in the morning and eating crow.

PRAYER A lot of people would do more praying if they could find a soft spot for their knees.

PREACHER, DEVOUT He could talk a whole bowl of mashed potatoes cold. In the country the preacher is often invited over for Sunday dinner. A really devout preacher is one who takes so long saying grace that the entire bowl of mashed potatoes turns cold. The most devout preacher of all can talk an entire turkey cold at Thanksgiving.

PREACHER, EXPERIENCED He can estimate the size of the collection within ten dollars just from lookin' at the crowd ❑ one country preacher said he was so experienced that he could count the collection in his mind just from hearing the coins dropped into the plate ◻ then there was the experienced Arkansas preacher who could tell if a counterfeit coin was dropped in the plate 'cause it had a different ring from all the other quarters

PREACHER, SMART He has the ushers pass the plate before the sermon. The larger the collection the less he speaks. Of course, such a plan only works when the congregation knows it in advance ◻ when visiting, he keeps one eye open when saying grace so the children don't beat him to the fried chicken

PRECARIOUS SITUATION Your pig's sucking hind tit. Occasionally an old sow would have more piglets than she had teats to accommodate, which meant one or more had to scramble for a place to suck. The baby pig unlucky enough to get the hind teat often had to squirm between mothers legs to get at the spigot. If mamma hog changed positions or rolled over, the baby pig between her legs was in danger of being thumped hard or,

worse yet, being flung across the barnyard. The same situation also existed for calves who had to sneak up on the mamma calf from behind and stick their head between her legs to get to the hind teat. In either case, having to suck the hind teat was a precarious situation.

Also, you got the cow staked next to the truck patch. If you stake an old cow next to your truck patch she'll eat most of the crop you intended to sell. In such a precarious situation, the cow gets a full belly but you lose money.

PRECAUTION Never eat anything that grows wild around the back porch. In the country, some folks don't always make it all the way to the outhouse when they have to relieve themselves. In fact, many have been known to make it just as far as the back porch, thus any food growing around the porch probably had some strange liquid fertilizer dumped on it.

PREDICTABLE No matter how warm the sunshine is, the cat will always have her kittens in the barn.

PREFERENCE Some people object to a fan dancer,

others to the fan ❑ every fish has its favorite bait ❑ I'd rather get under the porch and peck with the chickens (or I'd rather get a tin bill and peck with the chickens) than do that ❑ I'd rather give a camel an enema than do that ❑ I'd rather give a rattlesnake a root canal than do that

PREGNANT She was hung by a serpent ❑ she's got a big biscuit in the oven ❑ she looks like she swallowed her bowling ball

PREPARATION The best way to hold cattle in the winter is to do your sleeping in the summertime.

PREPARED He stays ready so he won't ever have to get ready.

PRESSURE If you got a rip in your parachute, it will show up under pressure.

PRESUMPTUOUS Just because you donated an organ to the church don't mean you can call the tunes to be played.

PRETEND Make out like, as in "He made out like he was a cowboy and tried to ride that wild horse." ❑ play like, as in "Why don't you

play like you're rich and lone me $20?"

PRETEND COWBOY He just found the hat.

PRETTY As a mortgage paid in full ❑ as a polished pearl ❑ as dollar cotton

PRIDE Every old crow thinks her chick is the blackest ❑ every old mother hen thinks her chicks are the best peckers ❑ pride is something that ain't hard to swallow once you chew on it long enough

PRIORITIES Don't chop firewood till you've built the fireplace ❑ you're looking for the thermostat when the roof is caving in ❑ a calf can't bawl and suck at the same time

PRISON, MINIMUM SECURITY Where you serve three years at hard tennis (or golf)

PRISONER Fun flies when you're doin' time.

PROBLEM Someone threw a dead cat down the well ❑ the only people without problems are in the graveyard

PROBLEM, LARGE He sat down in a bear trap ❑ he opened a can of worms and found out they were baby rattlesnakes. Ounce for ounce, the venom in a baby rattlesnake is considerably more dangerous than an adult snake. Fortunately, however, a baby rattler can't open his mouth wide enough to bite much.

PROBLEM DRINKER One that never buys ☐ Tommy Lasorda once said of Billy Martin, "When he reaches for a bar tab his arm shrinks six inches."

PROCRASTINATOR He never puts his best foot forward until he gets the other one in hot water.

PROFANITY Mark Twain said, "Under certain circumstances, profanity provides a relief denied even to prayer." What he meant by that was that sometimes it just feels better to tell someone to go to hell than it does to pray they don't make the trip.

PROFESSIONAL He takes time to sharpen his axe. A real pro would recognize the value of keeping a sharp edge on an axe because over the long haul it would make choppin' wood much easier. A non-professional would keep choppin' even when his axe got dull and would end up taking a lot longer to finish the job.

PROMISCUOUS *See Female, Promiscuous and Male, Promiscuous*

PROMISE The measure of a man is how many promises he keeps.

PROMISE, BROKEN There ain't no cement that will fix a broken promise.

PROPHECY I'd rather make a profit than be one.

PROSPECTS, GOOD He's got a good season in the ground, which means he's planted a good crop.

PROSPERITY Something business creates and politicians take credit for

PROSTITUTE A cheap spread

PROTECTION You can make the best scarecrow in the world but it won't do nearly as much good as a mean dog.

PROTRUDING Pooched-out, as in "His gut has gotten pooched-out since he went back to drinkin' beer and eatin' possum."

PROUD As a goat with four horns ☐ as a peacock in full

bloom, which means his tail feathers are fully open

PROVERBS, COUNTRY STYLE Proverbs have been around for about as long as folks have been talking. Every class of people, it seems, has their own versions and country folks are no exception. Here's a generous helping of some country style proverbs:

Trust in God, but tie your horse.

Watch your step when the chips are down.

Once you're on the ground don't worry about the horse throwing you.

You can shear a pig but you'll get a lot more noise than wool.

It's easier to plow around a stump than through it.

There never has been a horse that can't be rode or a cowboy that can't be throwed.

Crime don't pay, neither does farming.

If the boot fits, wear it.

A squeaking wheel gets the grease but a quacking duck ets shot.

You don't live longer in the country. It just seems that way.

Hold your chin up high, but keep your nose at a friendly level.

Don't let the grass grow between your toes.

You don't get to pick the members of the posse that'll chase you.

The farmer's curse: Chicken one day, feathers the next.

Never buy a horse from a milkman.

If you give a dance, you gotta pay the fiddler.

Don't kick before you are spurred.

You don't get lard unless you boil the hog.

A bucket under a bull will never be full of milk.

You can put hen's eggs in an eagle's nest but you'll still get chickens.

Hard work keeps the fences up.

Just because he's wearing boots don't mean he's a cowboy.

The longer the rope, the bigger the loop.

The wilder the colt, the better the horse.

Never get into a gunfight with an ugly man cause he ain't got nuthin' to lose.

A coyote will fool with chickens till he feels buckshot in his behind.

Eat all you can and can what you can't.

The girls all get prettier at closing time.

If you hitch a horse with a coyote, the wagon won't get pulled far.

No matter if you are in the frying pan or the fire, you're still cooked.

Even the smallest anvil won't float.

A nightmare can scare a cowboy more than any other horse.

A watched preacher never cusses.

Don't count the crop 'till it's in the barn.

A good horse is one that will stand without hitching.

No matter how tough the teat, the milk is still sweet.

Anything is possible if the Lord is willing and the creeks don't rise.

Never choose a wife by the glow of a neon light.

Make good or make room.

Dead ducks need no killing.

A man who keeps watching the horizon behind him has more his mind than scenery.

Given the choice between luck and intelligence, take luck.

Too many cooks spoil the chili (or gravy).

If you put all your eggs in one basket, take real good care of that basket.

The bird that is late finds the worm is already ate.

It's not the cough that carries you off, it's the coffin they carry you off in.

A man is is as good as he has to be, a woman is as bad as she dares to be.

PROVIDER, GOOD He keeps his smoke house greasy.

PRUDE She holds out like a Zane Grey heroine.

PSYCHIATRIST Nerve doctor

PSYCHIATRIST, CHEAP He uses a sleeping bag instead of a couch.

PUCKERED Like a wet sheepskin next to a hot fire

PUFFED UP Like a frog in a cream can

PUNCH, LIGHT A rabbit punch

PURE In his book *Texas Proud and Loud,* Boyce House included the definition: "Pure as the dew drop that sparkles on the tail of a Texas bull as he rises from his grassy couch and bellows in the face of the rising sun."

PUSH Mash, as in "You got to mash the button on the microwave to heat up your dinner."

Q

QUALIFIED He's earned his place at the bar.

QUALIFICATIONS, LACKING His bag of tricks has a hole in it.

QUALITY A good rooster will crow in any chicken coop ❑ a man is only as good as his nerve

QUALITY, FAIR Middling good ❑ fair average quality ❑ it ain't bad if you ain't used to much

QUALITY, GOOD You can't beat that with a hickory switch ❑ grade A good

QUALITY, LACKING He's a top water minnow, which is a minnow that, once on a fishing hook, swims around the top of the water instead of going deep where the fish are.

QUALITY, POOR Piddlin' poor ❑ it fell apart like a two-dollar wagon

QUANTITY, DECEIVING It ain't always the size of the load that counts. A handful of manure wouldn't be worth as much as a wagon load of fertilizer but a handful of diamonds would be worth more than ten truckloads of coal.

QUANTITY, LARGE A whole slew of ❑ a sight of ❑ a passel of ❑ Another forgotten word from out of the past is lavish, which means large quantity as in "We got a lavish of last year's calenders on hand."

QUARREL Cuss fight

QUARTER MOON Rustler's moon. Many rustlers preferred to ply their trade by the light of a quarter moon. A full moon was so bright, the thieves could easily be seen, and when there was no moon it was too dark to see the cattle.

QUICK AS An Arkansas preacher can spot a counterfeit quarter ❑ as the shake of a lamb's tail ❑ as wind from a duck's backside ❑ as a big minnow can swim a small dipper. A popular country saying is "quick as a minnow can swim a dipper" but the truth is there are some very small minnows and some large dippers and if you put those two together the speed would be a few milliseconds slower than a big minnow in a small dipper.

QUICK LOOK Give it a windshield inspection. In buying land, many people simply drive by and look at it through the window rather than getting out of the car and walking in the dirt.

QUICK TEMPERED He's got an easy wire to trip ❑ his trigger finger is always itchy or his trigger don't take much pullin'

QUICK TONGUE A man with a quick tongue had better have quick fists or a quick draw.

QUIET You could hear a worm sneeze ❑ you could hear the moon rise ❑ you could hear a pair of ants making love on a cotton boll ❑ you could hear your toenails growing *See also Be Quiet, Keep Quiet*

QUIET AS A sick sow in a snow storm ❑ as a coon stalking a crayfish ❑ as a worm's heartbeat ❑ as a sparrow in a hawk's nest ❑ as a cat burglar

QUIET TYPE He don't use much kindling to get his fire started, which means he is a man of few words but the words he does use generally count for something.

QUIET WORKER The hen that lays the biggest egg usually does the least cackling.

REMEDY, HOME STYLE — she could poultice the hump off a camel's back

R

RACEHORSE The only horse than can take a thousand people for a ride at the same time

RACEHORSE, SLOW It took that horse so long to finish, the jockey kept a diary.

RACCOON Always just a coon to a country boy

RADIATOR SHOP The best place to take a leak

RAGGED As a sheep herder's britches

RAIN, AFTER A DRY SPELL A sittin'-in rain, which means you are so happy to finally see rain that you go right outside and sit in it awhile.

RAIN, HEAVY Frog strangler □ a "clear up" rain, which is when you are in water clear up to the back of your lap □ it was raining horse apples and pig knuckles □ a log roller □ a fence floater □ a duck drowner □ tank destroyer, as in stock tank. On the farm, a really heavy rain may produce enough water to flood the place and wash out of any shallow stock tanks you might have □ the concrete turned to mud □ we had to jump into the river to keep from drowning □ raining bull frogs and heifer yearlings □ raining cats and dogs, which means you better watch out and not step in a poodle □ it was rainin' pitchforks and black cats

RAIN, INTERMITTENT A sputtin' and spittin' rain □ wasn't a runnin' rain, which means there wasn't enough water to run off the road □ a three-inch rain, as in there was three inches between each drop

RAIN, MODERATE A degreaser, which means it rained just enough to wash the grease off the road

RAIN, VERY HEAVY An anvil mover, as in "After that last rain last evening my anvil had been moved a foot and half." Any anvil, even a small one, is very heavy, so it would take a lot of fast-flowing water to move one. Even though that never happens, use of the saying produces the connotation that you got a lot of rain. To produce the connotation that you got an extremely heavy amount of rain you could say it was an anvil floater.

RAIN, SHORT Like an old-timers dance, it was soon over

RAIN, SOFT Angel tears

RAIN, SPRINKLING A Methodist shower, which is a reference to Methodists sprinkling when they baptize.

RAIN APPROACHING Comin' up a cloud ◻ the flies are swarming on the screen, which is said to be a sure sign of approaching rain storms

RAIN DROPS, LARGE Big drops mean little rain

RAINBOW, PARTIAL Sundog

RAINING HARD Like a cow taking a leak off a forty-foot cliff

RAINING WHILE THE SUN SHINES The devil is beating his wife.

RAINY DAY Good day to be in bed with a good book or someone who has read one

RAN Like a field mouse in an eagle's shadow

RANCH, LARGE Had to have its own zip code ◻ it's a two-horse ranch, which means you'd have to have two horses to ride across it in one day

RANCHER, RICH His cows ain't branded, they're engraved.

RARE AS A golden wedding anniversary in Hollywood ◻ as a mermaid in a stock tank ◻ as icicles in hell ◻ as wool in a beehive ◻ as a good-looking mail order bride ◻ as a pregnant nun pole vaulter ◻ as a wild rose in winter ◻ as a fat coyote ◻ as an all night rodeo ◻ as clean socks in a bunkhouse ◻ as a smile on an undertaker ◻ as a white crow ◻ as a dance at Baylor University. Dancing is not allowed at Baylor, a Baptist university ◻ as an honest fisherman (or politician) ◻ as a football bat ◻ as a smile on a Russian restaurant worker. When McDonalds and Pizza Hut expanded into Russia they had to teach their Russian employees how to smile instead of snarl at employees.

RARE BOOK One you loan to someone and get back

RARE MEAT I know a vet that could cure this critter ❑ this looks like you just knocked the horns and hooves off, wiped its behind, and put it on a platter ❑ I can still see the jockey's whip marks, which implies that the meat is not only rare but that it might not be prime beef

RATTLES Like ball bearings in a car door. A rancher once scraped up enough money to by a new Lincoln Town Car. He was really proud of the car but it did have a rattle in one door. He took it back to the dealer and they could not find anything wrong. After several more trips to the dealer, the door was removed and fully disassembled. Finally, a mechanic found a large, loose ball bearing in the very bottom of the door. The steel ball, which had obviously been placed inside the door when it was assembled had a small note attached which read: "So you finally found it, you rich S.O.B."

RATTLESNAKE Rattler, sidewinder

RATTLESNAKE, BIG So big it needed two coils

READY I'm primed and tightly wadded.

READY AS A rooster with his spurs up

REAL ESTATE DEAL, GOOD Got five years free on a four-year lease

REAR END Back porch

REAR END, LARGE Jug butted ❑ something nice to fall back on ❑ stern reality ❑ she's well-reared ❑ he couldn't sit down in a number three wash tub ❑ his rear end is so large when he gets up out of a chair it takes it half an hour to cool off ❑ looks a bag of nickles ❑ looks like fifty pounds of used chewing gum ❑ looks like two baby pigs under a bed sheet ❑ she's built like a black widow spider, which means she has a very large rear end and small legs and hands ❑ the back of her lap looks like two big cabbages in a tow sack ❑ his butt is bigger than a river bottom coon. Coons living along a river bottom are often better fed and thus plumper than most other coons.

REAR END, SMALL Looks a little hollow cheeked ❑ scarce hipped ❑ ol' sparrow butt

RECKLESS You're plowing too close to the cotton ❑ you're drillin' too close to the pipeline

RECONCILE, SOMEWHAT Bury the hatchet but don't forget where you dug the hole.

RECOVERED He hauled off and got well.

RED As the bottom stripe on a Texas flag ❑ as a dirt road in the Carolinas ❑ as a baboon's butt

REDNECK He's so country, his breath smells like cordwood.

REFORMED, SOMEWHAT He mended his ways but he used mighty thin thread ❑ he got painted into an amen corner but the paint was quick drying

REFORMER Someone who wants his conscience to be your guide.

REINCARNATION He believed in reincarnation so when he wrote his will he left everything to himself.

RELATED, SORT OF We're pea patch kin. This phrase evolved back when peas were a mainstay of many country diets. As Donnis Baggett explained in a column for the *Dallas Morning News:* "A system of informal farm co-ops evolved back when Texas was a rural state. Some families had more kids than land, and they needed more peas than they could grow. Some families had more acreage than kids, so they needed help to farm it all. Since the needs of one complimented the assets of another, a deal was struck. Two or three families would combine efforts on one garden and split the proceeds. Many of the families involved in these joint ventures were related to each other. And in cases where they weren't, pea patch romances often led to further mergers, takeovers, and stock splits. Hence the term, pea patch kin."

Also, we were weaned on milk from the same cow (cow cousins), which meant the families were close enough to share a cow but weren't officially related. An even closer version might be weaned by the same wet nurse.

RELAX Don't get your shorts in a knot ❏ don't get your panty hose in a pile ❏ don't get your dandruff up

RELIABLE As the sunrise

RELIGIOUS DIFFERENCE Dippers and sprinklers don't mix.

RELIGIOUS FREEDOM The right to go to church or to go fishing

RELIGIOUS PERSON, ALMOST The church he currently don't attend is Baptist. *See also Church Goer, Infrequent*

RELIGIOUS PERSON, DEVOUT He thinks the chicken came first 'cause God wouldn't ever taken the time to sit on an egg.

RELIGIOUS, BUT CHEAP He's a clink Christian, which means every time the collection passes him you only hear the clink of a few coins being dropped in.

RELIGIOUS, SOMETIMES A weekend Catholic. A person who was a little less religious would be an Easter Sunday Catholic. And the least religious of all would be a death bed Catholic, which means he only got religion when he thought he was gonna die.

You can substitute the religion of your choice but the implication is clear, the person involved is only religious some of the time.

RELUCTANCE I'd rather slap my mamma than do that ❏ I'd rather take out a polar bear's appendix with a pen knife than do that *See also Don't Want To; I Don't Care; Preference*

REMARKABLE PERSON He's got bodacious in his blood ❏ a real remarkable person is double bodacious

REMARRIED POORLY He divorced the devil and married a witch.

REMINDS ME Puts me in the mind of

REMOTE LOCATION About fifty miles past the resume speed sign

REPAIR, TEMPORARY Just gave it a lick and a promise ❏ whitewash won't strengthen the fence but it makes it look better when the preacher comes calling

REPEATING You've already treed that coon.

REPRIMAND Bring 'em down a notch or two ❏ cool 'em off a degree or two

REPUTATION A man is well known by the company he avoids.

REQUIREMENT If you give a dance you gotta pay the band.

RESCUED Snatched it out of the fire in the nick of time. Coals or grease can be used in place of fire.

RESEARCH *See Plagiarism*

RESEMBLES Favors ❑ takes after

RESERVE, LARGE He don't have an ace up his sleeve, he's got the whole danged deck.

RESIST TEMPTATION No matter how much you want to, never tell an IRS agent to kiss your butt.

RESOLVED We finally got to the bottom of the swamp and found the drain plug.

RESOURCES, INADEQUATE He has convertible taste and a pickup budget.

RESPONSIBILITY *See Accept Responsibility*

REST ROOM Sandbox

RESTRICTED It's difficult to run with the big dogs when you're chained to the porch ❑ I'm hog tied

RESTRICTION That cramps my style

RESULTS, POOR He did a lot of grinding but he didn't get much corn.

RETALIATE Give back as good as you got or better ❑ back cuss

RETIRE, EARLY Go to bed with the chickens.

RETIRED Pasteurized ❑ turned in his saddle

RIBS Smack bones ❑ steer staves

RICH He's got more money than me and God put together ❑ he's stiff in the heels ❑ he's got enough money to burn a wet elephant ❑ her kitchen has five rooms ❑ he even hired someone to stand around with his tongue out so he'd never have to lick his own envelopes *See also Wealthy*

RICH, BUT INEPT He tried to order a car pool for his Cadillac.

RICH CHILD He was raised in a floored pen. This comes from hog farmers who can afford fancy floored pens for their hogs.

RID Get shed of

RIDICULOUS As asking a politician to guard your wallet ❑ as building a bee hive next to a bear's den

RIGHTEOUS Doing good ain't no fun unless you're caught in the act.

RING Rang, as in: "I rang the bell, I heard the bell rang, or I gave her an engagement rang."

RIO GRANDE RIVER An early Texas settler once said of the river, "It is a mile wide and a foot deep, too thin to plow, too thick to drink." During prohibition, the Rio Grande was said to be the only river in the world that was wet on one side and dry on the other. It always pronounced as Rio Grand (without the river) and never as Rio Grand-ee.

RISES, FAST As gasoline prices in a Mideast crisis

RISK TAKING You're tap dancing in a mine field ❑ you're bathing with sharks. Donald Carter owns the Dallas Mavericks and he's had some anxious moments with one of his players who has violated the NBA substance abuse policy. Following the player's arrest, Carter lamented, ". . . this is what happens when you bathe with sharks. Sometimes you get bit." ❑ you're counting the cars in a funeral procession which, according to an old country legend, means you will be the next to be buried ❑ you're walking through a forest fire with a wooden leg ❑ you're kissing an ugly woman. If you kiss an ugly woman she'll tell the world and ruin your reputation with the other ladies ❑ as driving in a fog, especially if it is a mental fog *See also At Risk; Dangerous*

RIVER, DRY The fish raised dust swimming up stream ❑ the river had to be irrigated before the kids could go swimming

RIVER, SHALLOW A walkin' river. The Rio Grande between Texas and Mexico is said to be a walkin' river because in most spots, illegal aliens simply walk across it. In some places the river is so shallow, they can walk across without gettin' their feet wet.

Also, the lifeguards only have to know how to wade ❑ a hog crossin' river, which means the hogs are walking across it. Although hogs can swim, they don't like to. ❑ the water is so low the catfish are getting freckled, which means they are spending too much time in the sun

ROACHES, BIG As chocolate eclairs ❏ they're so big you have to have a huntin' license to kill 'em ❏ when Jerry Glanville was the coach of the Houston Oilers he was asked about the advantage of playing in the Astrodome. He replied that one advantage was the size of the cockroaches. It was his opinion that players from other cities had never seen roaches that big and thus were distracted from the game. As to how big the roaches were, Glanville claimed they were so big his players would ride them out to the team bus after a game.

ROAD, DIRT Arkansas asphalt

ROAD, ROUGH An Oklahoma freeway ❏ headache highway ❏ a corduroy road ❏ rough as a washboard ❏ a bad road will call the mile markers liars, which means it seems that miles are longer on bad roads

ROAD, SMALL A pig trail

ROAD, WINDING The road was so crooked a snake broke its back going around a corner.

ROAD TO SUCCESS Is always under construction

ROBBED They took everything but the fillings in my teeth.

ROBBER, INEPT He put his ski mask on backwards and tried to hold up a police station. *See also Crook; Thief*

ROCKING CHAIR Gives you something to do but it don't get you nowhere

RODEO Regardless of what they say in California, its pronounced row-dee-o.

ROOM, COLD Enough to use as a deer locker

ROOM, CROWDED There ain't enough room left for a shadow.

ROOM, LARGE You could drill a regiment in it.

ROOM, MESSY Looks like Willie Nelson held his last fourth of July picnic in there.

ROOM, SMALL You have to leave if sunshine comes in the window ❏ if you put the key too far into the lock you'll break the window ❏ the furniture is painted on the wall ❏ you can't cuss the cat without getting a mouth full of fur ❑ the dog has to wag his tail up and down instead of sideways ❑ you have to use a crutch and sleep standing up ❑ you have to go out into the hall to change your mind ❑ you couldn't pucker your lips

ROPE, LONG As a Georgia well rope ❑ long enough to hang all the wash in Tennessee on it

ROUGH AS As a rock seat in an outhouse ❑ as a peanut patty ❑ as a bed of broken rocks ❑ as a cat's tongue

ROUGH-HEWN Davy Crockett once described something rough-hewn as looking like it had been cut out of a gum log with a broad axe. Using a broad axe on a gum log would surely produce a rough-hewn appearance.

ROUNDUP Cow maneuvers

RUIN, IMMINENT The hogs are in the corn ❑ the little Dutch boy done pulled his finger out of the dyke ❑ the canker is in the flower. A canker is a destructive caterpillar.

RUINED (Ruint)

RULER Back scratcher

RUMOR Is like a check, never endorse it till you know it's good ❑ remember, a four-inch tongue can kill a six-foot man

RUNAROUND Gave me a song and dance ❑ he crawfished on me

RUNNER *See Fast Runner or Slow Runner*

RUNNING AROUND Cavortin' around like a fat pony in high oats ❑ gallivanting ❑ like a scared Mexican quail

RUNS FAST As panty hose in a briar patch ❑ as water through a sieve ❑ goin' like a house afire ❑ he runs like he was gingered up, which is a reference to the old (and highly illegal) practice of making a horse run faster by sticking some ginger in a very private spot just below his tail. The ginger will burn and cause irritation that the horse, in its infinite wisdom, will try hard to outrun.

RURAL We live so far out in the country we have to order our moonlight from Sears ❑ we live so far out in the country that they hold Sunday school on Monday night cause no one can get to the church by Sunday morning ❑ we live so far out

205

That Cat Won't Flush

in the country that we have to use a possum for a lap dog ❑ we live so far out in the country that nobody else even lives in our zip code ❑ we live so far out in the country we have to walk towards town to go squirrel huntin' ❑ we live so far out in the country that the sun sets between our house and the main road ❑ so far out in the country that you can't get there from here ❑ it's not the end of the earth but you can see it from there

S

SAVINGS AND LOAN OFFICER — he used to be the loan arranger, now he's the loan stranger

S

SACRIFICE Throw the virgin into the volcano ❏ throw him to the wolves

SAD Would make a glass eye in a jar shed tears ❏ would make you want to tune up your crier ❏ would jerk the tears right out of their little ducts ❏ would make an Italian statue cry

SAD MOVIE It brought a lump to my throat big as a fishin' bobber ❏ it's a two-box movie, which means you'll need at least two boxes of Kleenex to make it through

SAD AS A country song

SADAM HUSSIEN The Damn Insane

SADDLE SORES No one but your doctor and your sweetheart are ever gonna see the scars.

SAFE As a possum (or coon) in a hollow log. Although the dogs will try, the possum is usually safe inside the log so long as it waits for the dogs to leave before sticking out its head ❏ as an Alamo squirrel. There are several squirrels who live on the grounds of the Alamo in San Antonio, Texas. While the squirrels are not specifically protected, no one messes with them, perhaps because of the large security guards who always seem to be present.

SALESMAN, GOOD Could sell moonshine whiskey at a Baptist prayer meeting ❏ could sell clothes hangers at a nudist convention ❏ could sell sand to an Arab ❏ he could sell hot water in hell ❏ he could sell manure to a feed lot operator. A feed lot operator produces only two things, cows and manure ❏ he could sell carbon paper to Xerox ❏ he could sell left-handed screwdrivers ❏ could sell Bibles at an atheist convention ❏ he can talk you into debt

SALESMAN, MEAN He'd sell the whistle off the factory and nobody would know when to go home.

SALESMAN, POOR
Couldn't sell suntan lotion on a nude beach ❑ he couldn't sell feathers to a plucked chicken ❑ couldn't sell Malox on Wall Street ❑ he couldn't sell $50 bills for $10

SALOON, DANGEROUS
The Brawl of Fame ❑ a hold 'em and hit 'em joint ❑ where they check you for guns and if you don't have one they supply it

SALT PORK Cincinnati ham ❑ Arkansas chicken

SARCASM Barbed ire

SAUSAGE One of two things you should never see made. The other is a law.

SAVINGS AND LOAN OFFICER He used to be the Loan Arranger but now he's the Loan Stranger.

SAW TOO MUCH Got a double eyeful

SAY GRACE Ask the blessing

SAY THAT AGAIN Lick that calf again

SCARCE As horse manure in a two-car garage ❑ as pig tracks on a linen table cloth *See also Rare As*

SCARECROW, EFFECTIVE That's such a good scarecrow the crows brought back the corn they stole last year.

SCARED The butterflies in my stomach have butterflies ❑ scared the puddin' out of me (make up your own mind as to what puddin' means in this instance) ❑ she was so scared her panty hose were quivering

SCARY Made his hair stand on end and he was wearing a toupee ❑ I had goose bumps big as nickels ❑ gives me the hebejebes ❑ my underwear was creeping up like it had legs ❑ makes your fingernails sweat ❑ as a rattlesnake in your sleeping bag

SCARY SITUATION It's seat squirming time ❑ that made my butt pucker so hard I had to use a crowbar to get my jeans out of the crack ❑ that'll take the curl out of your hair or put a curl in your hair, take your pick

SCATTERED All over hell and half of Dixie ❑ like cannon balls at the Alamo (or at Gettysburg) ❑ like rice at a wedding

SCOLD Rake him over the coals.

SCHEDULE Dance card, as in "I can't see you till

Tuesday 'cause my dance card is full till then."

SCRATCHED UP He looks like he was sackin' bobcats and ran out of sacks ❏ he looks like he climbed through a barbed wire fence to fight a wildcat in a cactus patch *See also Bloody*

SCRATCHING Like a dog at a flea convention

SCRATCHY As burlap BVDs ❏ as tow sack bloomers

SCREWED UP You spit in your own hat ❏ you ripped your shorts on that one ❏ you dropped your drawers in the wrong parade ❏ you hollered come on when you meant sic 'em ❏ you stole a watermelon out of the sheriff's patch

SCREWED UP, BIG TIME You shot yourself in the foot with a cannon.

SEAMSTRESS, GOOD She uses a frisky needle.

SEARCH Look to hell and back ❏ turn over all the rocks

SEAT, SMALL A hug-me-tight seat, which comes from the days of the buggy when seats were notoriously small. If you picked up your best girl for a ride in the country, she

almost had to hug you tight to stay in the seat because there wasn't much room.

SECRETS Easy to hear, hard to keep ❏ something you tell only one person at a time

SEEMS 'Pears to me

SELF-CENTERED He don't think the cards were shuffled good unless he gets a good hand.

SELF-CONTROL The ability to not even try to keep up with the Joneses ❏ if you can't control yourself you can't control your horse

SELF-EMPLOYED Dangling on his own hook

SELF-MADE MAN Most men who are self-made are usually missing a few parts ❏ he may be a self-made man but he wasn't made with skilled labor

SELF-TAUGHT Jackleg, such as jackleg mechanic, jackleg carpenter, or jackleg brain surgeon

SENSE OF VALUE, POOR He sits in a $50 saddle on a $20 horse.

SENSITIVE Touchous, as in "He's might touchous about his new $10 boots."

SEPARATE THE GOOD FROM THE BAD Separate the goats from the sheep ❑ separate the chicken thieves from the preachers (or the chicken thieves from the chicken pluckers)

SERIOUS As a snakebite ❑ as a heart attack ❑ as a divorce ❑ as a barbed wire toilet seat

SERIOUS SITUATION It's cuttin' time, which comes from the act of cutting bulls to make them steers. For a bull, there ain't no situation more serious than cuttin' time.

SERMON The preacher feature

SERMON, LONG A growler, which means the preacher talked so long a lot of empty bellies in the congregation were beginning to growl. An empty belly hates a long sermon.

SERVING Helping

SET IN HIS WAYS He don't want to be confused by the facts.

SETTLEMENT We split the biscuit and both got a half, which means the argument ended when the bounty was divided evenly.

SEX A misdemeanor. The more you miss it the meaner you get.

SHAKE HANDS Press some flesh, as Lyndon Johnson said.

SHAKING Like a hen in a dust bath. When a hen decides to take a dust bath, she covers herself with loose dust and then shakes all over until the dust to thrown off. Anyone shaking like a hen in a dust bath would be shaking all over violently. *See also Nervous*

SHALLOW PERSON He's like a bass drum, he makes a lot of noise but there ain't much inside.

SHARE CROPPING Farming on the halves (or thirds or fourths, depending on the deal).

SHARP *See Knife, Sharp*

SHARP TONGUED He eats razor soup

SHACK, POOR A rattlesnake would be ashamed to meet his mother inside that shack.

SHE'S LEAVING She's wearing her "it's all over" coat.

SHINY As a diamond in a goat's butt. Donkey, coon, or

cat can be substituted for goat.

SHOCKED EXPRESSION You look like you just wet on an electric fence. On a pig farm near Lubbock, Texas a few years ago I was helping a friend tend to his hogs. Nature called and I asked where do I go to relieve myself. The friend pointed to a bush and said "water the plants." What he did not say was that his brand new electric fence ran just beneath that bush. Well, since water — any kind of water — is an excellent conductor of electricity, I soon learned the error of my ways. The friend swears I went eight feet straight back and landed with a thud in some pig manure. Thirty minutes later when I finally got my breath back, the friend also swore I had the most shocked expression on my face that he had ever seen. I have never doubted him.

SHOE HORN Slipper slide

SHOES, HIGH HEELS Stilt shoes ❑ calf enhancers

SHOOK UP As tequila in a blender ❑ as milk in a runnin' cow

SHOOT Uncork a shell

SHORT LIVED That lasted about as long as hoarfrost. *See Glistens*

SHORT PERSON He couldn't see over a sway-backed Mexican burro ❑ he'd have to stand on a step ladder to kick a grasshopper in the backside ❑ he's about tail high to a wooden Indian *See also Small Man; Male, Short*

SHORT TIME About as long as you can stare at another woman before your wife slaps the snot out of you ❑ about as long as you can stare at another man before your husband gets nervous ❑ about as long as you can stare at a cold beer without taking a swig

SHORTS, TIGHT *See Jeans, Tight*

SHOTGUN As Justin Wilson from Louisiana might say, "A twice barrel shoot gun."

SHOTGUN WEDDING, FORMAL They painted the shotgun white.

SHOULD NOT You hadn't oughta do that.

SHOULDER HOLSTER An ace in the armpit

SHOVELER, EXPERT He fills up the back end of the shovel first, which implies he jams the shovel all the way into the dirt, which is the most efficient way to use a shovel.

SHOW OFF She's wearing a white hat in the show ring. Most contestants in a horse show wear black or brown hats. Anyone wearing a white one is thought to be purposely calling attention to him or herself.

SHREWD He could go into a revolving door in the section behind you and beat you out.

SHRIVELED UP Like a 200-pound raisin (or prune)

SHRUNK Drawed up, as in "When she washed my new shirt it drawed up so much I didn't recognize it for a shirt."

SHUT UP Put a stob in it ❑ check your tongue ❑ put a lid on your voice box and screw it closed

SHY As an old maid skinnin' a pole cat

SICK I was so sick that there is folks in a cemetery feelin' better ❑ the doctor said if I got any worse he'd have to change my prescription to embalming fluid ❑ my nose is running like a tourist who drank Mexican water ❑ I got the whistleberry thumps and the back door trots ❑ I've got the green apple nasties *See also Ill and Ill, Gravely*

SIDEWAYS Slaunchways

SIGHT, IMPAIRED His glasses lenses are so thick they look like the bottoms out of Coke bottles.

SILK A material invented so women could be seen naked in public.

SIMILARITIES, NONE *See No Similarities*

SIMPLE An easy row to hoe ❑ an easy fish to clean

SIMPLE MINDED Like a goose, he wakes up in a different world every day ❑ he don't know scat from scout ❑ he don't know a hawk from a handsaw ❑ he don't know spit from shinola *See also Dumb, Ignorant, Stupid*

SINGER, HIGH VOICE She sings notes so high, you'd swear she had her hair caught in a wringer.

SINGER, POOR They call him "gate mouth" 'cause he sings like a swinging gate with a rusty hinge ❑ he can carry a great tune but he can't unload it worth a damn ❑ after he carries a tune it has fingerprints ❑ no one knows what he did with the money his mother gave him for singing lessons

SINNER, REFORMED From now on, the only thing he'll be guilty of is singing too loud in church. That pretty well means he has ruined his bad reputation.

SIPHON HOSE Oklahoma credit card

SISSY He had to live at home while he went to college 'cause he was still bein' wet nursed ❑ suffers from wimplash ❑ he's got little red hearts on his shorts

SITUATION, DELICATE A blonde hair in the butter ❑ a fly in the buttermilk (or ointment)

SITUATION, PERPLEXING It's too slow for possum and not fast enough for coon.

SITUATION, POOR He's like a Missouri mule, no ancestry and no hope for posterity.

SITUATION, REVERSED Now the horseshoes are on the mule ❑ now the boot is on the other foot

SITUATION, SENSITIVE We got a skunk under the church.

SIZE DON'T COUNT Even the meanest bull has to defend himself from flies.

SIZZLED Like a lizard stuck by lightning

SKEPTIC A person who believes that something which looks like manure, smells like manure, and tastes like manure might be custard pudding.

SKEPTICAL Wouldn't believe that even if God and half the disciples swore to it and the governor of Mississippi notarized it. (The governor of any state you like can be substituted for Mississippi.)

SKIN SPECIALIST Itch doctor

SKINNED UP Skint ❑ he looks like a strawberry patch. Strawberry, in this case, refers to the superficial skin wounds you get when you slide a little too hard on some rough ground ❑ he looks like he was drug over three miles of gravel road by a runaway horse *See also Face, Skinned Up*

SKINNY MAN If he was in the circus, they could shoot

him out of a shotgun instead of a cannon ❏ he ain't nuthin' but breath and breeches ❏ he don't carry a key to the front door 'cause he just crawls through the keyhole ❏ if he played hide an seek he could get lost behind a clothesline pole ❏ if he was a little taller you could use him as a cane pole when you went fishing ❏ he's so skinny he inspects oil wells from the inside ❏ he has to walk past a place twice to cast a shadow ❏ he looks like an earthworm with the guts slung out ❏ when he works out his bones sweat ❏ when it rains he can run between the rain drops and not get wet ❏ you could use him for a tomato stake ❏ he's so skinny he has to wear flippers in the shower to keep from going down the drain *See also Male, Skinny; Thin*

SKINNY WOMAN She could walk through a harp and not strike a note ❏ if she blushed real bad, she'd look like an upside down thermometer ❏ if she was an artist's model everyone would draw stick people ❏ she wears a thread bikini (as opposed to a string bikini) ❏ if you were in bed with her you'd have to shake the sheets to find her ❏ if she turned sideways and closed one eye she'd look like a needle *See also Female, Skinny*

SKIRT, SHORT A deep water skirt, which means she can wade in deep water without getting her skirt wet

SLEEP LIKE A BABY People who say they sleep like a baby don't have one.

SLICK As polished ice ❏ as an eel dipped in axle grease ❏ as snot on a glass door knob ❏ as oil on ice ❏ as a bull snake dipped in hot butter *See also Politician, Devious*

SLIPPERY Go back to Slick

SLOP BUCKET Slop jar ❏ thunder bucket

SLOW DOWN Hold it down to a gentle promenade ❏ whoa up a little or give them whoa reins a good jerk ❏ put the flaps down ❏ throttle back on the afterburner ❏ test your anchor

SLOW DRIVER He's a one-man traffic jam ❏ he thinks every day is Sunday ❏ she's a two-shifter. In the old days, most cars came with three-speed manual transmissions. As you accelerated, you shifted to a higher gear as the speed increased. Some folks, especially little old ladies on their way to church, never went fast enough to shift into third gear so they were two-shifters.

SLOW PERSON He's so slow you have to set out some stakes to see if he is moving ❏ he couldn't catch a fat dog hooked to a leash ❏ he moves slower than cream does when rising in butter-milk ❏ he moves slower than a flea abandoning a dead dog (The poor ol' flea just don't want to admit he's lost his meal ticket.) ❏ he couldn't even catch the caboose on a gravy train ❏ he's movin' slow as a short legged turtle in a molasses spill *See also Moves, Slow*

SLOW POKE A dust eater. On a cattle drive, anyone bringing up the rear (riding drags) had to eat a lot of the dust kicked up by the herd in front of them. Only the slowest cowboy would ever ride behind the herd.

SLOW RUNNER On a good day he could out run a glacier or a new born colt.

SLOW WITTED He don't know manure from moth balls which is why his closet smells funny and his tomatoes died ❏ it takes him an hour and a half to watch "60 Minutes"

SMALL Pissant sized ❏ no bigger than a nubbin (John Wayne's favorite) ❏ as a landlord's heart ❏ about as big as a bar of soap in a boom town bordin' house. During the great oil booms of the 1920s and 1930s, boarding houses were notorious for supplying very few amenities at very high prices. After a few dirty roughnecks got a turn at one bar of soap, there wasn't much left for the rest of the crew. *See also Eggs, Small*

SMALL HEAD He could look through a keyhole with both eyes at the same time.

SMALL MAN He'd have to stand on a step ladder to look a Pygmy in the navel. *See also Male, Short*

SMALL TOWN *See Town, Small*

SMELLS BAD As a wet javelina pig ❏ as bad as an Easter egg in July ❏ would drive buzzards off a road kill ❏ as bad as a mildewed saddle blanket on a sore-back horse that was rode three-hundred miles in August

SMILE One smile from a pretty girl is worth ten from a bartender ❑ the world's best face-lift

SMILE, BIG She smiles so big, she smears lipstick on her ears ❑ as a politician in a runoff ❑ as a game show host

SMILING Like a dead hog in the sunshine. This saying originated from hogs that were butchered and laid out in the yard of the packin' plant. When the sun got hot, the skin on the hog's face would draw up, giving the impression that the dead hog was smiling.

SMOOTH As butter in molasses

SNACK A tide over, as in "That candy bar'll tide me over 'till dinner."

SNAKE, LARGE Big as a fire hose

SNARLS Like a Russian restaurant worker

SNORES LOUD Enough to knock wallpaper (or paint) off a wall

SNORING Callin' his hogs ❑ laugh and the world laughs with you, snore and you sleep alone

SNOW, DEEP Elbow deep to a ten-foot wooden Indian ❑ the snow was so deep around the cabin that we had to sit down on a shotgun and shoot ourselves up the chimney to get out

SNOW, HEAVY Looks like there was an explosion in a feather pillow factory ❑ the angels are puttin' new feathers in their pillows

SOBER As a corpse

SOCIAL LIFE, LACKING A nun in a convent has a better social life than I do.

SOFT AS The inside of a calf's ear ❑ as a baby's kiss

SOLDIER, DEDICATED If he died with his boots on, they'd be polished.

SOLUTION, TEMPORARY You're just patching a crack instead of fixing the foundation ❑ your just puttin' Coca Cola in the transmission. Used car dealers are notorious for having temporary solutions to fix large problems with used cars. A little Coke in a slipping transmission gums up the works for a while and make it seem like the car is fine. Other temporary solutions are sawdust in a slipping rear end and Ivory soap on a leaking gas tank.

SOLVED THE MYSTERY We treed the coon.

SOON Directly, as in "I'll get it done directly."

SOPHISTICATED He can quote Shakespeare without crediting it to the Bible.

SORE Stove up ❏ I feel like a cow that was milked by Captain Hook ❏ I'm as sore as a porcupine with an ingrown quill ❏ I got a kink in my get along, which is a little worse than a hitch in your get along or being down in your get along

SOUND, GOOD Like the pitter patter of little feet going home.

SOUND, OMINOUS A gunshot in a graveyard ❏ the Budwiser whistle, which is the whistling sound a beer bottle makes when thrown across the dance floor in a honky tonk. You can substitute most any brand of beer you like but please only domestic brands, since imported beer is not a real favorite in honky tonks.

SOUND, THUD Like a bull rider landing on his back

SOUP, THICK As Mississippi mud

SOUR Enough to pucker a hog's butt

SOW BELLY MEAT Arkansas or hillbilly chicken

SPANK Ruffle his tail feathers ❏ give him a one-handed salute

SPEAK FRANKLY Tell it like it ought to be.

SPEAK KINDLY A sharp tongue might cut your throat.

SPEAK SOFTLY The softer you speak, the less wear and tear you put your tongue through.

SPEAKER, EXPERIENCED He can give directions without using his hands ❏ a really experienced speaker can describe a pretty girl in detail without using his hands. Go ahead, try it. *See also Advice for Speakers*

SPEAKER, LONG WINDED He goes around the pig twice to get to the tail, which means it takes him a long time to get to the point.

SPEAKING ENGAGEMENT, DIFFICULT You're fightin' the food. If you have to give a speech while the audience is eating, you will lose 'cause no one can compete with food.

SPECIFIC *See Be Specific*

SPEECH, TOO LONG Keep it short 'cause the mind can only absorb what the backside can endure ❑ if the cook uses shortening, you should too

SPEEDING Like a bat out of Georgia

SPELLER, POOR He never learned to spell 'cause the teacher kept changing the words.

SPEND TIME WISELY A policeman can catch more thieves watching a chicken coop than he can watching a saloon.

SPENDS A LOT She lives her life based on three principals: spend till the end, buy till you die, shop till you drop ❑ Visa is considering puttin' her picture on every new card they issue

SPENT All petered out

SPINELESS As a burlap sack ❑ as a Kleenex ❑ as a bowl of spaghetti

SPIRITED He's got a lot of gumption ❑ she's mighty feisty

SPITTER, EXPERT Could spit tobacco into the neck of a swingin' bottle ❑ he could spit tobacco juice through a new broom and not get a single straw wet.

SPLATTERED Like a country cow wettin' on a city sidewalk

SPORTS The perspiring arts ❑ jockdom

SPOUSE, FAT He's got more meat in his bed than he does in his smokehouse.

SPREAD OUT Like dishes at a church social

SPREAD QUICK As a wildfire in dry grass ❑ as a rumor in a retirement home

SPREAD RUMORS Talkin' out of school *See also Gossip*

SPRINGTIME Struttin' and gobblin' time

SPRINGY As curb feelers on a '48 Dodge

SQUEAKS Like springs in a fat woman's bed

STALLING You're just spittin' on the handle ❑ standin' around like a wet tree

STANDARDS, LOW If girls were rated on a scale of 1 to 10 with 10 bein' the best, his idea of a perfect 10 would be a 4 carrying a six-pack of beer.

STARCHED SHIRT Petrified shirt

START TROUBLE Pull the plug on tranquility.

STARTLED Like he was hit with a church stick, which is a long stick with a fox tail on one end that is used to tickle people who have fallen asleep in church.

STATISTICS, MEANINGLESS It don't make any difference if the average depth of the river is five feet or five inches once you're drowned ☐ Baseball legend Bobby Bragan had some words for folks who fool with statistics to develop percentages. He said, "Say you were standing with one foot in the oven and one foot in an ice bucket. According to the percentage people, you should be about perfectly comfortable."

STATUS QUO Blackie Sherrod of the *Dallas Morning News* once quoted a country preacher as saying that status quo was Latin for "the mess we is in."

STAY CLOSE Stick to him like varnish on a dresser.

STAY TILL THE END I'm gonna stay till the last dog dies.

STAYED TOO LONG Overstayed the invitation, such as they invited you over for supper and you stayed for breakfast ☐ they stayed till the last pea was out of the dish

STEAK, TENDER This steak is so tender I don't see how it held the cow together.

STEER The difference between a bull and a steer is that a bull has his work cut out for him and a steer has had his works cut out.

STICKING OUT Like a cow catcher on the front of a switch engine

STICKS Like melted gum to a horse's tail (or tennis shoe) ☐ like spaghetti sauce to a silk tie ☐ like stink to a skunk's tail

STICKY As Georgia blacktop in July

STIFF As a tow bar ☐ as cordwood ☐ as an Italian marble statue

STILL As a rat in the light of a floodlight. Deer, possum, or rabbit can be substituted for rat.

STINGS Like rock salt in your butt. Anyone who has ever tried to steal watermelons from a patch guarded by a farmer armed with a shotgun loaded with rock salt knows exactly how much the salt stings when it hits your backside. If you haven't experienced the sensation, you can trust me on this one — it stings.

STINGY The only thing he ever gives is advice ❑ he'd only give you the sleeves off his vest ❑ he won't even give his wife an argument ❑ if he don't share his whiskey let him catch his own horse, which means if someone drinks all the whiskey by himself, he'll get good and drunk and probably need some help to catch his horse *See also Frugal; Miser*

STOOD OUT Like a tall man at a funeral

STOP HIM Spike his cannons, which means drive an iron spike into the touch hole on the breech of a muzzle-loading cannon. Once a cannon has been spiked it is useless, so the artillery has been stopped from doing any more damage.

STOPPED SUDDENLY He stopped quicker than a barefoot bowler. In bowling, the approach to the lanes is very slick so, with the proper shoes, you can slide to the foul line when making your delivery. If you tried that barefooted, you would definitely come to a sudden stop the moment you tried to slide.

STOUT As a Mexican plate lunch ❑ as mare's breath *See also Breath, Bad*

STRANGE PERSON His biscuits ain't golden brown ❑ he's a few bricks short of a full load ❑ he's a few cards short of having a full deck ❑ he ain't wrapped too tight ❑ he's wired different than the rest of us ❑ his tractor don't get much traction ❑ he ain't workin' with a full string of lights *See also Acting Strange, Crazy, Idiot, Odd Person*

STRANGER We ain't on borrowing terms ❑ don't know him from Adam (or her from Eve) ❑ Blackie Sherrod of the *Dallas Morning News* once wrote, "I wouldn't know him if he walked into this very room and played 'Come to Jesus' in whole notes on a bagpipe."

STREETS, CROOKED San Antonio streets. It has been

said that the streets of San Antonio, Texas were laid out by a drunk Mexican on a blind mule in a sandstorm.

STREETS, POOR
Oklahoma streets. It has been speculated that the asphalt used to pave streets in Oklahoma has less tar in it than a carton of cigarettes.

STRONG, SILENT TYPE
He bores with a deep auger.

STRONG AS A new well rope

STRONG PERSON He can throw horseshoes when they are still attached to the horse □ he could knock a tank off its tracks □ he could throw an anvil across the Grand Canyon at its widest point

STRUTTING Sashayin' □ flapping elbows like a young rooster in love with his own voice

STUBBORN As a blue nose mule □ he's like a hog, you got to hit him on the snout with a stick to get his attention □ he refuses to buy life insurance so everyone will be sad when he dies □ as a two-headed mule □ treat a stubborn man the way you would a stubborn mule you're fixin' to corral. Don't try to drive him in, just leave

the gate open a crack and let him bust in.

STUCK As a dollar bill in a miser's wallet □ as a cat in a mud bog

STUCK UP Her nose is so far up in the air she could drown in a thunder storm □ her nose is so far up in the air a sparrow tried to build a nest in her nose

STUDENT, POOR They had to burn down the school to get him out □ he was only in school for two terms, Johnson's and Nixon's (any two terms can be substituted) □ fighter Rocky Graziano once said, "I quit school in the sixth grade because of pneumonia. Not because I had it but because I couldn't spell it."

STUDENT ATHLETE The only things he can pass are a physical and a urine test.

STUPID MAN He saw some baby pigs sucking on mamma and thought they were blowing her up □ he opened a tall man's shop in Tokyo □ he'd change the oil in a rented car □ he's so stupid he'd get in a squirting contest with a skunk □ his head is full of stump water □ he don't have the sense God gave a screwdriver □ he don't have enough brains to fill up a gnat's ear ❑ he's got about as much sense as last year's bird nest ❑ if you put his brains on a butter paddle, you wouldn't have enough to smear on a mosquito's back ❑ his pilot light went out ❑ he was born ignorant and went downhill ❑ he just gargled at the fountain of knowledge ❑ he tried to hide behind his wife's skirt and she was wearing a mini skirt ❑ he'd hold a fish underwater to try to drown it ❑ he's about half as smart as Trigger the wonder horse ❑ he thinks Johnny Cash is change for the pay toilet *See also Male, Stupid*

STUPID WOMAN She don't know if she's washin' or hangin' out ❑ she thinks Joan of Arc was Noah's wife ❑ she's so stupid she can't pluck a chicken 'cause she can't find its eyebrows ❑ she planted Cheerios tryin' to grow doughnuts ❑ she thinks marshmallows grow in marshes ❑ if she had twice as much sense she'd be a halfwit ❑ she built a snow man and then brought it inside so it wouldn't get cold *See also Female, Stupid*

SUBMARINE CREWMAN Bubble head. A crewman of a nuclear submarine is a glow-in-the-dark bubble head. There was once a couple of country boys from West Texas who joined the navy and volunteered for submarine duty because, they said, they'd seen enough wide-open spaces to last three lifetimes.

SUBSTANDARD It ain't up to snuff

SUBTLE, NOT VERY He's about as subtle as a rhinoceros in heat ❑ that's about as subtle as a poke in the eye with a sharp stick

SUCCEEDED He kept his head up and his overhead down ❑ if you itch for success don't stop scratching ❑ never let the sun catch you in bed if you want to amount to anything

SUCCEEDED, ALMOST He finally got to the top of the ladder but it was leaning against the wrong wall ❑ his ship came in but it docked at the wrong pier

SUCCEEDED, PERHAPS Got his ends meeting but they are tied with a slip knot.

SUCCESS Is the result of backbone, not the wishbone ❑ when yearning meets earning ❑ being able to tell the truth at your high school reunion ❑ to be a success you have to jump at opportunities as quick as you do conclusions

SUCCESSFUL PLAN It went off without a hitch.

SUCTION, GOOD Could pull a Pecos cantaloupe through an irrigation pipe ❑ could back start a Harley Davidson ❑ got more suction than a bucket full of ticks

SULLEN As a mule in a mud bog ❑ if he ever smiled it'd crack open his face like a watermelon that fell off a wagon

SUNBURN, BAD His head looked like a beach ball ❑ turned him into a crispy critter

SUNRISE Sunup

SUPERFICIAL Shallow rivers and shallow minds freeze first.

SUPPORTING CAST Even the best song wouldn't sound so good without the minor keys.

SUPPOSE SO Reckon so

SURE THING A closed savings and loan would reopen just to loan money on it ❑ you can bet the baby's milk money on that ❑ if you

gamble on a good deal you'll end up with a good deal less, which is another way of saying there ain't no such thing as a sure thing, unless you're talking death and taxes

SURPLUS We got more of them than we had buggy whips in the 1920s. Thanks to Henry Ford, the automobile was an instant success; so much so that many vendors were caught with a large surplus of buggy whips that suddenly no one seemed to want. Any merchant who had more of something than he had buggy whips was really overstocked.

SURPRISED As a nearsighted porcupine trying to make time with a cactus ❑ as a car-chasin' dog that caught one

SURPRISED OATH *See Oath*

SURPRISING That'll put a kink in your hair ❑ that set me back on my heels

SUSPICION He dresses too good to be a Bible salesman, which is a reference to old-time door-to-door Bible salesmen. They never had much luck and thus were never dressed too well. You would, therefore, be highly suspicious of anyone that was well dressed and claimed to be a Bible salesman. ❑ I think we got a one-armed man in the game. Country folks are just naturally suspicious of a one-armed man in any sort of game because they seem to win more often than they lose.

SUSPICIOUS He don't trust his own memory ❑ he only believes half of what he sees with his own eyes ❑ as a country boy who found tennis shoe tracks under his wife's window. Since country boys don't usually wear tennis shoes, he'd naturally be suspicious that someone else was pickin' fruit off his tree *See also Skeptical*

SWEAT A waste of good beer ❑ something a hard working housewife has to put up with and her lazy husband don't ever see

SWEATER, TIGHT She fills up that sweater like hot wax fills up a candle mold *See also Jeans, Tight*

SWEATING Like a heifer in heat ❑ like a hog butcher after a frost ❑ like a Mississippi cotton chopper on election day

SWEEP Run a broom over it.

SWEET As a mother's kiss when you're sick

SWEET POTATO PIE New-ground pie

SWIMMER, POOR The only time he gets near water is when he uses it as a chaser.

SWOLLEN UP Like the head of a horse that was snake bit on the nose ❑ swollen up like a poisoned pup

T

TOWN, SMALL — the town was so small the "Reduce Speed" and "Resume Speed" signs were on the same pole

T

TACTFUL If he was a doctor, he could give you a shot and you wouldn't feel the needle ❑ he can step on your boots and not mess up the shine

TAKE A BREAK Shade up

TAKE A CHANCE You can't make an omelet without breaking some eggs ❑ you can't steal second base and keep one foot on first ❑ you have to go out on the limb if you want the best fruit

TAKE ACTION Texas Agriculture Commissioner Jim Hightower said, "The water won't clear up till you get the hogs out of the creek."

TAKE AIM Fill your sights ❑ get your cross hairs on it

TAKE CARE OF YOUR OWN BUSINESS FIRST You better clean your finger before you point it at someone else ❑ clean your own barn before you complain about the smell coming from your neighbor's barn

TAKE IT EASY Cool your saddle some.

TAKE OVER Get the drop on 'em.

TAKE THE SHORT PATH The farther you ride, the longer it is back.

TAKING A CHANCE You're leading with your chin ❑ you're under a tall tree and a thunder storm is brewing ❑ you're buyin' a tired horse. This is a reference to the old horse trader's trick of taking a spirited horse out for a long ride just before offering him for sale to someone. The horse would get tired and settle down long enough for the deal to be made but anyone buyin' a tired horse was taking the chance that once the animal got his wind back he'd be just as hard to handle as ever.

TALK NICE You get more hogs in the pen by throwing corn cobs instead of rocks.

TALK, MEANINGLESS He's got a good line but there

ain't no clothespins on it, which means he's got a lot to say but not much of it is worth holding onto.

TALKATIVE If a cat tried to get his tongue he'd eat it fur, purr, and all ❑ she could talk the loincloth off a wooden Indian ❑ she is like the sky, the only time she is quiet is when she is blue ❑ she could talk the legs off a baby grand piano ❑ his tongue is tied in the middle and waggin' on both ends ❑ she can talk tomatos out of a can ❑ if silence was golden he couldn't earn a plug nickle ❑ he's a man of few words but he uses them often ❑ he could talk for half an hour after he told you all he knew ❑ she can talk till you're blue in the face ❑ she could talk the ears off a brass monkey ❑ he has enough tongue for five rows of teeth ❑ she's got a tongue like a bell clapper

TALKER, GOOD (ALMOST) He's got a silver tongue but it is only plated.

TALKER, PERSISTENT She's like an echo, always gets in the last word.

TALKER, PERSUASIVE He could convince his wife she doesn't look good in mink ❑ she could talk the devil into an amen corner

TALKER, SLICK He uses words so polished you could skate on them.

TALKING BIG You're spreading more manure than all the cats in Mississippi could cover up.

TALKING TOO MUCH His mind is on vacation while his mouth is working overtime.

TALKS FANCY He's silk tongued.

TALKS SLOW It takes him three and a half hours to describe a two-hour movie.

TALKS TOO FAST She can talk fast enough to confuse God.

TALKS WITHOUT THINKING Shoots from the lip ❑ he thinks by the inch and talks by the yard (which frequently makes you want to move him by the foot)

TALL AND SKINNY His Adam's apple drops six inches when he swallows ❑ he looks like two eyes mounted on a cane pole

TALL PERSON The angels in heaven have to cut his hair and the devil polishes his boots.

TALL TALE Highly embroidered story ❑ never let the truth stand in the way of a good story

TALL TALE, TEXAS STYLE The difference between a fairy tale and a Texas tale is that a fairy tale begins with "Once upon a time" and the Texas tale begins with, "You ain't gonna believe this."

TAN, PARTIAL A farmer's tan. Farmers spend a lot of time outside and they generally wear a shirt under their overalls. They almost always a have a deep tan on their neck and their forearms, which makes them look partially tanned when they take their shirt off.

TANGLED UP Like a bushel basket full of wire coat hangers ❑ like a tackle box full of loose fish hooks. A man in South Carolina once had a tackle box so full of tangled fish hooks that he gave up ever trying to sort them out. Instead of throwing the whole mess in the trash, however, he came upon a stroke of genius. He sent the box, tangled hooks and all, to an old geezer who had the reputation for being a miser. At last report, the old man had spent more than two years working on the tangled mess and only had a handful of hooks to show for the effort.

TASTE, GOOD She put a good scald on it ❑ it'll make your tongue slap your brains out (or slap an eyeball out) ❑ if it was any better, I'd rub it in my hair ❑ so good it'll make your teeth shake ❑ that'd make you want to slap your granny

TASTE, BAD That tastes like rinse water from a Chinese laundry ❑ like diluted wallpaper paste ❑ like runoff water from a packin' plant ❑ would harelip a hyena ❑ that tastes worse than a salmon, onion, and smoked sardine pizza, which was a delicacy Pizza Hut invented when they expanded into Russia. They believed the sardines and onions would be palatable for the Russian people, which may speak volumes about Russian taste.

TASTES, SIMPLE I was weaned on corn bread and iced tea.

TAXES Are like golf, you drive hard to get to the green and end up in the hole

TEACHER, GOOD An educator once said that the

three things to remember when teaching are: 1. know your stuff, 2. know who you're stuffing and, 3. stuff them elegantly.

TEACHER, POOR He couldn't teach a chicken to peck.

TEETH, MISSING He has so many teeth missing he talks with an echo.

TEETH, STRONG She could bite a chunk out of an anvil (or a railroad rail).

TELEPHONE OPERATOR Call girl

TELEPHONE STATIC There's a dead cat hangin' on the line somewhere.

TELL HIM OFF Tell him how the cow ate the cabbage ❑ give him a tongue whippin'

TELL ME MORE Put some more kindlin' on that fire.

TELLING THE TRUTH You ain't just whistlin' Dixie.

TEMPER TANTRUM A running, or wall-eyed, or squalling fit

TEMPER The only thing you can lose and still have ❑ he's so well-tempered that he can lose it three or four times a day and not run out

TEMPORARY As a movie set ❑ as a cloud ❑ as affection from a fallen angel

TEMPTATION A character check

TENDER LOVING CARE A year of nursing don't equal a day of sweethearting.

TENNIS PLAYER, STRONG He can knock the fuzz off the ball.

TENSE He's wound tight as a pea vine through a picket fence ❑ his nerves are tighter than rope clothes lines after a soakin' rain ❑ his nerves are as tight as a gut stretched between two pups ❑ he was so tense he had to slap himself to sleep

TENUOUS He's got a shaky caboose.

TEQUILA (Ta Kill Ya) Mexican gasoline

TEST HIM Try him on for size.

TEXAS (Tex-iz) A state of mind

TEXAS WEATHER The weather in Texas proves that God has a sense of humor. Harold Taft, of Channel Five in Dallas/Fort Worth, once reported on some strange events related to the Texas weather. When he finished the report, Mr. Taft sort of shook his head and commented: "Texas weather will do anything to get into the news."

THANK YOU NOTE A bread and butter letter

THAT EXPLAINS IT Ah, that accounts for the milk in the coconut, which is an expression used when something you don't understand, like how the milk gets in the coconut, is finally explained.

THAWED Unfroze it. A child once offered the following grace: "Lord bless this food and the person that unfroze it."

THERE IS STILL TIME It's only thunder, which means it has not started raining yet so there is time to finish the job. In his book *If I Tell You a Hen Dips Snuff,* Don Bowman used the expression "Cut your peaches, girls, thunder ain't rain."

THICK HEADED If he got shot between the eyes, it'd take the bullet half an hour to make a hole.

THICK SKINNED If he ever had to have an

operation, the doctor would have to use a chain saw.

THIEF He'd steal the straw out of a widow's broom ❑ he'll take anything but a hint ❑ he'd steal a hot stove and come back for the smoke ❑ someone who can find things before you lose them *See also Crook*

THIEF, EXPERT He can steal your shadow.

THIEF, FAST MOVING He was traveling so fast he didn't have time to pack his real name.

THIEF, SNEAKY If you yawned, he'd steal your chew of tobacco (or your gold fillings if they were loose).

THIEF, STUPID He held up a bus load of Las Vegas tourists on the way home ❑ he couldn't even steal a kiss from an old maid

THIGHS, LARGE Ol' thunder thighs, which means her thighs are so large that it sounds like thunder when they bang together as she walks.

THIN As a whisper ❑ as a bat's ear ❑ as an ant's eyelash

THIN BUT STRONG He's sneaky strong, which means

he's a lot stronger than he looks.

THIN PERSON If he turned sideways, you could paint stripes on him and use him for a yardstick ❑ he don't even have enough meat on his bones to qualify for a class project in anatomy school ❑ his body don't look lived in ❑ he's so thin he has to get out of the tub before he pulls the plug so he won't go down the drain ❑ if he stuck out his tongue and turned sideways he would look like the world's largest zipper *See also Male, Skinny and Skinny Man*

THINGS HAVE CHANGED As James B. McSheehy said, "The roosters have come home to roost."

THINK ABOUT IT Let's whip the devil around the stump awhile.

THINK AHEAD Don't wait till the alarm goes off to start building the fire escape ❑ set your pace by the distance left to go and not by the distance already covered

THIRSTY As a mud hen on a tin roof ❑ as a cowboy in a new dry town, which means the cowpuncher hasn't had time to find a local bootlegger

THREAT I'm gonna hit you so hard that it'll raise a knot on your head so big you'll have to stand on a step ladder to scratch it ❑ I'm fixin' to cut you three ways, high, wide, and deep ❑ I'm gonna hit you so hard you'll wear out bouncing ❑ I'm gonna tie you in a knot and hang you on a fence ❑ I'll beat you like a tied up goat ❑ I'll hit you so hard your kids will be born shaking ❑ I'll turn you ever which way but loose ❑ knock you into the middle of next week ❑ I'll hit you so hard you'll get stopped for speeding when you go through the next county ❑ I'm gonna slap you nekkid ❑ I'm gonna pinch your head off and tell God you died ❑ your ox is about to get gored ❑ I'm fixin' to knock the stuffin' out you ❑ I'm gonna break you like a bad habit ❑ I'm fixing to dot your eyes ❑ I'm gonna rid the ground of your shadow ❑ I'm gonna whip knots on your head faster than you can scratch 'em ❑ I'm gonna get on you so hard, you'll have to set fire to your shirt and smoke yourself out from under me to get away ❑ I'm gonna stomp a mud hole in you and walk it dry ❑ I'm gonna open a can of whupass and pour it all over you ❑ if you mess with me you'll wake up in a coffin ❑ I'm gonna whip you before God gets the news

THREE Rs Education: readin', rittin', and 'rithmatic ❑ Ranching: riding, roping, and 'rangling ❑ Marriage: romance, rice, and rocks

THROAT Gozzle, as in "I got some deer meat stuck in my gozzle and like to choked plumb to death."

THROW Chunk, as in "I wouldn't trust her as far as I could chunk her."

THROW DICE Ford 'em (as in shake, rattle, and roll)

THUNDER The angels are bowling ❑ so loud it knocked me out of the shower

TIGHT AS A $10 face-lift ❑ as a clam with lockjaw ❑ as a fiddle string ❑ a leather jock strap when it's wet ❑ as last year's long johns or bikini ❑ as a steel spring bustle ❑ as next year's budget

TIGHT FIT Fits tight as a duck's (or cow's) foot in a mud bog.

TIGHTWAD He's so tight if you threw him in a river he wouldn't make a bubble

'cause he wouldn't give up the air ❑ when he throws a party the beer flows like sap out of a tree ❑ he can make a nickel go so far that the buffalo gets sore feet

The best definition in the world came from Edwin Pope, the legendary sports writer for the *Miami Herald*. He was speaking about another newspaper legend, Furman Bisher of the *Atlanta Constitution:* "Swimming was invented," Pope said, "when Furman Bisher came to a toll bridge." *See also Frugal, Miser*

TIME TO GO Put the chairs in the wagon. On the frontier, chairs were often in short supply, so when families went calling they often carried their chairs so they'd have a place to sit. When the man of the house announced, "put the chairs in the wagon," everyone knew it was time to go home. ❑ Time to put the bricks in the buggy, which relates to the old custom of placing heated, wrapped bricks in the floor of the buggy to keep the feet warm during a trip.

TIMID Has the personality of a custard pudding ❑ he's got the guts of a butterfly ❑ the only bull he'll ever take

235

by the horns is the one on a can of Schlitz Malt Liquor

TIRED I feel like an empty shuck ❏ I'm played plumb out ❏ too pooped to pop ❏ I feel like I was run down, run over, and wrung out through a little bitty wringer ❏ I could sleep on a barbed wire fence without a blanket ❏ my get along has got along all it can ❏ as a North Carolina 'sang hunter. To hunt 'sang (ginseng root) you have to walk a lot of miles over rough terrain while fighting off bugs and snakes and you just can't do it without getting real tired. In *You All Spoken Here,* Roy Wilder, Jr. included this quote from one hunter, "To harvest one pound, a man must walk not less than twenty miles over a two-day period, and in the process kill three rattlesnakes and ten copperheads."

TIRES, WORN Those tires are so thin you can see the air inside.

TO EACH HIS OWN Even a buzzard is cute to another buzzard ❏ a cow chip is a buffet to a fly

TOAST, BURNT Cajun style toast.

TOES, LARGE Nut crackers. There is a man in Mississippi who claims that when he goes out to hunt pecans, he always goes barefooted. That way when he finds a nut, he picks it up with his toes and cracks it open at the same time, so when he puts it in his gunny sack it is ready to shell. Believe it or not.

TOGETHER We're swimming in the same swamp.

TOLD A SECRET He put a bug in my ear.

TOLERANCE Ability to listen to a fish story and keep a straight face

TONGUE TIED I got my tongue wrapped around my eye teeth and I can't see what I tryin' to say.

TOO CLOSE TO THE PROBLEM When you're sittin' in it you don't smell it.

TOOK OFF Like a cut cat

TOOTHLESS A dog without teeth chews careful.

TOUGH AS A knot in a pine board ❏ as a cast iron washtub ❏ as a bunkhouse (or campfire) steak ❏ as a wagon load of wet rawhide *See also Hard As*

TOUGH JOB Like trying to drive a swarm of bees through a snow storm with a hickory switch

TOUGH MAN He uses barbed wire for dental floss

TOUGH SPOT The toughest spot of all is when you have to face the music with your nose to the grindstone and your back to the wall.

TOUPEE His hair ain't home grown or his home grown hair was grown in someone else's home.

TOWN, BORING I spent three weeks there one weekend, which means the town is so small and boring that a weekend seems like it is three weeks long ❑ A soldier from San Antonio was once transferred to a small base somewhere out west and he always claimed he did a two-year tour there one month.

TOWN, POOR You can hear anything except the jingle of change and the fryin' of bacon ❑ the only thing you hear after dark is the hardening of arteries

TOWN, RURAL It's located miles and miles from the middle of nowhere. *See also Rural*

TOWN, SMALL So small they had to widen the street to put a stripe down the middle ❑ if anyone turned on an electric blanket, the street light would go out ❑ the street sweeper uses a Hoover vacuum ❑ nothing but a wide place in the road ❑ they only need one department store Santa Claus ❑ where there ain't much to do but plenty of people to talk about it when you do it ❑ the only thing that goes out after 10 p.m. is the lights ❑ the "slow down" and "resume speed" signs are on the same pole ❑ the last time they held a boxing match, both fighters had to use the same corner ❑ a fixin' to town ❑ they don't even have a cannon in the park ❑ so small no baby arrives unexpectedly ❑ in Pyote, Texas, they have a sign which says Entering Pyote on one side. On the other side it reads Leaving Pyote.

TOWN, STRICT The young girls can't buy a bra without a prescription.

TOY A play pretty

TRACKER, GOOD He could track a minnow through a swamp.

TRADE, POOR He offered me a squash for a quarter horse.

TRAPPED Like a lizard under a cow patty. If a lizard happens to be in the wrong place when a cow gets rid of yesterday's oats, he is surely trapped ❑ like a minnow in a bucket ❑ like a kid's toy in a blister pack. Anyone who has ever tried to open a blister pack knows that whatever is inside is truly trapped ❑ like a wasp inside a window ❑ like he was pennied into his room, which relates to the prank of trapping someone in a room by using a roll of pennies to keep the door from opening

TRAVELER, POOR His idea of a long trip is havin' to walk halfway round the camp fire to get to the handle on the coffee pot.

TRIAL Where your fate lies in the hands of twelve people who weren't smart enough to get out of jury duty.

TRICKY AS Trying to braid a mule's tail

TRIED BUT FAILED He did a lot of stirring but he didn't make no gravy.

TROUBLE Is like muddy creek water. Be patient, don't stir it up, and it will soon clear ❑ it's easier to borrow trouble than it is to give it away ❑ it's cut a switch time ❑ it's woodshed time *See also In Trouble*

TROUBLE, BIG TIME You're trapped on a high bridge by an unscheduled train. In the old days, the easiest way across a big river or deep ravine was the railroad bridge. Even though crossing the bridge was usually prohibited, a lot of people would simply learn the schedule and then cross at times when no trains were due. However, since the bridges were just large enough for the train, if you happened to be about halfway across the bridge and an unscheduled train suddenly appeared, you were, indeed, in big trouble.

TROUBLEMAKER Boat rocker ❑ the one who is always looking for trouble usually hopes he don't find any of it

TROUBLES Are like babies, they grow if you nurse them

TRUE AGE Women won't admit it and men won't act it

TRUSTWORTHY He's a good man to go to the well with ❑ he can carry the key to the smokehouse ❑ you could trust him to count the collection in church

TRUTH Some say country folks have such a high regard for the truth that they use it sparingly so as to not use it up, which is why country folks never let the truth stand in the way of a good story. Harry S. Truman, an original Missouri mule, once said, "I never did give anybody hell. I just told the truth and they thought it was hell."

TRY IT Run it down the well and see if it holds water.

TRYING THE IMPOSSIBLE You're trying to work in two lion cages at the same time. That saying came from a man in Kansas who added that the use of lions was an indication that trying the impossible usually did not work and often met with disastrous results, such being eaten by one of the lions.

TRYING TIMES Times are most trying when you aren't.

TURKEY FRIES *See Calf Fries and Brave As*

TURN OVER Tump over, as in "Billy tumped over his milk and the cat lapped it up."

TWILIGHT First dark

TWINS Womb mates

TWINS, UGLY The lee twins, ugly and homely

This space is for your favorite sayings.

U-V-W

WATER, HIGH — the water got so high we were catching catfish in the kitchen mousetrap

U

UGLY As a fresh foaled moose ❑ as the west end of an east bound mule ❑ as the back side of a mud fence after a hard rain

UGLY BABY He's so ugly, his mother made him put on an Elvis mask before she'd nurse him ❑ she was so ugly, the stork had to get drunk before he could deliver her ❑ he was so ugly, when his daddy saw him he grabbed a shotgun and went down to the zoo to kill a stork ❑ he was so ugly his mother took him everywhere she went so she wouldn't have to kiss him good-by ❑ his mother had morning sickness after he was born ❑ his mother had to be drunk before she'd breast feed him which explains why, 15 years later, he thought Jack Daniels came from cows.

UGLY CHILD If she ever gets kidnapped they'll never put her face on a milk carton 'cause it would ruin the milk business ❑ so ugly he ought to sue his parents for damages

UGLY ENOUGH TO Clabber a mud hole ❑ to gap lightning ❑ to make your eyes fog over ❑ enough to scare a maggot off a bloated buffalo carcass

UGLY MAN He has to soak his clothes in catnip to get the cat to play with him ❑ he was shot through the ugly forest and bounced off every tree ❑ as a mud fence in a rainstorm ❑ he's got a face that would sour buttermilk ❑ as a stump full of worms ❑ if he was an armed robber, he wouldn't need a ski mask ❑ has to slip up on a mirror to shave ❑ he could look like a baboon by shaving and taking off his hat

UGLY WOMAN If she was hangin' on a Christmas tree naked, no one would open their presents ❑ she didn't get a full helping of looks ❑ she wasn't hit with the ugly stick, the whole danged tree fell on her ❑ her face looks like a tow sack full of turnips ❑ she couldn't get a date if she was cooking naked for a deer camp, troop train, football training camp, lumber camp, or cattle drive ❑ whenever her husband goes out on the town he always takes her picture with him so he'll know to stop drinking when she gets good looking *See also Female, Ugly*

ULCERS What you get from mountain climbing over mole hills

UNABLE TO ANSWER Don't start me to lyin',' which essentially means don't ask me that question 'cause if I answer it I'll have to tell you a lie.

UNATTRACTIVE The reason she's unattached is 'cause she was put together sloppy.

UNAVOIDABLE No matter how high a bird flies, he still has to come back down to earth to get something to eat ❑ you can't get around it, teeth and memory weaken with age

UNCHANGEABLE You can put a French nightgown, high heels, and pink lipstick on a jackass but you still wouldn't want to sleep with

it ❑ you can cut off a dog's tail and ears but he's still a dog ❑ you can paint lead gold but it's still lead ❑ you can take the boy out of the country but you can't take the country out of the boy ❑ you can take the boy out of the playground but you can't take the play out of the boy ❑ a crooked tree will never straighten its branches

UNCLEAN She hadn't bathed in so long all the flies stayed on her side of the pickup.

UNCOMFORTABLE As a barbed wire G string

UNCONTROLABLE You can't tell how far a frog will jump by the color of its hide

UNCOORDINATED He can't shuffle dominos ❑ he couldn't guide a plow across a little bitty garden ❑ he can't plow and chew tobacco at the same time ❑ can't shower and sing at the same time ❑ he can't walk and breathe at the same time ❑ his egg got shook, which means he has been uncoordinated since birth ❑ he couldn't even twiddle his thumbs

UNDECIDED He didn't swim or sink, he floated ❑ it's hangin' fire, which is a reference to a breech loading cannon that has a fire in the breech but hasn't gone off

UNDERESTIMATED You're callin' an alligator a lizard.

UNDERTAKER Someone who always lets you down or the last man on earth to let you down ☐ someone who plots your future

UNEDUCATED GUESS He used the WAG system, which is a wild assed guess. *See also Educated Guess*

UNEMPLOYED He has so little to do and so much time to do it in.

UNEXPECTED As a seagull in Colorado ☐ it just came out of the blue

UNFAITHFUL She won't even dance with the one that brung her.

UNFINISHED JOB That's a kiss without a squeeze.

UNFRIENDLY They don't put their horses in the same corral.

UNGRATEFUL He never said "kiss my foot" much less thank you.

UNHAPPY AFFAIR This has been about as cheerful as a coroner's inquest.

UNKNOWN Don't know who in blazes it is ☐ don't rightly know ☐ ain't got the foggiest notion

UNLUCKY If he'd been a dog on Noah's ark he would have ended up with both fleas ☐ he could get a cavity in a porcelain crown ☐ he's been in more holes than a grave digger during a small-pox epidemic ☐ the hind tit is the only one he's ever sucked ☐ if he read a self-help book he'd get killed by a misprint ☐ if he bought a flower shop, they'd outlaw Mother's Day ☐ if he found a peep hole in a nudist colony fence, the only thing he would see would be his wife ☐ if Dolly Parton had been his mother, he'd have been a bottle baby ☐ if he started selling light bulbs the sun would stop setting *See also Born Loser*

UNMARRIED He never got married 'cause mothers don't trust him too far and fathers don't trust him too near.

UNMOTIVATED The only thing he ever did on his own was get dandruff.

UNPOPULAR He was voted most likely to have an autopsy or to end up as a specimen in an anatomy class ☐ whenever he plays horse, someone else plays the front end and he plays himself ❑ he could run for election unopposed and lose ❑ if you ever need someone to push into the creek, he'll do

UNPREDICTABLE He changes his mind as often as a windshield wiper changes sides ❑ you can never tell which way a pickle will squirt. Tomato, orange, or lemon can be substituted for pickle with the same results.

UNPREPARED You ain't got all your dogs barking.

UNPRODUCTIVE You're driving rusty nails in a new board.

UNQUALIFIED He couldn't pass muster.

UNRELATED As chalk and cheese ❑ as a bull and a ballerina

UNREPAIRABLE As a broken window pane

UNROMANTIC As a seasick bride ❑ his idea of eating out is a picnic in the garage

UNSOPHISTICATED He can't tell whether the symphony orchestra is playing or just tuning up ❑ he just come into town on a

load of cantalopes. Watermelons, turnips, cordwood, or manure can be substituted for cantalope.

UNTRUSTWORTHY He's the kind of person you like to see cause you wouldn't want him behind you ❑ she keeps secrets like a politician keeps promises ❑ as a jaguar with a rabbit ❑ you'd be better off to trust a rabbit to deliver a head of lettuce ❑ A man from Austin, Texas advises: "Never trust a cow with white eyelashes, a walleyed horse, or a woman in black underwear."

UNWANTED As a snake at a garden party ❑ I need that about as much as I need a boil on my butt ❑ as a frog in the water can ❑ as a cow chip in the punch bowl at a wedding reception ❑ I need that as much as a dead horse needs flies ❑ I have about as much need for that as a hog does a Sunday hanky

UNWELCOME As a quitter on a trail drive. According to country legend, there wasn't any room on the chuckwagon for a quitter's bedroll.

UPSET As the young lady whose clothes were stolen while she was skinny dippin' ❑ he's got his tail over the dashboard. If a horse got his tail over the dashboard of a buggy, he'd try to run away ❑ his nose is out of joint ❑ he's got a clod in his churn *See also Angry; Female, Angry; Male, Angry*

URINATED He shook the dew off the lily ❑ he drained his lizard ❑ he watered the bushes (or the horses)

USE YOUR HEAD An old buck will stay alive a lot longer by using his brains instead of his antlers.

USEFUL AS A lock on the outhouse door ❑ as a long sermon on a cold Sunday morning. The church is always warm as a depot stove, so on a real cold Sunday morning the longer the preacher talks, the longer you get to stay inside and keep warm ❑ as a pullin' chain at calf time. If a cow is having trouble delivering a calf, cowboys use a pullin' chain to give her a hand so to speak. Without a pullin' chain you have to let nature take its course.

USELESS AS Hair on a barbershop floor ❑ as a needle without an eye ❑ as a well without a bucket. If you've ever been real thirsty and come up on a well only to discover there isn't a bucket handy, then you know a well without a bucket is nothing but a big useless hole in the ground.

Also, Useless as a bathtub without a drain plug ❑ as a barbed wire fence full of knot holes ❑ an outhouse on a submarine ❑ as an udder on a bull ❑ as a crocheted rubber glove ❑ as a fork at a soup convention ❑ as a shotgun with a bent barrel ❑ as combat boots at a track meet ❑ as a pump without a handle ❑ as a marriage license to a tom cat ❑ as an egg-sucking dog ❑ as a one-legged hurdler ❑ as a ticklish fan dancer ❑ as a wedding dress to a sow ❑ as two buggies in a one-horse town ❑ as gossip that ain't worth repeating ❑ as a kiss over the phone ❑ as hair curlers to a bald man

V

VACILLATE Crawfish

VACUUM Dust sucker

VAIN He wouldn't go to a funeral unless he could be the corpse ❑ he even checks his toupee for gray hairs ❑ she'll walk down lover's lane holding her own hand ❑ I wish I could buy her for what she's worth and sell her for she thinks she's worth

VALUABLE As the front door key to Fort Knox

VALUE Secondhand gold is as good as new ❑ As Mark Twain once said, "A used diamond is better than no diamond."

VALUE, POOR The cheapest oats are the ones that have already been through the horse once.

VALUES, HIGH Don't make yourself a dog for the sake of one bone.

VEGETARIAN David Brenner said it best by far, "A vegetarian is a person who won't eat anything that can have children."

VERY Down right, as in "He's down right bodacious."

VET, GOOD He could cure a bear skin rug.

VICE PRESIDENT According to John Nance Garner, the vice president is "A spare tire on the automobile of government."

VINDICTIVE As an IRS agent

VIP Tree shaker

VIRGIN Piece de resistance ❑ she's pure as the driven snow. Of course, the opposite is "pure as the driven slush" as Tallulah Bankhead once described herself.

VISITOR, INFREQUENT He comes around about as often as Elvis does.

VOICE, DEEP His voice is so low you can smell socks on his breath ❑ his voice is so deep he has to wear an athletic supporter for a chin strap

VOICE, POOR Her voice sounds like a Sears buzz saw cutting through a cast iron skillet ❑ she sounds like she has one foot in a bear trap ❑ she makes Roseanne Barr sound like an opera star ❑ if she had to sing for her meals she'd starve to death

VOICE, ROUGH His voice sounds like a rusty gate hinge

VOTING Lyndon Johnson once said, "We don't care how they vote so long as we get to count 'em."

W

WAIT Keep your shirt on for the men and keep you bra on for the ladies

WAITING Just sittin' on the well, which is a country expression that means you're waiting for an oil or water well to come in.

WALK, SEDUCTIVE She's got more moves than Allied Van Lines ❑ I'd rather watch her walk than eat chicken fried steak ❑ If she was in a harness she'd make plowin' a pleasure. This is a reference to the old days when plowing was done by walking behind a plow all day and the only scenery was the back end of a flea bitten ol' mule.

WALK CAREFULLY Like a chicken with an egg cracked

inside ❑ like you're tryin' not to wake the twins ❑ like you were walkin' through a feed lot wearin' a brand new pair of white shoes

WALK SOFTLY Cat foot it

WALKING Ridin' shanks mare

WANDERING If you wander around like an unbridled pony you'll never get to the end of the trail.

WAR SONG The bridal march

WARM As a road lizard ❑ as worm dirt ❑ as a baby chick in a wool basket

WARM EMBRACE An all-squeezin hug

WARNING If you go out and break both legs, don't come running to me ❑ keep the cat off the piano keys or you'll have bad luck ❑ I'm gonna pull you through a knot hole so you can relive the moment of your birth ❑ you're stinkin' for a whippin' ❑ you're aimin' for a maimin' *See also Advance Warning; Threat*

WASH Do, as in "If you'll do the dishes, I'll take you to a moving picture show."

WASHING Suds busting

WASTE OF TIME A kiss over the phone is like a straw hat, it ain't felt ❑ you're looking for feathers on a goat ❑ a wild goose chase ❑ like whistling at a pregnant woman

WASTED EFFORT *See Effort, Wasted*

WASTEFUL As a loaded beer truck going over a cliff ❑ as a cyclone hitting a law school during summer vacation ❑ you're burnin' three lamps and there ain't a ship in sight

WASTING MONEY You can put a silver bridle on a jackass but he's still a jackass ❑ you're fritterin' away your bankroll

WASTING TIME A man from South Carolina said, "You're fishing with a straight hook" to mean wasting time. Which raises the question, If you took a fish hook and straightened it out would it still be a "hook" or would it be a worm harpoon? ❑ you ain't ever gonna find a watermelon in a pumpkin patch ❑ you're beatin' your head against a brick wall ❑ you're preaching to the choir ❑ you're salting the ocean ❑ you're peeing on a forest fire (or trying to put it out with a tea cup) ❑ you're ironing with a cold iron ❑ you're tryin' to catch butterflies in a basketball net ❑ whippin' a dead horse ❑ you're trying to get the river to run over the bridge ❑ you're tryin' to plow in concrete ❑ you're just sittin' there rustin' ❑ you can give a pig a bubble bath but you'll still have a pig ❑ you're grabbin' at sunbeams ❑ you're whistlin' in a graveyard. A lot of people think if you whistle while walking through a graveyard that the ghosts and goblins will be scared away. Not true. If the ghosts are gonna get you, they'll get you regardless of what you do, so whistlin' is wasting time.

WATCH OVER Mind, as in "Will you mind the kids while I go to the store for diapers?"

WATCH WHAT YOU SAY Keep an eye on your tongue ❑ mind what you say ❑ never use sharp words in case you have to eat them later

WATER, DEEP The water was about ankle deep if you were standing on your head ❑ the water got so high we were shooting ducks in the parlor ❑ we were catching catfish in the kitchen mousetrap ❑ the water was so high that the turtles crawled out of their shells and used 'em for life boats *See also Creek, Flooded*

WATER, MUDDY The catfish had to swim backwards to keep from getting mud in their eyes.

WATER, SHALLOW Wouldn't float a kitchen match (or a toothpick) ❑ I've seen dew deeper than that ❑ I've sweat more water than that after mowin' the lawn *See also River, Shallow*

WATER, POOR You have to chew it up before you can swallow it.

WATER COOLER Swamp breeze air conditioner

WAVERING Waffling

WEAK PERSON All his starch is in his shirt ❑ he couldn't even pull off his own hat if he was caught in a whirlwind ❑ he's about as strong as a sick kitten

WEALTHY She's got so much money she uses an imported anaesthetic instead of a local ❑ he has so much money, when he goes out to celebrate he paints the town multicolored instead of just red

WEARY As a kitten walking in fresh mud

WEATHER CHANGE COMING The prairie dogs are building banks. When prairie dogs build up the banks around the mouth of their holes, it is thought to be a sign that heavy rains are on the way ❑ the cattle are drifting toward the fence, which means a blue norther is coming. When cattle sense a severe weather front is coming they naturally begin to drift away from the weather. They will drift till they come to a fence and then bunch up in a tight group and hope for the best ❑ we're in for some weather, which usually means a storm of some sort is on the way. This prediction is often made by someone with arthritis who can sense the coming weather change in his or her afflicted joints ❑ after the storm the weather is "fairing up" when it begins to return to normal

WEATHER DETERMINATION Call in the dogs and see if they're wet so we'll know whether or not it's raining outside.

WEATHER TIPS If it starts to rain and the chickens run for cover, it won't rain long. If the chickens stay put and continue to peck while it rains, you are in for a long wet spell. The reason is if it's only gonna rain for a short while, the chicken won't want to get wet. On the other hand, if it's gonna rain for a long time, the chicken knows she's gonna get wet sooner or later so she might as well keep eating ❑ thick shucks on corn mean a hard winter is coming *See also Texas Weather*

WEATHER, HOT AND DRY Sick dog weather, which is a reference to a sick dog's nose being dry and hot instead of cold and wet as usual.

WEATHER, COLD It's hog killin' time. In the rural west before the days of deep freezes, meat was kept in a smokehouse. The hogs generally weren't butchered until the first cold snap signalled winter when the temperatures would be cold enough to keep meat longer.

WEATHERMAN, POOR The only thing he can predict correctly is darkness at night.

WEIGHT GAIN He's gained so much weight his appendix scar is now more then a foot wide.

WELCOME I'd appreciate that as much as Travis and the boys would have appreciated a gattlin' gun or two at the Alamo.

WELL ACQUAINTED I know him better 'n I know my old broom.

WELL BEHAVED He got a double portion of manners.

WELL ENDOWED He's a bank walker, which comes from the days of skinny dipping when the boy with the biggest equipment would walk the bank to show it off ❑ a four-button man, which means he is so well endowed he has to loosen four buttons on his jeans to relieve himself. A one or two-button man would not be as well endowed ☐ when he's tired, he leaves three tracks ☐ when he went out for the football team he had to use a gunny sack and bailin' wire for an athletic supporter

WELL ENDOWED, NOT When he went out for the football team he had to use a peanut shell and a rubber band for an athletic supporter.

WENT BAD Went back on his raisin', which is often said of preacher's kids who turn out bad.

WENT CRAZY He went hog wild ☐ he come unbuckled ☐ his common sense come unraveled like the seam in a cheap suit ☐ he sprang a leak in his crankcase ☐ he ripped a hole in his marble sack ☐ that joker went wild *See also Crazy*

WENT HOME Went back to the barn

WESTERN GIRL An angel with denim wings and a golden halo for a hat band

WESTERN WINE Chateau Bubba

WET As the bottom of a stock tank ☐ as an old woman's hanky after a sad

movie ☐ enough to bog a snipe

WHAT DID YOU SAY? Come again?

WHATEVER Whatsomever

WHEELBARROW Georgia buggy

WHEN ALL IS SAID AN DONE Lou Holtz explained it best with, "When all is said an done, as a rule, more is said than done."

WHIPPED He whipped me like a red-headed stepchild.

WHISKEY A strong drink that makes other people interesting ☐ confidence water. The right amount of whiskey will make you believe you're an eight-foot-tall, bulletproof gift God gave to the women of earth ☐ it's easier to put up with the smell than it it is to listen to it ☐ whiskey talks loudest when it is let loose from the jug ☐ the stuff that makes you tipsy also makes you tip your hand *See also Liquor*

WHISKEY, GOOD It's smooth as a moonbeam

WHISKEY, POOR Tastes like something that came out of a jackass with a kidney problem ☐ worm medicine, which means it ain't good for drinking but it will kill your worms ❑ tastes like the scum off pond water

WHISKEY, STRONG
Stealth juice, which means after a few drinks you think you can fly and no one can see you ❑ strong enough to take the moss off your teeth ❑ that'd cause a baby bullfrog to spit in the eye of a great white shark ❑ it'll remove warts from people you have to look at ❑ antifogmatic, which was a popular country term for whiskey around the turn of the century. It is included because it's a great word that should not be forgotten altogether.

WHISTLING WOMAN
According to an old country saying, a whistling woman and a crowin' hen will come to a bad end.

WHITE As skin under a bathing suit

WHORE Mattress buster

WHO'S IN CHARGE Who's skinning this cat? Who's runnin' this railroad?

WIDOWED, THREE TIMES She wore out three dashers but never had but one churn. The number of dashers (husbands) can be

changed to suit the needs but the number of churns is always one.

WIFE Your better half ❑ somebody you used to catch in your arms but now you catch in your pockets

WIFE, GOOD I wouldn't trade her for twelve acres of pregnant red hogs

WIFE, IDEAL A virgin with the experience of a New Orleans flatbacker that can stay on a diet and live within a budget.

WIFE, SMART She had her husband's part of the marriage ceremony changed to "I will love, honor, obey, and give up fishing and drinking" ❑ she knows how to make a man out of a jackass and vice versa

WIFE, UNDERSTANDING She gives you all the rope you want but she never forgets how to tie a hangman's noose ❑ Lee Trevino said his wife doesn't care what he does when he's away so long as he doesn't have a good time.

WIFE, UNFAITHFUL A baby got caught in her trap, which means the lady had a baby but the father was not her husband ❑ you can't buy a wedding ring small enough to stay on her finger which implies that whenever she goes out, the wedding ring comes off ☐ she didn't figure her husband would miss one or two peaches off the tree

WIFE, WASTEFUL She can throw more out the window with a teaspoon than her husband can carry in the door with a shovel.

WIFE, UGLY *See Husband, Ugly*

WIFE, WASTING HER TIME She's tryin' to make a heel toe the mark.

WIGGLE Like a maggot in hot ash

WILD AS A peach orchard boar

WILL A dead giveaway

WILL POWER, LACK OF His will power suffers from generator failure.

WILLINGNESS If you want butter, you gotta be willing to churn the milk.

WIMP He could be kicked to death by a grasshopper.

WIND, STRONG It's blowing like perfume through a high school dance ☐ blows through you like you're wearin' crocheted

underwear ☐ the tomatos wouldn't grow 'cause the wind kept blowing the sunshine off the vines ☐ you could spit in your own eye ☐ it blew so hard it knocked John Wayne off his horse at the drive-in movie ☐ blowin' hard enough to turn a prairie dog hole inside out ☐ blowin' so hard a chicken layed the same egg three times ☐ so hard it blew the feathers off an eagle ☐ In West Texas the wind blows so hard they use a piece of iron for a kite and some trace chain for a tail. They also use an anvil connected to a steel pole with a log chain as a weather vane. The wind stopped blowing one day in Lubbock, Texas and it took everybody two hours to learn how to walk straight up.

WINDBAG He could blow up the Goodyear blimp.

WINK Is as good as a nod to a blind mule

WINNER The bell ringer

WISDOM Making the most out of what comes and the least out of what goes ☐ a double portion of horse sense

WISDOM VERSUS FOOLISHNESS A wise cowboy learns by watchin' others get thrown, a fool has to taste the corral dirt for himself.

WISDOM VERSUS EXPERIENCE Wisdom comes from good decisions, experience comes from bad ones.

WISE MAN Holds his tongue when arguing with a woman, a fool, or a drunk

WISH May all your kids be born nekkid ❑ may the wind at your back never be your own

WISHBONE Pulley bone ❑ a poor substitute for backbone

WOBBLED Like a drunk on a bicycle ❑ like a model A Ford with a flat tire ❑ like a red wagon with three wheels

WOMAN, ATTRACTIVE *See Female, Attractive*

WOMAN, MAD Hell on high heels *See also Female, Angry*

WOMAN SPURNED She woke up on the wrong side of the will.

WOMAN'S WORK Woman's work is never done if she asks her husband to do it.

WOMEN Are like cow patties, the older they are the easier they are to pick up ❑ are not like horses because the wilder they are the easier they are to pet

WON'T WORK That dog won't float ❑ that dog won't hunt ❑ that chicken won't lay ❑ that bucket wouldn't hold water in a monsoon ❑ that motor won't crank

WON, BARELY We out sorried 'em, which means neither team played well but somebody has to win.

WOOD, QUICK BURNING Breakfast wood. Some wood, like dry pine, burns very quickly allowing only enough time to cook breakfast and not enough time to cook a large meal like supper.

WOOD, SLOW BURNING Supper (or dinner) wood. Some wood, such as oak and hickory, burns slow and thus provides enough fire to cook an entire supper.

WORD, VERSATILE In the country language, one of the most versatile words is reckon. It can be used for suppose, think, guess, believe, calculate, presume, expect, know, imagine, assume, and speculate among others.

WORK HARD If you want your dreams to come true, don't oversleep ❑ it's better to have two tired arms than one empty stomach ❑ you can't climb the ladder of success with your hands in your pocket ❑ you're better off to be bent from hard work than crooked from trying to avoid it ❑ as a sugarmill jackass ❑ as a sled dog

WORKED LATE When I went home I met myself coming back to work (which frequently happens if you write a book).

WORKER, GOOD He keeps his corner up, which means he keeps his property in good order or he does his share of the work ❑ he's active in the harness ❑ he works so hard he has to be careful not to drown in his own sweat ❑ he's hell on leather, which means he can wear out a saddle or a pair of boots real quick 'cause he works so hard ❑ if you give him a job to do you can color it done

WORKER, POOR The only time he holds his end up is when he sticks his head in the sand ❑ he's all back and no brain ❑ when he walks up it's about the same as three good men leaving ❑ he won't last till the water boils. After killing the hogs, the carcass is boiled in hot water. Anyone who didn't make it

till the water boiled wouldn't be around long.

WORKER, QUIET *See Quiet Worker*

WORKERS The wagon pullers ❑ the infantry (or the Indians)

WORKING HARD As a little train on a big track

WORRY HIM Like a banty rooster worries a bulldog ❑ drop him in the grease and let him feel how hot it can get in the kitchen

WORRIED, A LOT She's worried all the way to the bone.

WORRYING He's walking a hole in the carpet.

WORTHLESS It ain't worth a Continental damn ❑ not worth a plug nickel ❑ not worth the spit on a postage stamp ❑ ain't worth a tinker's damn

WORTHLESS AS A moral victory. It might make you feel good for a short while but it don't change the standings ❑ as sour manure ❑ as a pickle barrel full of feathers ❑ as last year's calender ❑ as a dead possum's tail *See also Useless As*

WORTHLESS GROUP A sorry lot

WORTHLESS PERSON
Ain't fit to roll in the slop
with the hogs ❑ he's too
dumb to work and too lazy to
steal

WRINKLED As a cheap suit
in a cheaper suitcase ❑ as a
burnt boot ❑ as a boiled shirt
❑ as a washboard ❑ the only
thing he has that ain't
wrinkled is his teeth ❑ he
has so many wrinkles, he
has to screw on his hat

WRITER, POOR She'll be
in real trouble if she tries to
write anything more
ambitious than a grocery list
❑ his hero died in the preface

WRITES SMALL Could put
the Bill of Rights on a
matchbook cover

WRONG That cat won't
flush!

X-Y-Z

YES — does a 10-foot chicken lay a big egg?

X

X RAY Bone picture

Y

YAHOO A rowdy buckaroo

YANK Jerk to a country boy

YANKEE For a lot of southern country boys there is no such thing as a Yankee. There are only damn Yankees. Being one of those southern country boys, I was ten years old before I knew damn Yankee was two words. For a lot of folks from the south you're either a Southerner or you're a Yankee, which explains why some country boys refer to people from Colorado, California, or Canada as Yankees. Other than damn Yankee the only other descriptive phrase printable is Northerner.

YELLOW Pale green to country boys who speed through a traffic light on yellow

YELLS, A LOT He's a hollerin' master ❑ she yells more than a little leaguer's mother

YES Does a cowboy's socks stink? ❑ Does a cat lick his back side? ❑ Does a mule eat corn? ❑ Does a bear sleep in the woods? ❑ Is a frog waterproof? ❑ Dan Jenkins may have said it best in *Baja Oklahoma* with, "Does Dolly Parton sleep on her back?"

YESTERDAY The tomorrow that got away

YOU CAN DO IT Even a brown and red hen can lay a white egg ❑ the smallest dog can bury the biggest bone ❑ a small horse can throw a big cowboy ❑ There is a sign in the locker room of the Texas Rangers which proclaims, "You can if you believe you can."

YOU'LL REGRET IT You'll wish you hadn't done it.

YOU'RE LATE You missed the blessing, which is a reference to someone arriving for dinner after the blessing had been asked but before all the food was gone.

YOU'RE WELCOME You bettcha, which is a good country response when someone says thanks.

YOU'RE WRONG You got another think coming, as in "If you think I'm gonna go to the dance with you, well, you got another think coming" ❑ you're pullin' on the wrong string, which may be a reference to the old-time country carnival game where you paid a nickel and then pulled a string to see what prize you won. More often than not the prize wasn't worth anywhere near a nickel.

YOUNG He's still wet behind the ears ❑ he ain't been weaned long

YOUR CHOICE Whatever trips your trigger, melts your butter, or pulls your string ❑ grab a skinnin' knife, grab a leg, or grab your butt and haul yourself outta here.

YOUR PROBLEM It's your possum so you skin it ❑ it's your itch so you scratch it ❑ it's your kid so you whup it

YOUR RESPONSIBILITY If your dog trees it, you gotta eat it ❑ you can't get some other dog to do your barking ❑ you got to learn to butt with your own head

YUPPIE BATTLE CRY Don't give me any more cheese, just let me out of the rat trap, which means forget the perks, just let me go to the country where life is simple and the biggest decisions are whether to plow or go fishing.

YWCA Heifer club

Z

ZEBRA An umpire horse

ZERO Ought, or nuthin', as in "They whupped us 40 to nuthin.'

ZIPPER Barn door ❑ match starter. If nothing else is available you can almost always strike a match on your zipper but its best if you exercise caution so you don't start a fire that might be double painful to put out.

ZIPPER, OPEN Your cotton is blooming, which means your zipper is open and your white briefs are visible to any who might want to look ❑ it's snowing down south ❑ XYZ, which translates into check your zipper

THE END Period, stop, and quit. That's all he wrote folks.

This space is for your favorite sayings.

Bibliography

Alpern, Lynne, *Oh, Lord, I Sound Just Like Mama.* (Atlanta: Peachtree Publishers, 1986).

Alstad, Ken, *Savvy Sayin's.* (Tucson: Ken Alstad Company, 1989).

Atwood, E. Bagby, *The Regional Vocabulary of Texas.* (Austin: University of Texas Press, 1962).

Benthul, Herman F., *Wording Your Way Through Texas.* (Burnet, Texas: Eakin Press, 1981).

Black, Donald C., *Handy as a Hip Pocket On A Hog.* (Dallas, Texas: Taylor Publishing Company, 1989).

Bowman, Bob, *I Ain't Sure I Understand Everything I Know About This.* (Lufkin, Texas: Best of East Texas Publishing, 1985).

Bowman, Bob, *If I Tell You a Hen Dips Snuff . . . .* (Lufkin, Texas: Best of East Texas Publishing, 1981).

Claiborne, Robert, *Loose Cannons and Red Herrings.* (New York: Ballantine Books, 1988).

Eaton, Dian, *Is It True What They Say About Dixie?* (Secaucus, N.J.: Citadel Press, 1988).

Funk, Charles E., *A Hog On Ice.* (New York: Harper Colophon Books, 1985).

Funk, Charles E., *Horsefeathers & Other Curious Words.* (New York: Perennial Library, 1986).

Mitchell, Steve, *How To Speak Southern.* (New York: Bantam Books, 1976).

Mitchell, Steve, *More How To Speak Southern.* (New York: Bantam Books, 1980).

Moore, Jack S., *The Official Redneck Handbook.* (Houston: Larksdale, 1983).

Bibliography

Powers, Nick, *Speakin' Suthern Like It Should Be Spoke.* (Lindale, Georgia: Country Originals, 1975).

Russel, Kay and Jones, Nancy, *Texas Talkin'.* (Burnet, Texas: Eakin Press, 1981).

Smith, Diann S., *Down Home Talk.* (New York: Collier MacMillan, 1988).

Syatt, Dick, *Country Talk.* (Secaucus, N.J.: Citadel Press, 1980).

Syatt, Dick, *Like We Say Back Home.* (Secaucus, N.J.: Citadel Press, 1987).

Weaver, Ken, *Texas Crude.* (New York: E. P. Dutton, Inc., 1984).

Wilder, Roy E. Jr., *You All Spoken Here.* (New York: Penguin, 1984).

Index

THIS DOG'LL
HUNT

AN ENTERTAINING TEXAS DICTIONARY

INTRODUCTION BY ANN RICHARDS, TEXAS STATE TREASURER
WALLACE O. CHARITON

This Dog'll Hunt

The ultimate Texas dictionary! *This Dog'll Hunt* contains thousands of the popular Texas sayings so common in the language of the state. All entries are arranged in the familiar dictionary format so the material is easy to use. As a bonus, many interesting quotations and stories are included to make this a dictionary that everyone will want to read and find difficult to put down.

This book is an absolute must for anyone who wants to talk like a Texan or to simply understand what a Texan is saying. *This Dog'll Hunt* is the perfect choice for anyone searching for that unique gift for a friend or relative "up North."

1-55622-125-8 • **$12.95**   1-55622-126-6 • **$14.95**
softbound • 300 pages • 6 x 9   hardbound • 300 pages • 6 x 9

Texas Wit & Wisdom

This book is a friendly, entertaining collection of stories, anecdotes, amusing quotations, funny signs, some classic Texas jokes, and even some surprisingly sound advice from the often wacky but always wonderful world of Texans. Features in *Texas Wit and Wisdom* include the bumper sticker hall of fame, amusing T-shirt slogans, and some interesting photographs. This book is a true classic collection of Texas hilarity.

1-55622-135-5 • **$9.95**
hardbound • 256 pages • 5 1/2 x 8 1/2

Texas Highway Humor

In the beginning, it was happy trails. Then some dummy invented the horseless carriage and things haven't been the same since. As ribbons of concrete spread over the horse trails, so did the fun and frustration. This book explores some of that highway fun, both past and present. Included are unique pictures of strange vehicles, early gas stations, convenience stores, the evolution of the stop light, unusual roadside signs, the Texas billboard hall of fame, unusual accidents, strange things seen when driving, and much, much more.

1-55622-176-2 • **$10.95**
softbound • 140 pages • 5 1/2 x 8 1/2

Rainy Days in Texas Funbook

This book is a new entertainment package that is perfect for occupying kids on those rainy days when they can't go outside to play. All the material is presented to subtly teach youngsters something about Texas history while they are entertaining themselves.

Rainy Days in Texas Funbook contains a wonderland of easy-to-do projects including word search puzzles, do-it-yourself jigsaw puzzles and mobiles, some emergency coloring book pages, a Texas flag construction kit, connect-the-dots pictures, and so much more.

1-55622-130-4 • **$9.95**
softbound • 120 pages • 8 1/2 x 11